5

# Marine
# Inboard Engines

ALSO IN THE MOTORBOATS MONTHLY SERIES

*Practical Motor Cruising*
Dag Pike
ISBN 0 229 11827 5

This first title in the series breaks new ground in that it avoids the formal approach and instead takes the motor cruiser owner (both novice and experienced) by the hand to show them the ropes of *practical* motorboat handling and management.

Distilling 40 years of experience in all types of powered craft from motor cruisers to offshore powerboats and even lifeboats, Dag Pike explains how planing and displacement boats behave, how to handle them skilfully in all conditions in harbour, on rivers and at sea, describes what makes them tick and advises how to get the best from them.

Pike explains that the key to good boat handling is preparation and planning – and having something in reserve for when things go wrong. Knowing your boat, learning about the weather, the sea and how it behaves, matching the speed to the conditions and knowing how to navigate effectively will all contribute to help you become a proficient and safe motorboat skipper – and, most importantly, to enjoy it!

*Fast Boats and Rough Seas*
Dag Pike
ISBN 0 229 11840 2

This is a more advanced follow-up to *Practical Motor Cruising*, and is designed to explain advanced handling techniques for fast boats. With a very practical emphasis, Pike covers high speed handling as well as operating techniques in rough weather, all based on personal experience.

*Fast Boats and Rough Seas* begins with an analysis of how waves are formed and their effect on the boat. Pike then looks at hull shape as related to speed and seaworthiness, controlling the boat, crew comfort, navigation under difficult conditions, power requirements, equipment and fittings for high speed, and emergency procedures. Lastly he considers weather changes and describes tactics for avoiding the worst of storm conditions.

Throughout, Pike's approach is wholly practical, as one would expect from such a highly experienced seaman. Even experienced skippers and crew will welcome this book and value its sound advice, from preparation through to emergency procedures.

*In preparation*:

*High Speed Navigation*
Dag Pike
ISBN 0 229 11859 3

# Marine
# Inboard Engines

## Petrol and Diesel

## LORIS GORING

**ADLARD COLES**
8 Grafton Street, London W1

Adlard Coles
William Collins Sons & Co. Ltd
8 Grafton Street, London W1X 3LA

First published in Great Britain by
Adlard Coles 1990

*British Library Cataloguing in Publication Data*

Goring, Loris
  Marine inboard engines: petrol and diesel.
  1. Boats. Engines
  I. Title  II. Series
  623.8'72

ISBN 0-229-11842-9

Typeset by Ace Filmsetting Ltd, Frome, Somerset
Printed and bound in Great Britain by
Mackays of Chatham plc, Letchworth, Herts

# Contents

# Acknowledgements

Without the help of the marine engine manufacturers, this book would not have been possible. In particular, I would like to thank the following engine manufacturers who have patiently helped by providing a high input of technical information as well as supplying a number of the illustrations: Deutz/Mermaid; The Ford Motor Company; General Motors, Detroit Engines Division; Mercruiser; Perkins Diesel Engines; Sabre Marine; Volvo Penta; Watermota; as well as all the other engine manufacturers mentioned in the text. In addition, I would like to thank Lucas CAV and Bosch, who supply a major part of the fuel injection and electrical equipment that is used worldwide on marine engines, and Self-Changing Gears for their help with the gearbox section.

My thanks are also due to Emrhys Barrell, editor of *Motorboats Monthly*, who has given me help and encouragement over many years.

To all those who have cooperated, contributed or simply encouraged with the writing and illustrations, my sincere thanks.

# *Preface*

This book offers an introduction to the design and use of marine inboard engines, both petrol and diesel, which are used in pleasure craft.

Much of it has been written to encourage those with a limited knowledge of marine engines to understand first about general background, then specific design features and, finally, to offer pointers as to how engines are best looked after to maximise their service life. Chapters have many sub-headings so that the reader can locate them quickly from the index.

Pitching the technical level of the text so as not to baffle the newcomer or bore the old-hand is always a difficult task but I hope I have been able to maintain a satisfying balance. Again, I hope my American readers will forgive me for once again using the word petrol for what we all know is really gasoline!

We must never forget that the prime aim of boating is pleasure. An engine that is ill-maintained may spoil that pleasure, if not actually put the lives of the owner and crew into real danger.

The owner should get more out of this text if it is used alongside the *Owner's Manual* for his particular make of engine. The basic knowledge this book endeavours to offer can then be practically applied. When you start doing the simple basic work on the engine yourself it should give you a real sense of achievement – and greater enjoyment of a splendid hobby.

Loris Goring
Brixham, Devon

# 1   Getting to know marine engines

Most of us realise that to be a competent skipper a basic knowledge of a marine engine is essential. Although most would acknowledge that the safety of boat and crew is the foremost reason for this, surely value for money and buying an asset with low depreciation must also be considered.

In an age where the car has come to dominate our civilisation there are still many owners who have been lulled into a false sense of security by increased reliability and longer periods between servicing an engine. It is not necessary for a car owner to know what is under the bonnet; the breakdown services can be called if anything goes wrong.

There will be serious trouble for both engine and skipper if the same attitude is brought to boating. Faults are more likely to develop in marine engines – not because they are less well made than car engines but simply because they are operating in almost alien conditions and in a hostile environment which is only too ready to take advantage of ignorance and neglect. Long periods between use do not help.

Thankfully, there are many exceptions to the uninterested owner. Many of us have sharpened our wits and mechanical skills caring for motorbike or car engines and the knowledge gained is often directly applicable to marine engines. Sadly, there is also ample proof from rescue statistics that there are far too many boat owners who rely on neglected engines which are in poor mechanical condition. Even worse are owners who fail to do the simplest of things such as filling the fuel tank.

Figures from all branches of rescue organisations which actually provide a service to save life and not boats are available for all to see. For rescue organisations – US Coast Guard, HM Coastguard,

Air Sea Rescue Services and Royal National Lifeboat Institution – the foolish skipper is bad news indeed. It must be said that many marine rescues never even become statistics because helpful yachtsmen and fishermen help boats that otherwise would be in distress. The great majority of rescues are necessitated by engine breakdown or running out of fuel.

Safety must be a primary reason for a skipper to look after his boat engine. This may be obvious where the sea is concerned, but even on a flooding river or weir an inland boater needs to be certain that engine failure will not put the boat and the life of the crew in jeopardy.

Most of us will be adequately spurred on to proper engine maintenance by the very considerable savings that can be made by carrying out repairs and maintenance ourselves. The vast majority of us own modest boats and have to keep an eye on running expenses. Regular maintenance prolongs the life of any engine and avoids the punitive damage to our pockets that is inflicted if a major mechanical disaster occurs through neglect.

Not all of us are born mechanics but by reading the engine manufacturer's manual most people will find that basic DIY maintenance is well within their scope. Many of us who are really keen on our hobby get a great deal of pleasure simply tinkering about with engines – we take pride in keeping them spick and span. This can be a great advantage, for it is easier to spot when things are going wrong on a clean engine and it is far more pleasant to work on.

Don't worry about how good a mechanic you are at this stage, for in the text I will detail some repair jobs that can be done by the relatively unskilled mechanic. The time when major repairs are needed will often be delayed by regular routine servicing, especially at fitting out time and when an engine is laid up for the winter.

For those mariners who hate car engines, the same feeling is more than likely to be transposed to the engine in their boat. There is hope for a lost soul like this and he might be saved yet! Fear of the unknown may be the root of the problem. If his boat is to remain safely tied up to the marina berth like a maritime caravan, he is missing out on the real fun of boating – getting under way and going places on the water.

Basic knowledge about the boat's engine will often save a great deal of money in another way. If an owner cannot bring himself to hold even a screwdriver, his ability to pinpoint a fault or job that needs doing on the engine is an asset – he can at least point out what is needed to the mechanic so that time and money are not wasted. A mechanic's time is wasted simply in getting to a boat; if some idea can be given of the spare parts needed this can save him a double journey. A mechanic's time is expensive so the more of it you can save the smaller the bill will be.

Knowing roughly how many hours might be involved in work and being able to understand a written quotation for the parts and expertise an owner is paying for helps put the mind at rest. It does little for an owner's nervous system if he gets involved in acrimonious dealings or even the law courts. A mechanic's time charges are easier to understand if an owner is used to working on a boat engine doing simple things. Working in the confines of a cramped engine space takes far longer than it would if access were easier and this has to be paid for. This brings me to an important aspect of boat mechanics – engine spaces.

## Engine rooms – or (more likely) engine spaces

It would be great if we could all boast that we had engine *rooms* where engine maintenance could be done in comfort. The reality is that the vast major- ity of us have boats where engines are cramped into the smallest space possible. While the cynic might say this is to allow the boat salesman to boast ten berths in an 18-foot boat, we all know that compromises in design are necessary. Just ensure that the engine has a fair share of the inter- ior space at the designer's disposal and that there is reasonable access to all parts for servicing.

I believe that one of the main reasons why marine engines are neglected is that just as Count Dracula probably dreaded the change into a bat keen on blood transfusion each moonlit evening, we dread the change from gin-sipping human into the greasy orang-utan necessary to becoming a boat mechanic.

Undoubtedly there has to be bias in design towards human comfort and gratification, but equally the engine makes demands that really should be satisfied. It ought not to be a menacing liability we dread working on.

Look out for boats with solidly built furniture over the engine space, or with fixed engine hatch beams across the top so it is difficult, if not impos- sible, to adjust the rockers or do a de-coke. Beware the construction which makes the sides of the engine nearest the hull's topsides in a twin installa- tion almost impossible to reach. The practical per- son will think ahead and foresee engine servicing difficulties. Before buying, reject craft that will be difficult to look after. Look at the way engine hatches are hinged and supported. They are often extremely heavy, requiring rigid support systems to ensure they do not fall on fingers, especially when they have to be opened at sea.

The next question that must be decided is whether to have a diesel or a petrol engine.

## Non-mechanical differences between petrol (gasoline) and diesel engines

### SAFETY
The first major difference is the fuel used. Diesel fuel has a much higher flash point than petrol and is generally safer. Petrol is a highly volatile fuel which is highly explosive when mixed in certain quantities with air.

This danger has often given petrol marine engines a bad name for safety. Unfortunately, a boat's interior shape will encourage any fuel vapour or gas to be contained within it. Petrol vapour from spilled or leaking fuel can soon build up to explosive levels in bilges. To be fair, the real culprits for fire and explosion are poor installation practices and human error. Often it is not the fuel at fault so much as the boat builder and/or the owner.

Regulations exist in most countries to encourage if not legislate for boats to be built to safe standards. Sadly, ignorant owners either alter boats during a re-fit, or behave in such a way as to encourage disaster. We will be taking a much closer look at the safety of fuel systems, but there is little or nothing a book like this can do about unsafe owners.

The second difference between petrol and diesel is the relative cost of these fuels. Depending which part of the world you are in, this can have an important bearing on choice of engine. In Europe, diesel fuel is generally cheaper than petrol and if a boat is used for a great number of engine hours each year this can amount to a big saving. However, most pleasure craft, at best, only manage a couple of hundred engine hours each season so the saving may not be as big as first thought.

## CAPITAL COSTS

There are savings on capital outlay since most small marine petrol engines are cheaper to buy than a diesel engine of equivalent power. The cost differential should be watched as the large diesel production runs being created by the automotive industry are gradually decreasing the price differential. The manufacturing cost of a diesel engine is higher for a number of reasons, the chief one being that it has more precision engineering than a petrol motor. It works at greater pressures and has sophisticated fuel injection equipment compared to the lower pressures and comparatively simple fuel systems of a petrol engine. However, this does not include specialised racing/high performance petrol injection units that can be as sophisticated and expensive to build as any diesel engine and cost just as much, if not more.

*Noise.* The petrol motor is generally, power for power, quieter than a diesel engine. Noise levels are important for the comfort of the crew and, as we shall see later, much money has been spent on achieving quieter engines. Boatbuilders now use far more sound attenuating materials in construction than they did only a few years ago.

## TRENDS IN THE MARKET

In the past, diesel engines found no favour in racing crafts and very little with fast planing cruising boats as they had a poor power to weight ratio. In the late 1950s and 1960s when railways were declining rapidly and road transport was taking over, the creation of faster running, powerful diesels for road transport units enabled conversion to marine use and power for a growing generation of planing craft.

This trend has continued in the road transport market in both America and Europe, mainly as a result of government legislation to encourage heavier road transport. In turn, more efficient, lighter and more compact diesel engines have become available for marinisation – ideal power units for the fast planing craft whose popularity has shown no bounds in the world's pleasure boat market.

In the 1970s, concern began to grow for the world's finite fossil fuel sources. We saw both improved refining for better utilisation of crude oil and research to make both petrol and diesel engines more economical. Oil politics emphasised the need to develop fuel economy to a higher degree than was needed in the past. The modern fuel efficient marine diesel engine has been the outcome. Where petrol engines are concerned, much work was started in the 1970s to produce 'lean burn' units, causing less atmospheric pollution, and which ran on smaller quantities of fuel, at one time thought impossible to achieve. The automotive industry is still moving towards these goals, but for the moment, the marine petrol engine plays such a minor part in the total sales of marine engines in Europe that the new technology has had little or no impact (unlike in the USA). Even in the USA, however, there has been a powerful trend to use more diesel engines to power craft.

The domination of the market by fast planing craft is likely to continue as the automotive industry has put enormous emphasis on the development of even lighter and more compact diesel engines. These modern diesel engines are faster running, quieter and have power-to-weight ratios that are increasingly competitive with petrol units of similar power. They achieve high levels of pollution control without the expensive catalytic controls needed by petrol engines.

Another spin-off from the dwindling supply of fossil fuels has actually turned the wheel full circle. Seventy years ago experimental engines were being run on vegetable oils and mixtures of coal dust slurry. Perkins have once again been experimenting with similar fuels, but enthusiasm seems to wane when politicians make peace and greater oil reserves are found. Nevertheless, as the century draws to a close, the quest for power will only increase and we shall see the development of new engines and fuels. I often wonder if the many boats that never leave the marina (but which have windows full of potted plants) are secretly experimenting with vegetable fuel production that will, one day in the not too distant future, allow them to leave their berths under power.

## DEPRECIATION

Although the petrol engine costs less initially, it depreciates faster than a diesel engine of equivalent age and condition. Where petrol is relatively cheap and taxes light this is perhaps not so important, but where petrol is heavily taxed the prospective owner of a boat will tend to favour the diesel installation. Where fuel tax is high, the rate of depreciation on petrol engined boats is likely to be high, but this may not be so bad as it seems.

For the person desperate to get into boating, but who needs a fair sized craft, the comparatively low cost of a second-hand petrol engined boat might make all the difference between being able to afford to go boating or just dreaming about it.

For the buyer who, like most of us, forks out his last penny on a boat, it is important that such an expensive asset should be recoverable with a minimum amount of depreciation. In the 1970s and on occasions in the 1980s it was possible to sell a boat

for more than you paid for it. Boat production costs and variations in the world's economy soon put paid to this state of affairs. Owners need to be aware, if not wary, of depreciation factors and the choice between petrol and diesel is important.

## Mass production engines

Small volume engine makers do fulfil the needs of a limited specialist market. Small inboard petrol two-strokes such as the Vire and even the ancient Stuart Turner find a small market and are often able to provide a very personal service to owners. However, the really large volume manufacturers of marine engines such as Ford, General Motors USA, Perkins (UK) and Volvo Penta (Sweden) – to name just four, spread over the continents – do offer their customers certain advantages that must be considered when purchasing an engine.

These companies between them have several thousand dealers. It is only recently that Perkins and Volvo Penta have co-operated to market virtually the same engine developed by Perkins – the Prima. Likewise, Volvo Penta use General Motors' block for their new AQ 205 V-6 petrol engine. This large-scale international co-operation should provide ready access to spares and servicing.

The world-wide Ford Motor Company keeps a comparatively low profile in the marine market but in fact provides thousands of base engines for a great number of smaller firms to marinise. Appendix B lists companies that do this. Although it is not a practice I would endorse, spare parts for Ford base engines are usually obtainable through automotive sources – car and heavy transport outlets as well as marine dealers. No one wants to do the marine trader out of his living, but if an owner has a crippled engine that must be back in service swiftly, this is comforting knowledge. So, too, you will find that Volvo Penta use some GM blocks and Mercruiser the Italian VM for their 6-cylinder diesel outdrive shown in Fig 1. All owners should know from which basic engine unit their marine engine is derived. Obviously, the engine mariniser is needed for the special parts he provides. This brings me to a sensitive subject – marine engine spares.

## Marine engine spares

A factor every owner must consider when buying a new or used boat engine is the cost of spare parts. Spares for boat engines tend to be more costly than automotive ones. This is partly because volume sales of parts that have undergone extra processes to marinise them are small, and franchised dealers must make a living from these small volume sales during what is usually a limited sales season.

Costs vary enormously between rival makes for the same basic part. It is not unknown for a manufacturer to sell engines into production boats at little more than cost, but recover profits from the extra margin put on spares. *Caveat emptor*.

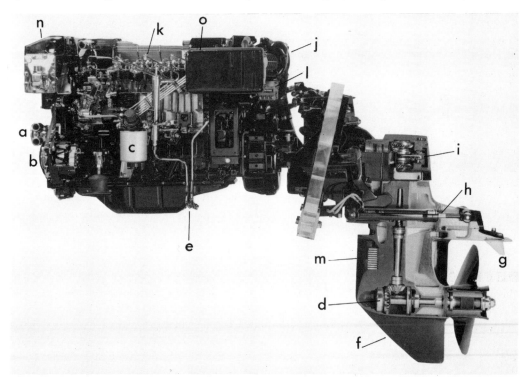

*Fig 1 The Mercruiser 636 0-TA Bravo Two diesel outdrive. This 6-cylinder 180 hp turbocharged aftercooled diesel engine is based on the Italian VM engine.*

KEY

(a) Impeller type raw water pump.
(b) Alternator.
(c) Oil filter.
(d) Heavy duty final drive bevel gears.
(e) Return oil pipe to sump from turbocharger and pipe to sump emptying pump (immediately below 'k' on the figure).
(f) Hydrodynamically designed drive housing which cuts down drag at speed.
(g) Adjustable trim tab.
(h) Power trim allows adjustment of trim by means of these hydraulically operated rams, which also absorb shock of impact from a submerged object.
(i) Mechanical cone clutch.
(j) Turbocharger.
(k) Injection nozzle with high-pressure pipe.
(l) Mer Cathode protection is an impressed current system that senses the electrical currents that cause electrolytic corrosion in the drive leg. It then impresses its own current to counteract and neutralise them.
(m) Raw water intake through leg.
(n) Fresh water expansion tank.
(o) Air cleaner.

On the other side of the coin, there is great danger for the penny-pinching owner buying counterfeit spare parts. From time to time such engine spares appear (sometimes packaged exactly like the originals) but often they are of grossly inferior specification. By using them an owner may not only wreck his engine but also find that any guarantee from the engine maker becomes totally invalid.

## Other factors an owner must consider

Another important factor which should influence engine purchase is the ease with which spares and service can be obtained. Even if you don't cruise great distances, there is comfort in knowing that you can obtain these things quickly and easily. The bigger manufacturers have world-wide appointed agents and service depots, but sometimes the smallest firms can pick and despatch spares as fast as the robots in larger warehouses. Talk to other owners and see how the local land lies.

Some large companies offer additional services when installing new engines. Their applications engineers will advise both designers and owners as to the best way to install their engines and often insist on inspection before accepting them into guarantee. This can be very reassuring.

When it comes to re-engining a boat there is sometimes a factory re-built replacement service available. A worn engine may be replaced, at reduced cost, by a guaranteed factory re-built engine which is usually as good as new. This service also applies to some of the better makes of electrical (starters and generators) and diesel fuel injection equipment bolted onto engines. Always enquire what back-up service a company is willing to provide as this can save both time and money.

## The two- and four-stroke principles

There are two basic operating principles which can be applied to both petrol and diesel engines.

The two- or four-stroke designation refers to the number of movements up and down the cylinder that are required to complete a full power cycle of the engine.

## PETROL TWO-STROKES

Fig 2 shows the principle involved in a two-stroke petrol engine. This is the familiar one found in the majority of outboard marine engines, and is still found in a few small inboard engines.

*First stroke.* On each direction of stroke the piston has a dual function – the volume above the piston being used for one function, the volume below for another. Thus, above the piston on the upward stroke the fuel/air mixture is being compressed while underneath the suction created is drawing more mixture into the crankcase chamber.

*Second stroke.* The fuel is ignited and the expanding gases drive the piston down until the exhaust point is reached. The volume below the piston is under compression from the underside of the descending piston and this drives new fuel/air mixture via a transfer passage into the upper part of the cylinder. This also helps drive out the exhaust gases.

The figure shows what is called a *cross flow* engine; the fuel/air mixture enters from one side and the exhaust is ejected from the opposite side. The designer is trying to achieve the best 'clearing out' or scavenging of the exhaust gases while at the same time obtaining the maximum amount of the clean fuel/air mixture into the cylinder to produce the power. An alternative method is to produce *loop scavenging*, which is as shown in Fig 3.

Lubrication of the two-stroke is dependent on having oil mixed in the fuel. This may be done either directly by mixing it with the petrol in the fuel tank in an exact proportion, or by automatically pumping it into the fuel on each stroke. This latter method is used on some modern outboards but, as the two-stroke inboard is a dying breed, it still uses the fuel/oil pre-mixes.

Oils have been developed especially for two-stroke lubrication to reduce ash and carbon deposits and, provided the correct ratio of oil to

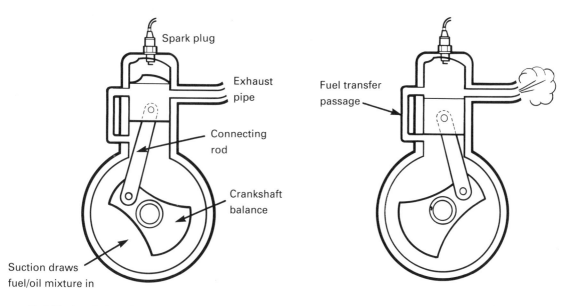

Spark plug

Exhaust pipe

Connecting rod

Crankshaft balance

Suction draws fuel/oil mixture in

Fuel transfer passage

*Fig 2 The two-stroke cycle.*

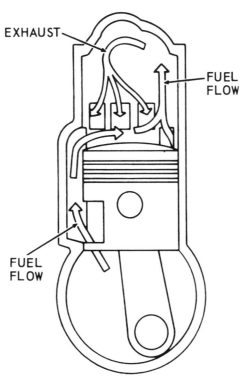

EXHAUST

FUEL FLOW

FUEL FLOW

*Fig 3 Loop scavenging of a two-stroke petrol engine.*

petrol is used, they cause less trouble than the straight oils did previously. When ordinary lubricating oils were used they sooted up plugs, put nasty deposits on them and generally misbehaved so that a two-stroke owner seemed always to have a plug spanner in his hands. You are not being kind to a two-stroke by giving it a little extra oil. The fuel is simply diluted so that there is less of the power producing element in the cylinder and the chance of long service life for the plug is jeopardised.

## TWO-STROKE FUEL CONSUMPTION

Because the two-stroke engine uses its fuel less efficiently than a four-stroke, combustion, exhaust and inlet take place almost at the same time. Its consumption is higher than a four-stroke engine, usually in the region of 0.8–0.9 imperial pints per hp/h, but as these small inboard engines are only used for auxiliary propulsion of small sailing yachts, the relatively high consumption is of little relevance.

## MAINTENANCE OF THE TWO-STROKE

One of the advantages of this type of engine is its simplicity. There are far fewer moving parts than in the four-stroke, and provided the spark is generated at the plug there is little to go wrong. The main maintenance points are:

1. Cleaning the plug/s.

2. Keeping the exhaust manifold clear of carbon.
3. Ensuring that seals are intact both in the crank-case and cylinder head areas.
4. Cooling is usually the simplest raw water system so only needs flushing out and leaving dry over winter. The water passageways may be preserved by using an emulsifying oil in the flushing water which leaves a rust inhibiting coating on the metal.
5. Cleaning petrol line, filter and carburettor.

Spares for ancient two-stroke inboards with magneto ignition can often be obtained from the Wipac Group, Buckingham UK or Lucas (UK), who made the SR series magneto.

## THE TWO-STROKE DIESEL ENGINE

Like the two-stroke petrol motor, the entire combustion cycle is completed in each cylinder for each revolution of the crank-shaft – two strokes of the piston, one upwards and one downwards, complete one revolution of the crank-shaft. The intake and exhaust parts of the cycle are then integral parts of the compression and power strokes. Unlike the petrol two-stroke, the lubrication is quite separate from the fuel and is the same as for a four-stroke engine. The general servicing needs are similar to a four-stroke engine.

Fig 4 shows the cycle as used in the General Motors Detroit range of two-stroke engines. This employs what is known as uni-flow scavenging: the incoming air from the blower moves in a single

*Fig 4 General Motors Detroit two-stroke diesel showing uni-flow scavenging.*

*Top*

1. Lower ports in cylinder admit exhaust scavenging air.
2. Mechanical blower supplies fresh air for scavenging and combustion. On the newer turbocharged range of two-strokes the blower can be bypassed at a predetermined cylinder inlet pressure to allow the turbocharger to take over so

that the air produced flows directly into the cylinder.
3. Exhaust outlets – the figure is based on the 71 Series engines, which have an extremely long history of development and production.
4. Unit-injection – both fuel pump and injector are built into a single element.

Four lower figures illustrate the two-stroke working cycle.
*1st Stroke (a) and (b) up the cylinder*
(a) Blower air finishes scavenging the gases immediately the lower

cylinder inlet ports are uncovered by the piston. (b) As piston continues travelling upwards and closes these inlet ports, the last volume of the blown air is compressed ready for combustion. *2nd Stroke (c) and (d) down the cylinder*
(c) Fuel is injected to produce the power stroke. (d) The exhaust commences, the exhaust valves opening and the burnt gases leaving the cylinder initially under their own high pressure.

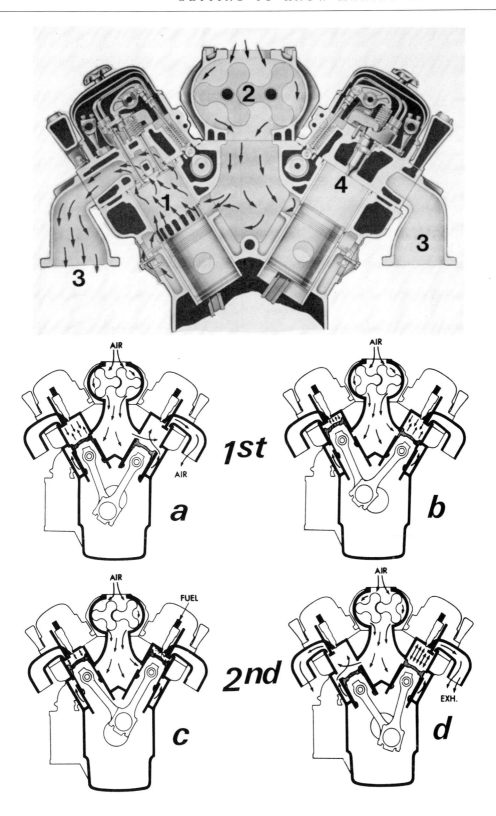

direction and helps in the ejection of the exhaust gases. A feature of the Detroit engines is the unit injector fuel system where each cylinder has its own combined fuel pump and injector built as one unit. Each is operated directly from lobes on the camshaft. This makes for not only an efficient injection system, but for a clean looking engine that does away with high pressure injection pipes that might rupture.

The two-stroke Detroits from the 71 Series onwards to the latest 400 hp 6V-53TI have been under development for many years. Although the sophistication of low-pressure blowing for scavenging and supplying combustion air does add cost, their engineering principles have many bonuses which, if cost is not a primary consideration, should make them of interest to any discerning owner or engine enthusiast. A classic engine of the same type that may occasionally be found is the Foden FD4 and FD6 Mk IV Series two-stroke marine diesel engine, which can still be serviced by Rolls Royce of Crewe nearly 40 years after the first one was produced.

## THE FOUR-STROKE CYCLE

This is by far the most common cycle found in both petrol and diesel inboard engine design. Fig 5 illustrates this. Although it is based on a petrol engine with a spark plug, for all intents and purposes, a diesel fuel injector could be substituted in the drawing. One other variation is the actual design of the cylinder head and piston, which will be discussed later, but the basic cycle is not affected.

*1st induction (downward) stroke.* The fuel/air mixture (petrol engine) or air (diesel engine) is drawn into the cylinder via the inlet valve by the suction created by the descending piston while the exhaust valve remains closed.

*2nd compression (upward) stroke.* The piston is ascending in the cylinder to compress the fuel/air mixture (petrol) or air (diesel). The swirling motion imparted to the charge is vitally important in the design to maximise the fuel/air mixture particle size in a petrol engine and to impart a motion

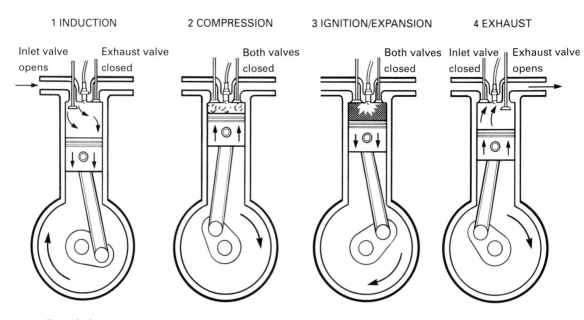

Fig 5 *The four-stroke working principle.*

to the air in a diesel engine so that the incoming fuel will be mixed to maximum effect.

*3rd ignition/expansion stroke.* The spark ignites the fuel/air mixture (petrol), or the fuel injector (diesel) injects the fuel into the hot air, which mixes with and then ignites it. Both gaseous fuel mixtures then begin to burn, expanding the air to drive the piston down. For the design engineer the way the fuel burns, the flame spreads and pressure increases within the cylinder are a constant and fascinating challenge.

The burn effects the service life of the engine, as well as economy – to mention just a couple of factors that must be kept under surveillance. Put simply, too rapid a pressure rise means harder wear on pistons and bearings, excessive heat and excessive fuel consumption. While many books talk about an explosion of the fuel mixture this is the last thing the engineer wants, since such a tremendously rapid pressure rise would damage the engine. Amongst many undesirable things it would probably burn pistons and valves, and damage bearings. Proper timing of the spark or the moment of fuel injection is vital to achieving a safe pressure rise within the cylinder.

*4th exhaust stroke.* The burnt gases are ejected from the cylinder as the exhaust valve opens. Among the many factors the engineer must consider are efficient gas flow for both incoming air/ fuel mixtures and ejection of exhaust gases. Both the incoming and exhaust gases should flow as freely as possible. Sadly, the contortions put into exhaust lines by a few boatbuilders often do nothing to help, and the applications engineer must insist that back pressure in the exhaust line is kept within reasonable limits. It also detracts from performance if exhaust manifolds and lines are not kept clear of carbon deposits. In racing engines, when extremely fast engine revolutions shorten the time cycle even further, the polishing of ports and tuning of exhaust lines does much to enhance performance.

## Cylinder configurations

Marine engines for the pleasure boat market vary from small single-cylinder units to twins, fours, sixes, eights and at the top end of the market 16-cylinder units. Theoretically you can think of engine power being produced as:

$$POWER = Torque \times Revolutions$$

Torque is turning power, and revolutions are the familiar r/min (revolutions per minute or rpm). You will notice that you may have either high torque and low revolutions or low torque and high revolutions to produce the same power. Thus, in the past, the safest way to produce power was to have enormous torque but slow rpm – the familiar canal boat 'thumper' where you could almost count the revolutions. A delightful sound in the right place, but certainly not what today's planing power boat wants. This type of boat has needs more akin to those of the modern car: fast acceleration, high r/min produced with modest torque. This is particularly fortunate as most engines, as we have already seen, are derived from automotive sources.

The power output has to be balanced against many more things besides torque and r/min. Engine balance is perhaps most important as far as we are concerned. The internal ('infernal' to sailing yachtsmen) combustion engine is subject to all sorts of forces which can make it run as smoothly as a sewing machine or vibrate like a jelly in an earthquake. The design engineer has to resolve revolving, coupling, multiple and reciprocating mass forces. Each type of cylinder configuration has particular advantages and disadvantages as far as these are concerned.

Some configurations are more difficult to balance out than others and all sorts of solutions such as counter rotating balance shafts are employed. The Sabb and Bukh single- and twin-cylinder diesels were excellent examples of what can be done with balancing shaft arrangements. We generally find that a twin is smoother running than a single and a four-cylinder engine is less smooth running than the six, but when buying an engine the following observations may be of interest. In addition to looking at the number of cylinders that produce the power, their configuration plays a vital role. As usual, there are advantages and disadvantages in each.

## IN-LINE CYLINDER CONFIGURATIONS

The benefits of in-line configuration may be summed up:

1. Simplicity – fewer parts.
2. Greater reliability – fewer parts to fail.
3. Good service life as there is usually plenty of room for large crankshaft bearing areas.
4. Excellent to install in a boat with minimum beam width and access to each side for servicing.
5. A six-cylinder engine is fully balanced.
6. Ideal for turbocharging (large bearing areas).
7. If thought is given, it is easy to provide excellent access to ancillaries on the engine's sides and top.
8. Easy to work on and service, parts should be less expensive due to simplicity of design.
9. Professional servicing and reconditioning charges should be lower than for other types as they are easier to do.
10. They can be canted over at the design stage to allow lower engine installation height.

## 'V' TYPE CYLINDER CONFIGURATIONS

These configurations from V4s to V6s and V8s offer the following benefits for engines of the same power output compared to the 'in-line' type of designs.

1. They can be made shorter in length and of more compact construction. Against this they are wider – something not always wanted in a boat engine compartment.
2. They are usually lower in height – an important advantage when they fit beneath a wheelhouse or cockpit floor.
3. They can safely achieve higher revolutions

owing to smaller cylinder dimensions. This means the swept volume can be smaller for the same power output.
4. Higher r/min. As we have seen this means lower torque therefore the drive train components (gears for timing, camshafts etc) can be lighter. It is usual, especially for normally aspirated engines, to produce a lighter engine than the equivalent 'in-line' one.
5. There is generally smoother torque throughout the speed range where engines use a greater number of cylinders.
6. Unitary cylinder design is possible so that a manufacturer can build a whole family of engines based on one basic cylinder unit. He can offer a wide choice in the power range and yet keep spare parts down to economic levels.

By comparing items, it is possible to see the advantages and disadvantages on which to base your own selection, but there is nothing to compare with taking a boat which is fitted with the engine of your choice on a trip. You will soon see how much noise and vibration it produces.

## The power you are buying

The prospective owner's interest in the power of the engine he is buying ranges from seeking the most economical and efficient powering of a particular boat to simply boasting about the enormous power output of the engines whose fuel consumption does little but make enormous furrows in the water and a hole in his pocket.

Many of us are obviously interested in the former, but we may have difficulty comparing the power from different makes of marine engine. There is presently a plethora of standards used to define the power output of internal combustion engines. Some of these are set out later, but it would cost a small fortune to buy them all, and it would still be difficult, if not impossible, to make sensible comparisons.

One might well ask why so many standards exist and which are the most relevant for the inboard engine buyer. As marine inboard engine production forms only a tiny part of the total volume sales of the engine manufacturers, we have until recently had to accept standards which have been solely or partially developed with industrial or road vehicle applications in mind. The governments of most of the major countries of the world have imposed their own standards and these differ widely in test specifications. However, the major engine manufacturing countries use four main standards: British Standards (BS), American Society of Automotive Engineers (SAE), German (DIN) and Japanese (JIS). The European Economic Community has contributed to the confusion by insisting on standards which must be equivalent to EEC ones or better. Countries which do not have their own standards adopt one of the major ones outlined above or the International Standard (ISO).

It would help if the many standards could be converted by sales staff from one to the other but this is usually quite impossible. Each standard has its own test conditions, such as air inlet temperatures, density and humidity, barometric and vapour pressures and fuel specifications. Again some standards quote power with (*gross*) or without (*net*) auxiliary power losses. Components like the generator and gearbox absorb power just to turn or churn oil round them so the output at the propeller shaft (Shaft Horse Power – SHP) is very different for gross and net power. There is also some difference in the power output from identical motors made on the same manufacturing line and the better manufacturers usually quote a manufacturing tolerance for engine power output, which may in itself be as much as ±5%.

It is vital when looking at different engines to compare power precisely like with like. Sadly, the ethical approach is not always adhered to by all salesmen (some depend heavily on the confusion these standards cause to secure sales). An example of this is when JIS and SAE J816 maximum gross power rating is quoted by some engine salesmen. In pleasure boat applications this rating is unrealistically high and could not be used in a normal installation to give the life and durability usually expected.

Standards are changed and superseded from time to time; thus BS 5514 has superseded BS 3109, BS 649 and BS 765. This is now the useful standard used when quoting gross power. Similarly DIN 6270A and DIN 6270B used by some European manufacturers defined intermittent and continuous operation power and this is now replaced by DIN 6271. Thankfully, SAE J245, J270 and J816 are now amalgamated and replaced by the single SAE J1349.

At present the standards of greatest interest to us are:

1. BS Au 141A – The performance of diesel engines for *road* vehicles. This standard is a good guide for engine power related to 'standard conditions' so that the variables due to differing test conditions can be eliminated.
2. BS 5514 and DIN 6271, which are derived from and identical to ISO 3046. There is at least some consensus here covering reciprocating internal combustion engines.
3. SAE J 1349 which, as we have seen, is the amalgamation of three SAE standards covering spark ignition and diesel engines and a power test code.
4. ISO 8665 – a standard for marine propulsion engines and systems for pleasure craft less than 24 m long. It covers power measurements and declarations. As it is very similar to ISO 3046 we can hope that it will be adopted on an international scale and that both BS 5514 and DIN 6271 can be aligned with it. Better still, marine engine manufacturers that claim part of the pleasure craft market could adopt it in their sales literature.

Never forget that the academic approach to engine power is brought home to roost when operating the engine under practical conditions. Presently, most owners of power boats are uncritical of the performance of their craft compared to that of their car. When buying a car, top speed and low fuel consumption are major selling points. Indeed, many countries have legislation which lays down precisely how fuel consumption should be measured at varying speeds; there is also consumer law to protect the customer against false claims. Presently, the pleasure boat customer is far more easy going. He is not too concerned with fuel consumption, or even speed, so long as the performance seems to be within a knot or two of the specification, or perhaps more accurately 'guesstimation' of the builder. How long this will continue, when boats are built on production lines like motor cars and the boating public becomes as discerning as the car owner, is open to speculation. In the meantime we may at least understand and use standards as they exist so that we really buy the economy, power and performance we want.

The kilowatt is now coming more into familiar use but in the meantime the following measurements of power are found in literature and it is useful to be able to convert them:

$$\text{Imperial 1hp} = 0.7456998 \text{ kW } (0.7457)$$
$$= 1.0139 \text{ PS or CV}$$
$$\text{or 1kW} = 1.3410221 \text{ hp } (1.3410)$$
$$\text{PS or CV} = \text{metric horse power}$$

## The propeller law curve

This is a curve (Fig 6) often shown on the engine manufacturer's sales leaflet power graph, and provided it can be interpreted correctly it can help an owner determine how much power he has in hand at any engine speed. It is useful when the curve can be used in conjunction with the specific fuel consumption curve to determine the most economic cruising speed and how much power is in hand at that speed.

The curve indicates the horse power which the propeller is capable of absorbing at various engine speeds. At 3000 r/min on the graph the propeller is absorbing about 20 kW, which is less than half the theoretical power (45 kW on a vertical line) that the engine could deliver at that speed. Obviously, it is assumed that the correct propeller is fitted to allow the engine to reach its maximum revolutions at full throttle thus absorbing the full power that the engine is capable of developing. As the throttle is closed the revolutions fall until idling speed is reached; the power decreases along the propeller law curve, not the full power curve.

The engine manufacturer's curve can only be taken as an approximate indication since it is impossible for him to predict the exact matching of propeller and hull form. The curve is influenced by the variables these two introduce. However, it is generally plotted in the proportion of the engine's speed, raised to a power of 2.8. This is purely an arbitrary figure as this index can vary between 2 and 3, i.e. square and cube law, but it is a reasonable approximation:

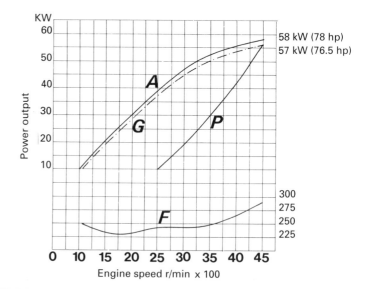

*Fig 6 Power and consumption curves for Perkins Prima M80T turbocharged marine diesel engine. Rating standard: BS Au 141A. Curve A = gross power output – engine without transmission. Curve G = net shaft power output with Hurth 250/3R 2.74:1 reduction gearbox. Curve P = propeller law shaft horsepower (2.8 index). Curve F = specific fuel consumption (prop law).*

$$\text{Propeller law power} = \frac{\text{Engine operating speed}}{\text{Engine governed speed}} \\ \times \text{SHP @ Engine governed} \\ \text{speed}$$

Note the reduction on the curve G, which shows power that is absorbed by the gearbox, usually in the region of 3 to 5% depending on its design.

Often a torque curve will be included. Torque is turning power, and a good engine for pleasure boat applications will usually have a nice flat curve showing that it produces even torque throughout its power range. If this curve is included, compare the point of maximum torque with the minimum point of the fuel consumption curve and note at what revolutions the engine is best used.

# 2 The inside and outside of an engine – recognising the parts

Helen might have had beauty that launched a thousand ships, but *you* have the eyes that might save a thousand pounds. The first stage of becoming a mechanic is simply to recognise the various parts of an engine that can be seen on the outside. The second stage is to know about some on the inside that can be reached easily and need only occasional attention. I am not talking about a total engine strip down, which usually requires expert knowledge as well as many specialised tools, the cost of which cannot be justified for work on a single engine.

## The outside of an engine

You cannot harm an engine by merely looking. Become accustomed to looking at your own engine in conjunction with the pictures usually found in the engine maker's *Owner's Handbook*. This is the start of gaining the basic knowledge and confidence that later will allow you to tackle jobs properly. When on another boat, or at a boat show, try to develop this recognition skill.

You will soon begin to notice that all engines, both petrol and diesel, are constructed from units which look remarkably alike and carry out similar if not identical functions. In fact some components on different makes of engine look alike simply because they are alike. These include spark plugs, fuel pumps and air cleaners – but there are usually important differences when it comes to their specification. Part numbers, often stamped on the component, are vital when determining the exact replacement model or parts needed for repairs.

For example, oil filters will vary in size from engine to engine. They do the same job, but the right replacement model must be purchased. Similarly starter motors, generators, cooling water pressure caps and many small items have common sources or are instantly recognisable for the job they do. We will discuss their function in detail later but, for the moment, let us study some illustrations and develop a mechanic's vocabulary.

Figs 7 and 8 are two views of a Ford 2720 Range 6-cylinder in-line intercooled marine diesel engine. Although this is a diesel engine, many similar parts, i.e. dipsticks, alternators, starter motor etc – marked (P) – are just as common to many four-stroke petrol engines. Each is discussed in greater depth later in the book.

## Exploded drawing of the Perkins Prima diesel engine (Fig 9)

*The crankcase.* This is generally the largest casting and houses the crankshaft and bearings which take the thrust imparted to them via the connecting rods and pistons. Usually it is of cast iron, but is sometimes of a light alloy. The casting process demands that vents, called core plug holes, are left in the casting. The design objective is to make the crankcase as stiff and as quiet as possible.

When a base engine is developed from the initial design stage as a marine engine, acoustic engineering analysis can be used to determine the best form of the crankcase and all the other 'bolt on' components to reduce engine noise. Rigidity under all normal running conditions is also developed to enhance bearing and crankshaft wear as

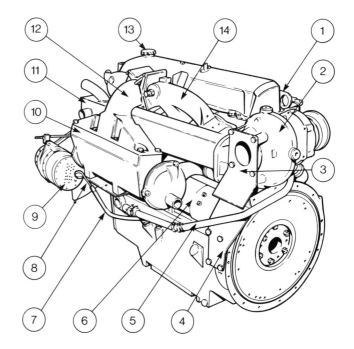

*Fig 7  Ford 2720 Based 6-cylinder intercooled engine. Port side view without gearbox.*

KEY

1. Lifting bracket (P).
2. Turbocharger.
3. Turbocharger support plate.
4. Turbocharger mounting bracket.
5. Turbocharger oil drain pipe.
6. Starter motor (P).
7. Oil dipstick tube (P).
8. Dipstick (P).
9. Alternator (P).
10. Intercooler for charge air.
11. Exhaust manifold (P).
12. Inlet manifold adapter.
13. Oil filler orifice and cap (P).
14. Inlet manifold (P).

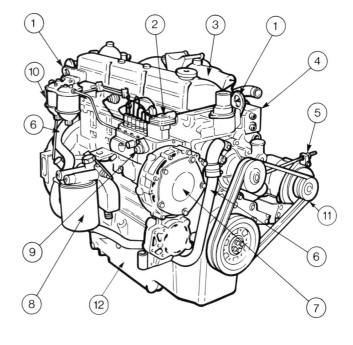

*Fig 8  Ford 2720 Based 6-cylinder intercooled engine. Starboard side view.*

KEY

1. Lifting bracket (P).
2. Boost control on end of in-line injection pump.
3. Air inlet manifold.
4. Water-cooled exhaust manifold (P).
5. Alternator drive belt adjuster (P).
6. Split flow water tube.
7. Injection pump timing aperture cover.
8. Oil filter (P).
9. Injection pump automatic excess fuel solenoid.
10. Fuel filter.
11. Water pump/generator drive belt and pulleys (P).
12. Engine sump (P).

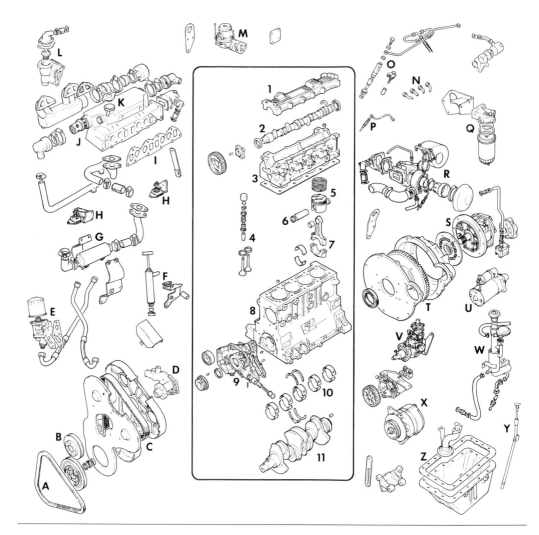

*Fig 9 Perkins Prima Marine T80 engine – exploded view showing main parts.*

A)  Rubber drive belt for alternator and water pump.
B)  Drive pulleys, top one for fresh water pump.
C)  Rubber drive belt for overhead camshaft.
D)  Fresh water cooling circulating pump.
E)  Canister oil filter.
F)  Sump oil emptying pump.
G)  Oil cooler (heat exchanger).
H)  Flexible engine mounting and brackets.
I)  Manifold gasket.
J)  Heat exchanger tube stack (fresh to raw water) in header

K)  tank.
    Header tank with fresh water
L)  filler and pressure cap.
M)  Thermostat and housing.
    Diaphragm fuel lift pump and isolating gasket.
N)  High pressure fuel pipes (not shown in full).
O)  Diesel injector and low pressure return fuel pipes.
P)  Heater plug for cold starting.
Q)  Fuel filter and mounting bracket.
R)  Turbocharger and inlet air filter.
S)  Gearbox.
T)  Flywheel with starter gear ring.
U)  Starter motor with solenoid on top.
V)  Injection pump.

W)  Oil filler assembly.
X)  Alternator.
Y)  Oil dipstick.
Z)  Oil sump and gasket.

*Outlined section of drawing*
 1.  Camshaft or rocker cover.
 2.  Camshaft.
 3.  Cylinder head with gasket below.
 4.  Exhaust and inlet valves.
 5.  Piston and piston rings.
 6.  Gudgeon pin.
 7.  Connecting rod – little end at top, big end at bottom.
 8.  Cylinder block casting.
 9.  Lubricating oil pump and pressure relief valve.
10.  Main crankshaft bearings.
11.  Crankshaft.

even an apparently rigid casting is not as perfectly rigid as one might think.

In the past, engineers produced over-heavy castings just to ensure that the crankcase was rigid and had sufficient metal to give many years of life even with the severest sea water corrosion taking place in the cooling water passageways. An excellent concept, but it added enormous weight. The Russell Newbury (Fig 10), still being manufactured, has about 55 lb weight for each horsepower it produces. Weight certainly does not matter in this type of engine which is designed for use in heavy displacement craft and, more particularly, traditional narrow boats.

This method of design is now anathema to the designer of a motor vehicle engine where a high power to weight ratio for quick acceleration is vital. Thus we find that the Perkins Prima weighs only about 9.6 lb per horse power. Fortunately, the high power to weight ratio of the modern engine fits very well into the modern boating scene which is dominated by fast planing craft. They need the high power and minimum weight to achieve and maintain the plane.

*The core plug* is produced as a necessary part of the crankcase casting process and the hole left in the crankcase is filled with a core plug disc to make the cooling water passages in the casting watertight. Today the plug disc is usually made from stainless steel, which withstands corrosion. In older engines it was often simply a mild steel disc. This

Fig 10 The Russell Newbury DM3. With a power/weight ratio of 55 lb for each of the 36 hp, the DM3, a slow running diesel managing 1,500 r/min, is a classic design that in the correct application such as a narrow boat could run for ever and perhaps a day. Note the convenience of hand starting, a side opening to the crankcase for easy access and the two-way oil pump for draining engine and gearbox. The drain cock, like the injection pump, is visible and placed very conveniently for servicing. The gear shift handle is now replaced by a cable-operated remote system.

may weep rust around its edges, but eventually it will corrode through and need replacing as in Fig 11. Sadly, engine makers seldom give easy access to the core plug, which gets hidden behind the bolt-on hardware round the crankcase or is even totally inaccessible within the bell housing where the gearbox is bolted.

*Drain cocks* are needed to drain down cooling water contained in the engine block. There are usually several on an engine and they may be found in the crankcase casting or on heat exchangers. Although they are usually made of brass, which withstands corrosion well, the small bore in the drain does get blocked with corrosion debris. When an engine is drained down for the winter the hole should be cleaned out as the water flows, then dried and sprayed with corrosion inhibiter both inside and outside the cock.

*The sump* is usually made of pressed steel, but it may be of a light alloy to save weight. It should not be allowed to live in bilge water, especially if made of light alloy, as this will seriously corrode the outside. Keep it dry on the outside and wiped down to remove oil drips.

The amateur will seldom need to get inside it for access to the main oil pump which is usually housed there. The sump may accumulate oil sludge which is deposited over a period of time, especially if a neglectful owner has left filthy oil in

it over winter. If this has happened, special proprietary flushing oils should be used to remove and then maintain the sump in reasonable condition. If an engine is new, just ensure that every last drop of dirty oil is pumped out and perhaps a flush given every four or five years. Although sump pumps allow easier emptying, if the sump plug can be removed without difficulty and the engine oil safely caught this will allow more of the dirty oil to drain out. The ability to drain the sump is related to the angle of installation and, when ashore, the resting angle of the hull.

While we all dread the thought of a sump plug falling out and subsequently losing the oil, it should not be over tightened. The plugs are usually of steel or brass and the latter can soon either strip its own thread or the thread it is being inserted into. Light alloy threads are vulnerable especially if the mechanic is over enthusiastic with a long handled spanner. Check that any fibre sealing washers on the engine or gearbox sump plugs are replaced.

*Pulleys and rubber drive belts* are needed to transmit some power from the crankshaft to drive various engine ancillaries. These usually include the electrical generator (alternator or dynamo) and a fresh-water circulating pump on a fresh-water (indirect) cooled engine. The nuts securing the pulleys should be checked for tightness and the rubber drive belt must be kept under just enough tension to drive easily without slip. If it is too tight it

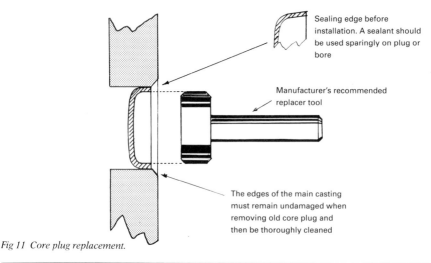

Sealing edge before installation. A sealant should be used sparingly on plug or bore

Manufacturer's recommended replacer tool

The edges of the main casting must remain undamaged when removing old core plug and then be thoroughly cleaned

*Fig 11 Core plug replacement.*

puts unnecessary strain on the bearings of the units being driven. If the thumb can depress the drive belt ½ in (12 mm) midway on its longest run, this will provide adequate tension for an alternator although the exact figure is usually given in the owner's manual. The generator mounting system is usually designed so that the securing nuts and bolts allow it to move through an arc which allows the belt adjustment to be made.

*The air cleaner.* Even though the air is generally cleaner in our environment than the land, particles of dust will have an abrasive effect and cause wear in certain components such as the piston rings and cylinders. My beagle used to shed enough hair at moulting time to provide a winter blanket for the engine, and some was always caught in the boat's air filter. The filters may be one of two basic types – oiled mesh or paper filter element. They are positioned just before the carburettor on a petrol engine and on the air inlet of either the manifold on a normally aspirated diesel or the turbocharger on a turbocharged engine. (See Fig 12.)

*Breathers.* When oil is being pumped round parts in an engine or gearbox, it can create increased pressure in the air contained within the space. Although the oil pressure is vital, the air pressure is not. Thus breathers are sometimes incorporated to equalise the air pressure inside with that outside. A typical case is the breather that connects a rocker box to the air cleaner. This not only equalises pressure, but also allows the engine to ingest its own oil fumes. A gearbox breather must allow the air to flow, but neither let the oil in the box out nor dirt in. Breathers and any linking pipes should be kept clean – if they become blocked they allow pressure to develop, which might force oil to be ejected where it is not wanted. Some breather pipes incorporate a helical wire spring to prevent crushing or kinks. Ensure that this has not been accidentally deformed.

*The exhaust manifold.* This is a complex casting with cooling water passages incorporated into it. The cooling water and exhaust gases are kept apart by metal and usually some end gaskets, but at such

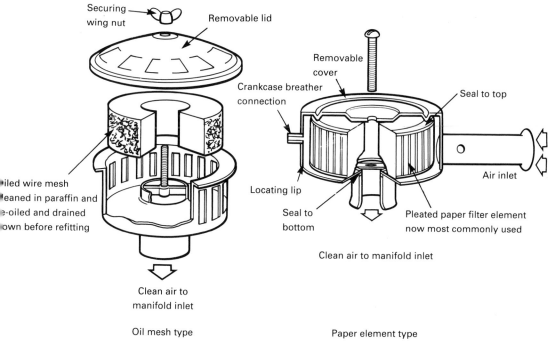

Fig 12 Air cleaners – paper and oil mesh types.

highly elevated temperatures corrosion is rife. The service life is usually good as plenty of thickness is cast into a manifold, but corrosion must be expected and looked for during maintenance. Fractures caused by frost damage or corrosion can allow water into the cylinders.

*The dipstick* allows a visual check on the engine oil and sometimes the gearbox oil. Check daily. (Some older types of diesel injection pump have a small dipstick as they are lubricated separately from the engine.) Usually there are two marks on the stick, the top one being for maximum level and the lower for minimum. These marks are calibrated to give a correct reading at any installation angle up to the maximum specified by the engine manufacturer. Some dipsticks indicate only one level up to which the oil should just reach. Overfilling can damage lubrication systems causing overheating, and sometimes too high pressure. This can damage oil seals.

## Unseen parts

Inside the engine – out of sight – are the most interesting working parts, and some need to be understood as they require attention from time to time. Understanding more about the inside of the engine should allow a buyer to appreciate what he is spending his money on as well as being able to recognise some of the parts which, when they wear, corrode or generally 'go wrong', will need serious mechanical attention.

*The rocker cover or cam cover* is to keep dirt and fingers away from the rocker gear or camshaft and the oil that lubricates it. The pressed steel cover usually has an oil filler hole in it and a screw cap. It may have a breather pipe stub where the breather pipe runs to the combustion air intake or air filter. This is to enable oil fumes to be ingested back into the engine rather than pollute the air in the engine space.

A couple of nuts secure it onto the cylinder head casting, but these must have some form of sealing

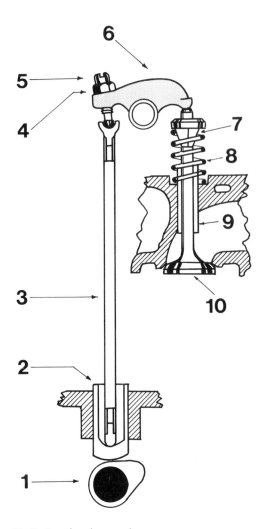

*Fig 13  A push-rod operated overhead valve mechanism.*

KEY
1. Camshaft lobe.
2. Cam follower. Both 1 and 2 can become grooved or pitted and cause noise.
3. Push rod. Can become bent and cause noise.
4. Rocker adjustment locking nut.
5. Rocker adjustment screw.
6. Rocker.
7. Spring retaining collets.
8. Valve springs (only one shown for clarity).
9. Valve guide.
10. Valve.

washer under them. A gasket, usually made of cork, is used between the cover and the head castings. As cork ages it can allow leakage of oil down the casting. The rear end is vulnerable when the engine is installed at an angle. A new gasket is fixed to the cover with a suitable cork-to-metal gasket adhesive. If there is a filthy black deposit on the inside of the rocker cover, it is worth checking that the oil used is up to its job.

## The valve mechanism (Fig 13) (for push-rod operated engines)

Under the rocker cover there are a mass of springs, inlet and exhaust valve shafts and a main rocker shaft on which the rockers run the length of the cylinder head casting. Each rocker has some means of adjusting the space that is left between the head of the valve stem and the underside end of the rocker or, on overhead camshafts, between the rocker and the cam lobe.

## VALVES

As the output of any internal combustion engine is directly related to the weight of air and fuel that it can burn in the cylinder, it stands to reason that the valves which admit the air (in the diesel) or fuel/air mixture (in the petrol engine) play a vital role in developing maximum power efficiently.

Normally, an owner will see little of a valve except its head, which has to have the space between it and the rocker adjusted. The poppet valve is now almost universally used and the majority of engines have just two valves per cylinder – one to let the air/fuel mixture into the cylinder in a petrol engine and air only in a diesel, while the other valve allows the exhaust gases to escape into the exhaust manifold.

They are subjected to absolute extremes of pressure and temperature and engineers give much thought to the design to give them a trouble-free service life. We are moving rapidly to a time when combustion efficiency to reduce environmental pollution is increasingly important, and increasing power to weight ratios are demanded which keep

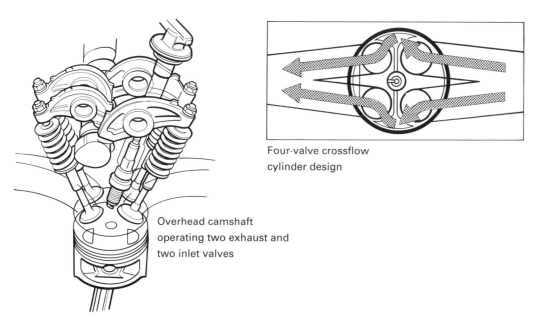

Four-valve crossflow cylinder design

Overhead camshaft operating two exhaust and two inlet valves

*Fig 14 Four-valve cylinder head operated by overhead camshaft and employing crossflow design.*

the physical size and weight of the engine small relative to the power produced. There is therefore a strong trend towards the use of four-valve cylinder heads (Fig 14) in the automotive industry. Undoubtedly, this trend will filter through to marine engines as automotive units are taken up for marinisation. Four-valve heads are certainly not new in marine engines and this trend is bound to be popular at the high-performance and racing end of the market.

The two-stroke diesel, as we saw on the GM Detroit engines, has the lower air ports uncovered by the piston so that the valves in its cylinder head simply exhaust the products of combustion. Thermal stress is greatly reduced when the combustion heat is shared between the valves and the whole of the cylinder head.

In small marine petrol two-stroke inboards (and outboards) there are no valves, both the inlet and exhaust use the piston to overrun the inlet and scavenge openings to effect the two functions. This makes for delightful simplicity but inadequate efficiency.

## THE EXHAUST VALVE/S

The exhaust valve always has a much harder life than the inlet valve as it opens when there is an extreme pressure gradient between the burnt gases in the cylinder and the exhaust manifold. The pressure is such that the gases can reach sonic velocities as they pass between the valve seat annulus and the valve itself. Theory is all very well but should highlight the need to keep the cylinder head cooling system in nothing less than first class condition. When overheating of the cylinder head occurs, distortion of the valve seating allows the high-temperature, high-pressure exhaust gases to blow by the valve and seat. This burns the valve head material – both valve seat and valve – which can permanently distort the cylinder head, making it impossible for the gasket to seal it to the block. This may allow cooling water into the cylinders.

## FOUR-VALVE HEAD DESIGN

If performance is the main criterion for an owner of a high-speed craft or racing craft then the four-valve high-performance engine is of obvious interest. However, for the majority of users, the lower cost and greater simplicity of the two-valve head must still be attractive. My caution is based on the fact that the design of a four-valve head, where two valves are used for inlet and the other two for exhaust gases, always pushes engineering further towards its limits. Cylinder head area is limited and must house twice the number of valves. The space or 'bridge' between each valve is cut down. In addition, either a spark plug or an injector must be housed in the same region. At the same time, sufficient machining metal must be allowed in the head casting to take these components while creating sufficient voids in the area for essential cooling water to be in close contact with the hottest parts where it is in greatest demand. This must be done without weakening the surrounding structure, or creating thin metal walls that will corrode quickly.

Keeping thermal stress within bounds is a major part of the design engineer's work. The difference in heat levels in parts of the engine can be extreme – from the cold raw water entering some parts of the cooling system to several hundred degrees Celsius round the exhaust valves. The different rates of expansion (on heating) and contraction (on cooling) must be taken into account at the design stage to provide suitable service life. It is for this reason that care is taken to prevent an engine overheating. When this occurs, we are pushing the design far too close to, or even well over, the limits that were originally determined by the engineer.

In the cylinder head itself there are huge differences in temperature and temperature gradient between the inlet valves which receive some cooling from the incoming charge air and the much hotter exhaust valves. As previously observed, when the exhaust valves open, the high pressure ratio across them may allow a minute sonic boom to take place in the annulus between the valve head and the seat. The temperature in the radius behind the valve head may be in the order of 800°C. Special metals for both seat and valve are used to cope with these extreme temperatures, but if valve seat distortion occurs and the valve no longer seats perfectly the blow by of the exhaust gases will burn the valve head material. In high-performance engines which are designed to cope with these problems the cooling system must still be nothing less than 100% efficient.

As with all engineering, there is a compromise to be made in every design but, as long as this is understood and appreciated, the excellent performance produced by the extra sophistication and cost of four-valve heads is surely justified.

## VALVE GRINDING

When engineers talk about regrinding the valves this is because over a period of time, despite the best metals being used along with special valve seat hardening processes, they get worn and burnt and fail to seal properly. Normally regrinding and refacing can refurbish a worn valve, but if the valve stem has become worn or the valve head warped so that regrinding produces a knife edge, then replacement becomes necessary. Knife edges may lead to breakage or create a hot spot that produces detonation – serious problems to be avoided.

The gradual conversion of petrol engines to run on lead-free fuels has posed particular problems where valves are concerned. This is because the lead produced compounds which act as a lubricant on the surface of the exhaust valve. Without the correct hardening treatment of valve seatings, the use of lead-free fuel could lead to serious valve problems. With new engines designed to run on lead-free fuels, this treatment is already given and the timing is retarded to match the octane rating of the lead-free fuels presently available. A few older engines may be able to have new valve seat inserts or even new cylinder heads but this is usually uneconomic. In the changeover period when both leaded and lead-free fuels are available, it is best for the individual to approach the manufacturer to check whether modifications are available.

On normally aspirated diesel engines the valve seats are usually at 45 degrees, but on turbo-charged diesels designers tend to favour 30 degrees, which provides a larger seating area and makes them better able to cope with higher seat loadings. This is because the turbocharged engine usually has a higher cylinder pressure and inferior valve guide lubrication. In a normally aspirated engine the induction causes a depression which actually sucks some oil down the valve guide stem. In a turbocharged engine, the induction air from the turbocharger is above atmospheric pressure, therefore less oil reaches the guide and stem. For these reasons, it is often found that normally aspirated engines need an oil control seal on the spring side of the valve while a turbocharged engine may manage without one.

## VALVE AND CYLINDER HEAD PROBLEMS

Horror stories about valves dropping into the cylinder and emerging from the side of the crankcase are true, but thankfully, this situation usually only occurs on racing engines which manage to lose the collet that retains the valve – perhaps when a valve spring breaks.

In old engines the springs may weaken. During a major rebuild they should be tested and if found to be weaker than the original specification they should be replaced. Another common problem occurring in old engines is worn valve guides and seals, which allow oil to enter the cylinder and increase oil consumption. Cylinder head reconditioning is a factory job and certainly nothing the average yachtsman needs to worry about unless he has a vintage engine to care for. One can usually find a local engineering firm which specialises in head reconditioning, and all the owner has to do is take the complete head to them.

As mentioned earlier, cylinder heads may warp from a true flat underside surface, making it impossible for the gasket to provide the high pressure seal needed. The head can usually be *skimmed* by a professional engineering company to reinstate the surface. Skimming is also a means used by some racing mechanics to increase the compression ratio. Care is needed when this is not required on an ordinary service engine. When a head has been skimmed it is not unknown for an extra-thick gasket to be used to restore the normal compression ratio and the correct clearance between the piston top and the valve.

## Rockers

Rockers are driven in one of two ways. In some designs (Fig 15) a camshaft low down in the main engine casting drives push rods which pass through the cylinder head casting to move one end of the rocker while the other end actuates the top of the valve stem. The springs return the rocker as well as pulling back the valve to close it properly in the cylinder head.

An alternative design is to have a single or twin overhead camshaft (OHC) to actuate the rockers. This is much favoured on high-performance engines where twin camshafts are used for the inlet and exhaust valves – these are directly descended from high-speed racing engines. The overhead camshaft saves very considerably on reciprocating weight and the number of parts needed. Smaller numbers of parts usually mean greater reliability, less weight and less reciprocating mass. Reciprocating masses such as the piston, tappets and push rods are a fact of life but a perfect engine could well do without them. Considerable

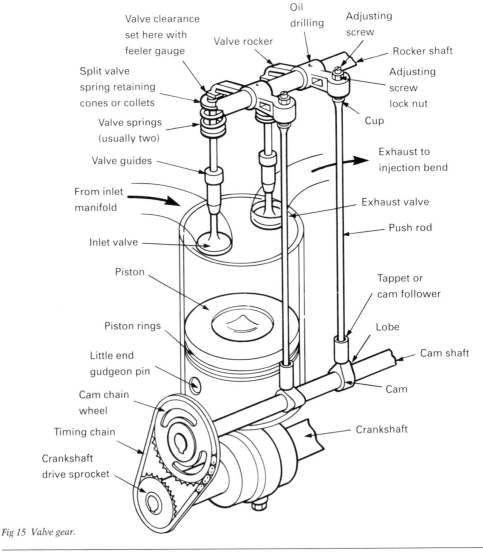

*Fig 15 Valve gear.*

energy is used in simply stopping a mass like a piston, connecting rod or push rod from moving in one direction and accelerating it in the other.

*Push rods* may take either tubular form with end inserts, or solid rods. The lower end that fits into the tappet or cam follower is ball shaped and at the top there is a ball shaped socket which fits the ball under one end of the rocker. It is possible for a push rod to be bent if a valve jams but this is fairly uncommon. Oil additives are much improved these days, but odd 'clicks' in the valve train should be dealt with before possible damage ensues.

## ROCKER/VALVE CLEARANCE

On either diesel or petrol engines, rocker clearance must be well maintained so that the valves are opened and closed correctly. Excessive clearance will not damage the engine – just the owner's nerves because of noise and lost performance. Too little clearance may not be noticed until the valves fail to close, first losing compression and power. We have already seen the damage caused if the exhaust valve is not closing properly.

Although amateur mechanics talk about setting or adjusting tappets, the tappets are normally never touched except in the circumstances outlined in the next section. Tappets transfer the movement from the camshaft to the pushrods, which then actuate the rockers. What is necessary is to adjust the clearance between the rocker and the valve. This clearance is necessary to compensate for linear expansion that is progressive throughout the engine's operating temperature range.

A few engines have hydraulic tappets which are self-adjusting and which require no work at all except during a major overhaul. The majority of both petrol and diesel engines have to have rocker clearance settings made at regular intervals and it is always necessary when a top overhaul of the cylinder head has taken place. Clearances should be checked each season and adjusted as necessary.

It is important to know when the rocker clearance should be set. Some engines, particularly petrol engines, demand that this is done when they are hot at normal working temperature, while diesels are set when they are cold. However, only the manual will confirm which method should be used as some engine manufacturers specify a sequence adjustment: once when the engine is cold, and a final one when it is hot.

The ambient air temperature has some effect on adjustment and, wherever possible, it should not be carried out in extremes of heat or cold. An engine that has to be adjusted when hot soon cools down in icy weather and vice versa.

## ROCKER ADJUSTMENT ARRANGEMENTS

Engineering to adjust the rockers varies between different engine makes and models. Some systems have an adjustable nut and lock nut on the top end of the push rod. BMW 6-cylinder petrol engines use an adjustable cam on the end of a forked rocker. With OHC systems there are again a variety of designs, each requiring a different method of adjustment. Specific details usually appear in the owner's handbook.

The most common arrangement for push-rod operated rockers is as shown in Fig 16, where the adjusting screw and locking nut is on the rocker itself. A small spanner to hold the lock nut, a screwdriver and feeler gauge are all that are needed to do the adjustment. The feeler should be a tight sliding fit – not so loose that it drops out of the gap and not so tight that the blades are bent when inserting it. If the screwdriver fits tightly in the head slot this helps prevent movement as the locking nut is tightened. As we only have two hands, when using these three tools care is needed to achieve the exact gapping. A more modern method is to use the specialised tool detailed in Chapter 10.

## PREPARING AND ADJUSTING VALVE CLEARANCE

Adjustment is easier if the cylinders are not under compression. On a petrol engine simply remove the spark plugs. On a few diesel engines which use hand starting the decompression levers can be lifted and the engine turned over by hand. Most modern engines do not have these, but if the adjustment can be carried out when the engine is cold the heater plugs (if fitted) or the nuts that hold the injectors in place can be slackened to relieve compression. Before you attempt to undo either of these be certain that no dirt can fall into the space between the main casting and the face of the unit you are slackening as this will prevent even tightening down when the procedure is finished. The alternative is to either turn the engine over on the starter or with a long arm spanner on the main front end crankshaft nut. Make certain the engine cannot fire up when using either procedure.

Before adjusting, each rocker must be fully off the cam or clear of the push rod cup so that it will rock to its maximum movement. Each rocker will achieve this position in sequence. On an in-line four-cylinder engine the number to be remembered is *nine*. If the front end furthest from the gearbox has No 1 cylinder, turn the engine in its normal rotational direction until No 1 valve is fully depressed by the rocker. Now adjust No 8 valve (1 + 8 = 9, the magic figure!). Continue No 2 valve depressed – adjust No 7; No 3 valve depressed –

adjust No 6; No 4 valve depressed – adjust No 5; No 5 valve depressed – adjust No 4, and so on.

With a six-cylinder in-line engine the magic number to apply is 13. When No 1 valve is fully depressed adjust No 12 and so on. Some ancient side-valve engines have no adjustment and a simple job such as I have just described becomes a major overhaul when the cylinder head has to be removed to extract the valve so that stem-ends and seats can be ground off or replaced as necessary.

*Cylinder head gaskets* affect the rocker/valve clearance. Before proceeding it is worthwhile checking that the cylinder head nuts are correctly tightened. This can only be done if you have a proper torque wrench in the tool kit, the manufacturer's torque figures and the sequence for tightening. On a new engine it is common to find that after a period of time – fifty hours or so – the cylinder head should be tightened down onto its gasket as well as the rocker clearance adjusted. Nuts must be tightened in a precise sequence as described in the manual. This is to ensure that the head is kept perfectly flat in relation to the main engine casting, and that the

*Fig 16 Adjusting overhead valve rockers. The feeler gauge should be a nice sliding fit. A ring spanner is best for tightening down the locking unit while the screwdriver has to be held so that the gap is not disturbed.*

firing stresses imposed by each cylinder, and the thermal loadings produced, are evenly spread over all the fastenings.

Some modern engines made by Volvo Penta have managed to eliminate a cylinder head gasket by precision machining of a lip and recess that makes a perfect seal without any fear of 'blowing', as occasionally happens with conventional gaskets.

Considering that gaskets work in the region of the highest cylinder pressures and temperatures, have water passing through them and are expected to keep a perfect seal as the engine expands and contracts it is hardly surprising that they occasionally fail. As already mentioned, rough running or a severe hydraulic lock may mean that the gasket has blown and water has entered the cylinder. Before taking the cylinder head off, check the previously mentioned sources of possible ingress. It is worth mentioning that if an oil cooler is employed on an engine the seal between the cooling water and oil can fail, which may account for some water being present, although most is likely to accumulate in the sump. Water in the cylinder is always a serious problem that must be dealt with immediately.

## VALVE TRAIN NOISES

During normal running there is an even noise from each of the valve trains – often referred to as 'tappet noise'. This is quite normal as there must be some working clearance between the tappet, push rod or cam and the rocker. However, you should listen for any extra noise that persists when the rocker clearance has been properly adjusted. This may be due to a number of faults, which should be investigated before they cause mechanical damage.

A weak or broken valve spring can put sufficient strain on the remaining one to break it and allow the valve to drop into the cylinder – with disastrous results. If a spring is suspect, with the engine still, use the wooden end of a hammer and push down on the valve head, trying to turn the valve with your fingers at the same time. Repeat on another valve and note any major difference.

If the springs are alright, on push-rod operated

trains start the engine and keep it ticking over. Use the hammer end to hold each rocker hard down in turn to isolate the faulty one. The unwanted noise should change or be eliminated altogether when the faulty rocker is located. Now look at the push rod area that is operating the rocker. A bent push rod will often oscillate and must be replaced.

Cams and tappets can become pitted and the extra 'clicks' may be irregular. The irregularity is caused as the push rod or tappet comes down in a different position on the cam, sometimes clicking, sometimes not. The removal of tappets can be a major job, necessitating the removal of the cylinder head, and even more complex if the camshaft needs renewal. The job is much easier with an overhead cam engine where pitting can be inspected more easily. Finally, that bothersome noise might be due to a sticking valve or damaged rocker on either the underside surface that contacts the push rod or on the valve top. With the engine ticking over, insert the feeler gauge to 'fill' the gap. If it is a valve that is sticking, the noise should disappear. If it is the surface of the rocker, you may have a wrecked feeler gauge with indentations in it! As the tool can be replaced less expensively than the engine, this is no great loss as you will need to renew the rocker, and it may well be that the whole set needs replacing at the same time. Only careful inspection can rule this out.

## Combustion chamber design

Both types of engine require fuel to be burnt economically and efficiently to cause minimum pollution from the exhaust gases.

The combustion chamber design for diesel engines can be divided into two main types:
1. *Direct injection* (Fig 17), where the fuel is injected directly into the chamber formed between the top of the piston and the cylinder head. Since complete mixing of the injected fuel and air must be completed in microseconds, some form of air swirl is needed. The air inlet port may be shaped to give the air swirl as it enters the chamber, but more

commonly the piston crown is cast in a scooped shape, which imparts swirl to the incoming air and fuel mist from the injectors.

2. *Indirect injection* designs (Fig 17) use a pre-chamber outside the cylinder head where the mixing and initial part of the combustion cycle takes place. As air under compression passes through the throat between the cylinder and pre-chamber, towards the top dead centre a high degree of motion is imparted to it, which is ideal for producing a rapid mixing with the injected fuel. The igniting and expanding gases then enter the cylinder head to complete the combustion process.

The advantage of the indirect system is that on small engines it is able to cope with a very wide speed range, is not quite so fussy about fuel quality, and has low exhaust emissions. Its main disadvantages are that the large wall area of the pre-chamber allows excessive cooling of the compressed air, making it necessary to employ heater plugs of one type of another to make starting easier. Fuel con-

sumption tends to be fractionally higher, but in boating this is not a factor that will really affect the smaller power range associated with engines using this system.

Larger engines and an increasing number of modern small units use direct injection. This system generally offers better fuel economy and less heat loss to cylinder head metal. It is less costly to manufacture and the modern injection equipment allows a greater speed range to be achieved. However, there is no 'best' system as the combustion chamber is only one of many design features that go into a marine engine.

## Cylinder liners

The cheapest way to produce a cylinder for the piston to run in is to machine the bore directly into the

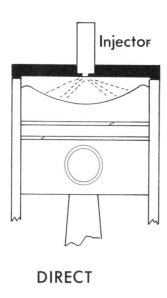

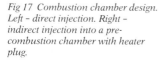

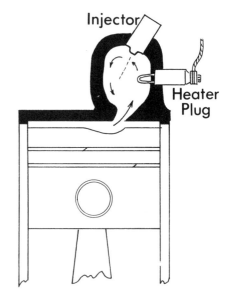

*Fig 17 Combustion chamber design. Left – direct injection. Right – indirect injection into a pre-combustion chamber with heater plug.*

engine block casting. This practice is successful with small power units. However, the majority of engines have the bores formed by liners which are fitted into the engine block. These may be one of two types :

*Wet liners* are pressed into the engine block and must have some form of seal at the top and bottom to seal the bore against coolant entry and firing pressures. One drawback that they have is that because their outer surface comes directly into contact with cooling water, they must be made thicker to withstand the corrosion that inevitably takes place. The early Perkins 4.107 marine diesel which had wet liners sometimes suffered cavitation erosion where the cylinder wall was eaten away, allowing coolant to flood into the cylinder. Cavitation erosion of the cylinder walls is caused when the liner vibrates in response to combustion shock or piston impact. The coolant responds to this in much the same way when the pressure over a propeller blade produces cavitation corrosion on the surface of the propeller. Modern engines tend to have closer fitting pistons and thicker liner walls with their outer surface made corrosion resistant by either chrome plating or ceramic spray. The use of inhibitors in the cooling system can also help but the wet liner is not, in my opinion, the best choice for any raw-water cooled engine.

*Dry liners*, as their name suggests, are forced into the cylinder block by an hydraulic ram and do not come into contact with the coolant. The engineering is more difficult since the outer circumference of the liner is in complete metal-to-metal contact with the block. The liner usually has thinner walls so that good heat transfer can take place and the bore may have to be refinished as some distortion may occur during 'interference fit' insertion. Some modern engines actually use an epoxy resin to glue the push fit bore into place. With this method, there is less chance of distorting the bore and machining time can be saved. The dry liner engine is generally much more rigid than a wet liner engine and this can make a contribution to longer service life of the reciprocating parts of the engine.

## The turbocharger

The turbocharger (Fig 18) utilises waste heat from the exhaust gases to drive a rotor on a common shaft, with a compressor at the opposite end. The idea is to increase the mass of air entering the cylinders by raising the air density. If more fuel is then injected into the air in the cylinders, increased power will result. The power increase can be quite phenomenal: the Perkins T6.3544 (Fig 19), for example, in its normally aspirated form produces 120 hp while its extreme turbocharged version can produce 250 hp – a 108% increase. Increases of as much as 450% occur when Sabre increases the 120 hp from the normally aspirated Ford base engine to 550 hp in their Sabre Marathon racing diesel, which produces this power at 2400 r/min.

In racing engines, the increase in work done per cycle has, as always, to be paid for. The increased brake mean effective pressures (BMEP) result in much stronger engines being needed to sustain a reasonable service life. Mechanical loads (piston, crankshaft, connecting rod and bearings) and thermal loading (cylinder head and valves) are increased and something has to be done to keep these within bounds. On racing diesel engines the compression ratio is lowered, the Sabre Marathon (Fig 20) runs on a meagre 10.5:1 compression ratio. This is quite a drop when you consider that most diesels run on a compression ratio of 15:1 upwards to 20:1.

Reduction in the compression ratio makes starting poor and devices have to be employed to make it possible for the engine to start at all. Sabre use the Start Pilot system referred to in Chapter 5. The Marathon also uses two-stage turbocharging (Fig 21) with twin aftercooling units after each turbocharger. Using the two Holset turbochargers in series enables a pressure ratio of 5:1 to be achieved (manifold air pressure 60 pounds per square inch) which is considerably higher than a normal turbocharge pressure ratio of about 2.3:1.

In the early days turbochargers were hopefully matched to engines strong enough to take them. Today engines are nearly always designed from the

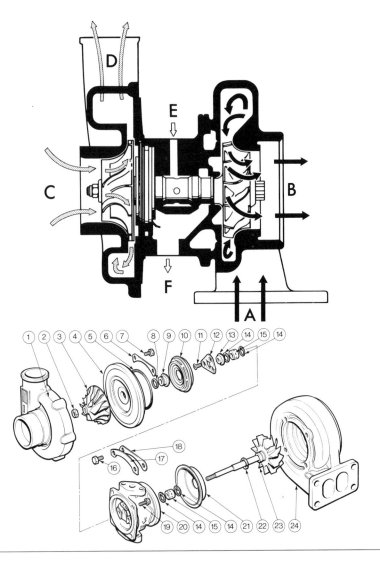

*Fig 18 Turbocharger – working principle and parts. The Holset turbocharger used on the Ford 2720 Series engines.*

**KEY**

*Top*

A) Hot exhaust gases from the manifold drive the turbine.

B) The exhaust gases then exhaust through the exhaust pipe/ silencer being cooled by a raw water injection bend fitted after the outlet.

C) Air from the air cleaner is fed into the compressor.

D) The compressed air is fed through the air inlet manifold to the cylinders where it can burn an increased amount of fuel compared to a normally aspirated engine.

E) Lubricating oil inlet from engine's pressurised oil supply.

F) Lubricating oil return to engine sump.

*Lower drawing*

1. Compressor-housing.
2. Locknut.
3. Compressor impeller.
4. Compressor diffuser.
5. 'SQ' ring seal.
6. Clamping plate.
7. Hex head screw and washer.
8. Seal (split ring).
9. Oil slinger.
10. Oil baffle.
11. Flat head cap screw.
12. Thrust bearing.
13. Thrust collar.
14. Circlip.
15. Bearing.
16. Hex head screw.
17. Lockplate.
18. Clamping plate.
19. Hex head set screw and washer.
20. Bearing housing.
21. Heat shield.
22. Seal (split ring).
23. Shaft and turbine wheel.
24. Turbine housing.

start as sufficiently strong base units which can be developed for both normally aspirated or turbocharged power units. This means that the normally aspirated engine may cost a little more than necessary, but this might well pay off in an extended service life.

The high power-to-weight ratio of the modern turbocharged engine has made it an ideal choice for the planing boat. What concerns me is that it is not always the ideal choice for every boating application. I would stress the need for an owner to match the power needs of his boat to engines best suited to fulfil them. Thus, the turbocharger is very carefully matched to the characteristics of a particular engine. At low speed, when the rotor is turning only relatively slowly, no boost is given at all. In fact, traces of smoke in the exhaust gas are often

seen as partially burnt fuel is ejected and wasted. If this engine is used on a sailing boat or slow boat that simply potters on or off a mooring, or is used for much of its life at low speed for fishing, the turbocharger does no work at all. It simply soots up and becomes an expensive liability. There is always a temptation for an owner to be beguiled into buying a turbocharged engine since, power for power, the normally aspirated unit is very much bigger and heavier than a turbocharged one. This may mean an extra inch or two in living accommodation space but unless this is really vital and the engine will be made to work hard, as for example in a hard driven motor sailer, the temptation should be resisted. It really is a matter of horses for courses.

*Fig 19 The Perkins T6.3544 (M) 6-cylinder turbocharged marine diesel engine.*

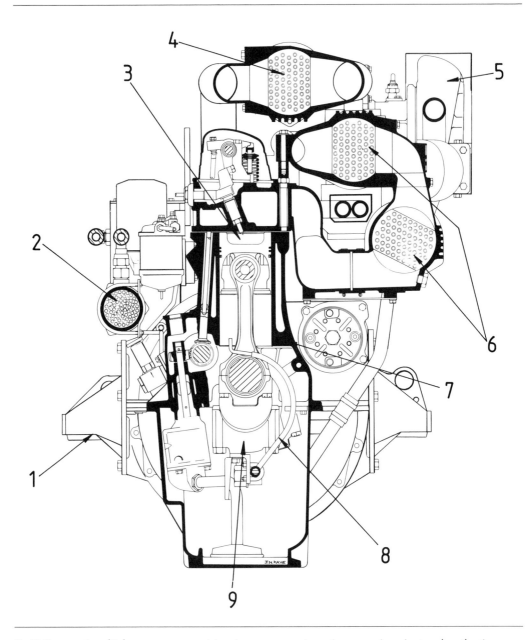

*Fig 20 Cross-section of Sabre Marathon diesel engine.*

KEY

1. Anti-shock mounts protect engine from damage in rough seas.
2. Oil cooler for engine oil, used both for lubrication and to remove heat from pistons.
3. Combustion chamber bowl in piston gives a compression ratio of only 10.5:1, in order to limit firing pressures.
4. Intercooler is used to reduce the air temperature after compression by the low pressure turbocharger.
5. Low pressure turbocharger compresses the intake air, which is then further compressed by the high pressure turbocharger.
6. Aftercooler uses two tubestacks in series to reduce the air temperature before it enters the engine.
7. Cylinder block has increased wall thickness to withstand high firing loads.
8. Piston cooling pipe delivers high pressure oil to nozzle, which sprays underside of piston crown.
9. Forged steel cap for main bearing resists high firing loads.

# TURBOCHARGER LUBRICATION

Lubrication is critical as turbochargers operate at anything between 90 000 and 140 000 r/min. It is usual for the bearings to be lubricated by oil supplied from the engine's main oil circuit. Since temperatures, particularly near the exhaust rotor bearing, are extreme, the oil must be able to withstand extreme oxidation conditions. Turbocharged engines usually have a special moderate or severe duty oil specification (American Petroleum Industry CC or CD classification upwards) to overcome this problem. As bearing clearances are kept to a minimum, the need for excellent oil filtration is important. Conventional labyrinth oil seals are used on the compressor and turbine ends of the shaft. If these fail, oil on the extremely hot exhaust end will result in an unhealthy outburst of smoke from the exhaust line. Provided the bearings are still intact, it is possible to motor home at very low speed.

To minimise the chance of this happening always ensure that bearings are treated with proper respect. Never start an engine with a turbocharger fitted unless you are certain that some new lubricating oil has reached the turbocharger bearings. It is easy to hold out the engine stop control and turn the engine over for fifteen seconds or so on the starter motor alone. This should enable oil to be pumped up into the turbocharger, although a good battery is essential for this. When stopping a turbocharged engine, always allow the engine to run for at least two minutes at low revolutions so that oil can cool the unit down and so reduce thermal shock.

Since the turbine and rotor are finely balanced units which rotate at high speeds, I would not recommend that the amateur mechanic do anything other than the simple maintenance prescribed in the owner's handbook. However, it is very important to keep the air filter clean. Restrictions in the air flow to the compressor induce pressure changes which may cause lubricating oil to be drawn in through the compressor oil seals. This often contributes to seal failure and will certainly cause extra fouling on the compressor blades, which will then need cleaning. Unless the owner's manual is specific about cleaning and advises on the approved cleaner for the job, it should be left to the professional.

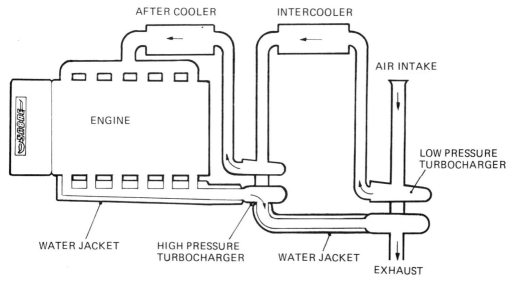

*Fig 21 Sabre Marathon two-stage turbocharger with twin aftercooling units.*

## INTERCOOLING THE CHARGE AIR

For the turbocharger designer, there are many difficult problems to overcome so that service life for both turbocharger and engine will be acceptable. The hotter the exhaust gases, the greater the power that can be extracted from them. This leads to a conflict since the density of the charge air decreases as it gets hotter: the very opposite of what is wanted if a greater weight of fuel is to be burnt to increase the power output. Excess heat must be contained so that the turbocharger bearings and turbine blades survive properly.

As air is compressed, it becomes warmer. Its temperature may also be increased by a high engine room air temperature and from the engine itself as it passes through into the cylinders. It is up to the owner to ensure that the engine space is kept cool by providing a proper ventilation system, but if the highest power output is to be achieved some form of combustion air cooling is necessary. This air charge cooling is sometimes referred to as aftercooling, and sometimes as intercooling, as it comes 'after' the turbocharger or 'inter' (between) the turbocharger and the inlet valve – but they add up to the same thing.

Air is passed through a heat exchanger where the transfer plates extract the heat using cold water as the transfer medium. This is usually the cold water from the raw-water side of the engine and it does its work in the intercooler before moving on to the engine cooling system itself.

As well as enabling an engine to achieve increased power, charge cooling has other benefits. The manifold inlet temperature of the air is substantially reduced and this effect is carried right through the combustion cycle, reducing the thermal loading and giving an increase in thermal efficiency. The brake mean effective pressure rises without an increase in the frictional losses within the engine. The pressure rise is, however, kept within safe bounds.

# 3 Fuel and fuel systems

Over seventy years ago, when slow running heavy diesel engines were emerging from their first phase of development, experiments were conducted to see if they would run on almost any liquid fuel that came to hand – including distillate petroleum fuels and their residues, crude oil, vegetable oils and even tar oils. The engines did run, but the fuels themselves created problems especially when diesel engine speeds increased and there was a growing demand for greater reliability and long periods between overhaul.

As time went by the demands of the environmental lobby were added. In the 1950s and 1960s the smell and smoke of diesel began to be unacceptable, and both the petroleum industry and the manufacturers had to work hard to make both diesel and petrol engines environmentally acceptable – no bad thing if you have ever suffered on a long leg of a cruise with diesel smoke blowing into the cockpit for hours on end. The problem of producing better fuels for internal combustion engines was helped by a world abundance of crude oils that could be more highly refined into distillates suitable for diesel engines. The problem was not so easily solved with the petrol engine, and legislation was passed in some countries to limit unacceptable emissions. Only of late have we woken up to the fact that lead in petrol contributes to air pollution as well as being a serious health hazard.

In recent years, the world has moved into an uncertain stage where it is believed natural oil reserves are finite. New exploration technology is able to recover new reserves economically, and this is still tending to cloud the inevitable truth.

It is anticipated that decreasing supplies of crude oil will, over the coming years, tend to depress the quality of diesel fuel oils. To balance this and maintain environmental standards there will have to be continuing research and development of diesel engine combustion systems to counter the decline. Similarly, while the automotive industry has been finding the technology to reduce emissions from automotive engines both difficult and expensive, marine petrol engines have been relatively unaffected. However, since most inboard engines, in both diesel and petrol form, are derived from automotive units, we will certainly expect to benefit from that field of development. Hopefully, all marine engines will become both socially and environmentally acceptable.

## Diesel fuel

While doctors say we are what we eat, so mechanical combustion engines reflect in their service life what they consume in the way of fuel. The oil companies in collaboration with engine manufacturers determine what characteristics the distillate must have if the engine is to work at maximum efficiency and at the same time have an acceptable service life.

Characteristics that are considered essential in a quality fuel may be summarised as follows:

1. *Good low temperature operation and starting.* While most of us give up boating in the northern hemisphere winter, we are all too often aware of yet another cold winter day when public and road transport fails because the diesel fuel has waxed up and blocked the fuel system. The refiners can determine the waxing point (CFPP = cold filter

plugging point) which differs from country to country. At the time of writing, this is fixed at $-15°C$ in the UK.

For those insisting on winter boating there are two remedies available to prevent diesel fuel waxing. First there are a number of proprietary additives, such as 'Silkolene Lo-Freeze', available that can be added to diesel fuel in a prescribed quantity. For the small quantity of fuel a boat is likely to consume in frostbite motoring this is the least expensive method. The second method is to install a Lucas CAV D-WAX or Racor Thermocoil or Thermoline diesel fuel heater which raises the temperature of the fuel taken from the tank as it passes through them. They are totally automatic in operation once switched on, easy to install, and need no maintenance other than ensuring that the electric cables are in good condition.

In diesel fuels, the cetane number of the fuel is a measure of its ignition quality or tendency to ignite in the diesel combustion chamber. We will look more closely at this later, but a high cetane number and increased volatility reduce starting time and cold smoke emissions.

2. *Minimal wear.* Simple neglect and corrosion do far more to destroy a marine engine than the fuel used. The need to use only top grade fuel oil may be better understood if we know what destructive elements are found in even the best diesel fuel distillates.

Wear is a combination of corrosion and abrasion. The products of combustion include water vapour, carbon dioxide and sulphur oxides. There are presently strict limitations on the sulphur content of diesel fuel, but these standards may well deteriorate and will only be maintained if future environmental legislation pegs them to acceptable limits. In the meantime, condensation temperature (or dew point) varies with the gas in the cylinder and sulphur content of the fuel. When it is higher than the temperature of the cylinder walls, carbon dioxide and sulphur oxides will combine in a solution of corrosive acids which attacks any metal parts with which it comes into contact. Later, we will see how lubricating oils counteract this type of corrosion.

Abrasive wear is associated with the friction of moving parts, with taking aboard contaminated

fuel, poor fuel filtration, or the production of harmful carbon particles that destroy oil films in the combustion system before they can be filtered out. Abrasive matter can be carried into the engine from the air intake. Cleaning and maintaining air filters is essential.

3. *Minimal deposits.* Carbon is a natural product of the combustion process, and its safe removal is a function of the lubricating oil and filtration. However, deposits do occur and we should be aware of likely locations so that the maintenance schedule copes with them before breakdowns occur.

Poor injector maintenance may be the cause of nozzle deposits. This leads to poor atomisation of fuel, a poor burn in the cylinder, injection nozzle dribbling and, at worst, injection nozzle blockage.

As the engine ages and wear takes place, there is a greater tendency for combustion gases to blow by the piston rings. These increase ring wear and may well gum up the rings and stop them working efficiently.

Although they are not a major problem now, exhaust gases can still foul the turbocharger. At over $450°C$ there is a tendency for combustion products to build up rapidly on the turbine blades. To minimise this, turbochargers should be kept within their safe working temperatures. Sadly, few owners realise when they are actually overloading them as they do not have a pyrometric sensor in the exhaust line connected to an exhaust temperature gauge. Restrictions in the air supply caused by a clogged air filter will increase the temperature in the turbine and contribute to blade fouling.

Always ensure that the air filtration to the turbocharger is thoroughly clean with no extra obstructions in the connecting ducting. Turbocharger fouling may be aggravated by fuel contaminated with salt water, over lubrication in the cylinder produced by poorly fitting or severely worn piston rings, and badly adjusted injection equipment over fuelling the cylinders.

## Fuel quality for diesel and petrol (gasoline) engines

Most of us give little or no thought to the job when filling the fuel tanks so long as we get the right fuel in the tank. It is not unknown for yachtsmen to fill their tanks with the wrong fuel and this kind of contamination must be remedied immediately. While some may say that a small amount of petrol in a diesel tank can be tolerated, I would suggest that, as the safe limit cannot be accurately defined in a particular situation, it is best to empty the tank and refill correctly.

For both the engine designer and owner, fuel quality is very important as it will affect power output, starting characteristics and the service life of the engine.

### DIESEL FUEL

The British Standards Institution and the American Society for Testing and Materials have two important specifications relevant to marine diesel engines. BS 2869 Class A1 and ASTM D-975 1-D support a light distillate which is intended for automotive engines so marine engines derived from this type of base unit will also be suited to its use. BS 2869 Class A2 and ASTM 2-D are slightly heavier distillates commonly used by the truck industry. While the engine manufacturer specifies which fuel should be used in his engine, it is important for the owner to realise that the poorer grades of diesel fuel often have a high sulphur content. In this case, the lubricating oils used in the engine will normally have a higher alkaline content to neutralise the higher levels of sulphuric acid produced. Keep to the oil specification that matches the grade of fuel being used.

Engine manufacturers must keep an eye on these standards which vary from time to time as crude oil supplies, politics and the world's diminishing supply affect them. As owners there is little we can do except to try to obtain the best matched fuel we can for our engines. This presently is no problem in the West when cruising locally, but for

long distance cruising some countries do not conform to these standards and offer sub-standard fuels.

## Tests to determine standards of ignition quality

Both petrol and diesel engines are designed to use a specific quality of fuel which will burn correctly in the cylinder. To ensure consistency of the recommended fuel, the fuel companies determine the ignition quality by comparing the blend with a low and a high ignition quality reference fuel.

In the case of diesel fuels, the two fuels adopted for this reference standard are $n$-cetane which has low ignition quality, and $\alpha$-methylnapthylamine which has high ignition quality. If a fuel is matched to the ignition quality of a blend of say 50% $n$-cetane and 50% $\alpha$-methylnapthylamine then it is said to have a Cetane number of 50. Generally, diesel boat owners have no need to worry about cetane numbers since few if any alternative blends are available at the dock-side. In petrol engines, the ignition rating is more important.

In petrol engines, the low ignition quality reference fuel is heptane and the high one $iso$octane, hence when the blend is compared to these two an octane number is arrived at. In fact, there are two methods still used to determine the octane rating – the research method and the motor method; the latter produces a more severe result (a lower octane rating). Using the correct fuel is more important in a petrol engine since the wrong one may produce 'pinking' – an unwholesome noise from the combustion chamber caused by pressure waves set up by an extremely rapid rate of inflammation. It must not be confused with detonation, which is actually an explosion that, if allowed to persist even for a short time, can wreck a piston as well as damage other parts of the combustion space and bearings. If either of these conditions occurs, immediate action should be taken to determine if the correct fuel is being used, and to check mechanical aspects, especially the ignition timing. An over advanced spark causes the fuel to ignite far too early, before the piston reaches top dead centre. This means that for the last part of the stroke it is under extreme adverse pressure, imposing excessive loads on the connecting rod and main bearings.

## Leadless fuels

The USA has had legislation for a number of years to limit pollution by the use of lead-free fuels and although most of the world is now in a changeover period, some confusion is bound to exist. As mentioned in Chapter 2, it is important for the owner to approach either his dealer or engine manufacturer to determine which models have already been engineered to take the new fuels. In the changeover period, European distillers are having to provide both normal leaded fuels and lead-free ones. Economics dictate that as the leaded varieties need to be offered in a full range of octane values, the unleaded ones must for the time being be limited.

In the UK, at the time of writing, two grades of unleaded petrol are offered for sale. The first to BS 7070 was with a minimum Research Octane Number of 95 (Motor Octane 85), and the latest a 'Super' grade of RON 98. Soon there will be an unleaded 91/92 RON grade available, which will replace the present 2-star (90 RON) leaded fuel (now being phased out). Leaded grades will continue to be available for some years to come, with 4-star (97 octane RON) being the most commonly available type. In the USA two unleaded grades are on offer, but as a general rule – from 1987 onwards – most car engine manufacturers have been developing and manufacturing engines that will run safely on reduced lead or unleaded fuels. European marine derivatives should have no problem converting, while US engines are already well advanced into the new era. From October 1989 all automotive engines in Europe must run on unleaded fuel so the marinised ones will quickly follow.

A word of warning is necessary regarding some unleaded fuels that do not conform to BS 7070. These may contain ethyl alcohol and methanol.

Problems occurred in the USA when unleaded fuels were doped with alcohols, for although these additives can increase the octane rating of petrol they have the ability to dissolve certain types of plastic – including some resins used in moulding GRP and items like fuel lines. In addition, methanol is entirely unsuited to the marine environment. It is hygroscopic and absorbs water, which can then separate out from the base fuel. The EEC leadless fuels will not contain alcohols in their specification.

We might expect to find that first-generation leadless fuel engines with their retarded timing will increase fuel consumption marginally and have lower power. This is not necessarily so as much work has gone into combustion chamber design on the automotive engines. Most pleasure boat engines run for so few hours each season that the power reduction caused by the new fuels is minimal and the effect will not be noticed by the average owner.

## Fuel handling

All fuels need handling with care to ensure that when they are taken aboard they are not spilled into bilges or onto surfaces where they can soak in to produce a fire hazard. Although diesel fuel is less dangerous than petrol, it is emphasised that every fuel should be treated as a possible source of fire or explosion and due safety precautions should be taken.

Contamination during fuelling is an ever present problem and cleanliness is vital. Not much can be done about fuel supplies that are contaminated before they are brought aboard except to complain to the company supplying them. However, this is far too late as far as safety is concerned.

Likely contaminants are water, rust and dust (which enters tanks through breather pipes), mainly transferred from shore-side installations. Water may contaminate both shore and boat tanks through condensation of water vapour on tank surfaces, and through faulty tank caps and filler orifices. When boats are laid up it is vital to ensure that rainwater which may lodge on the deck is not forming pools over the deck filler orifices as few are really water-tight in this situation.

Diesel fuel tanks sometimes suffer from a form of contamination caused by bacteria breeding on the interface between the diesel fuel and water. This growth can block fuel lines and filters. Regular tank cleaning to remove water and the use of biocide/conditioner proprietary products will inhibit growth and should be used if this problem occurs.

## Fuel tankage

Fig 22 sets out some of the basic requirements for a safe, efficient fuel system on a boat. Larger craft will undoubtedly employ multiple fuel tank systems using changeover valves and pumps to supply a central or day tank. The basic requirements still stand – although it will be essential to have a set of operating instructions that can be under-

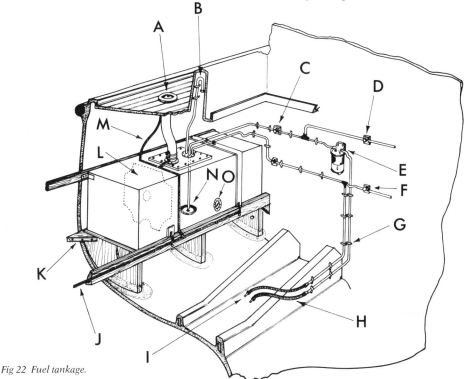

*Fig 22 Fuel tankage.*

KEY

A) Watertight deck filler.
B) Tank breather with flame trap on end, protected from water ingress.
C) Emergency fuel shut-off valves, either accessible or designed for remote operation.
D) Fuel tank changeover option valve.
E) Primary fuel filter/ agglomerator to separate out water.

F) Low-pressure return pipe fitted with valves which allow diesel fuel to be returned to correct tank or to the single tank in use when one is contaminated.
G) Fuel pipes well supported and clipped in place.
H) Flexible fuel lines always used to connect fuel pipework to the engine.
I) Flexible connection from engine to return fuel line (bleed-back line) from a diesel engine.

J) All parts of system electrically bonded to a ground plate.
K) Tanks must be very firmly fixed to the boat's structure.
L) Tanks must have the correct baffles fitted for their size.
M) Isolated metal fittings on the fuel system must still be bonded.
N) Fuel take-up pipe must not be at the bottom of the tank.
O) Tank to have an accurate fuel contents gauge on tank or remote reading gauge fitted.

stood by any person who might, in an emergency, need to operate the system. If this is not done a simple emergency may well be compounded into a disaster.

## TANK MATERIALS

It is important when fuel tankage is built into a boat that the correct materials are selected. Materials used should give protection from fire and contamination hazards. Table 1 gives details of suitable materials for both petrol and diesel fuels, but many local authorities have more specific regulations which it would be wise to seek out and comply with if you are not to break the law.

## TANK CLEANING

It is dangerous to clean fuel tanks without proper precautions to prevent the accidental ignition of explosive vapour that will accumulate in an empty tank space. Nevertheless, as a vast number of the rescue emergencies that occur at sea are directly attributable to engine failure and fuel problems in particular, the cleansing of the fuel tanks should be regarded as a chore that should be carried out approximately every three years.

This is best done when all fuel can first be pumped out into shore-side drums which will then themselves become a fire hazard. Store them carefully. Fuel line connections to the engine are then disconnected from the tank. A strong solution of water and Shell Teepol or Deb Marinol (a safe biodegradable marine detergent) should be used to flush out the tank. This job is often a nightmare and may be totally neglected when tank access is difficult.

If a tank is provided with a good-sized top access cleaning plate sufficiently large to get an arm into, a fluffless rag may be used to dry the inside. Finally, when you are quite certain there are no lurking vapours emerging from porous surfaces such as you might find with GRP, use a domestic vacuum cleaner set up as a blower to blow air through the tank to dry it thoroughly. Never use any electric motor driven suction or blower to dry a tank unless you are quite certain there is no fuel vapour present, or ensure that the machine is an approved spark and gas proof type which is safe for the job.

A fuel tank should have been tested to withstand a minimum of 5 lb per square inch pressure and have a plate affixed to it to demonstrate this.

TABLE 1. Tank materials

| | Petrol | TVO/kerosene | Diesel |
|---|---|---|---|
| Stainless steel | S | S | S |
| Copper/brass | U (Gum) | U (Gum) | U (Chem) |
| Galvanised iron | U (Chem) | U (Chem) | U (Chem) |
| Mild steel[1] | S | S | S |
| Tinned steel | S | S | S |
| Nylon/polythene | SR (Fire) | SR (Fire) | SR (Fire) |
| Light alloy | S | S | S |
| Glass reinforced plastic[2] | U | SR (Fire) | SR (Fire) |
| Flexible tanks[3] | SR (Fire, chafe) | – | SR (Fire, chafe) |

KEY

S = Satisfactory
U = Unsatisfactory (reason)
R = Risky material *not allowed for petrol by most authorities*
Gum = gummy deposits form that block the fuel system
Chem = Chemical reaction with fuel concerned
R = Serious risk of fire as material melts, burns, or will chafe
[1] = Only the outside of the tank should be painted to minimise corrosion
[2] = GRP tanks should be moulded only in isopthalic resins and used where legislation permits for diesel fuel. On no account should petrol containing benzine, ethyl alcohol or methanol be used in a GRP tank
[3] = Available but *not* recommended by author

## Tank accessories and pipework

### DECK FILLERS AND ELECTRICAL BONDING

As already mentioned, a deck filler should have a tight-fitting cap that is watertight. Check any gasket under the cap and if it is grease compatible use a thick grease on it to prevent ingress of water. Wipe excess grease off the top so that it does not trail all over the pristine deck! The filler must always be located outside any coaming so that spilled fuel can never get inside the boat or into the bilges where it could form an explosive vapour. All parts of the fuel system, especially metal ones separated by plastic fuel piping, must be bonded. Part of looking after a system is to check that bonding straps are in position and have excellent connections to the metal parts they are bridging.

### BREATHER PIPES AND TERMINALS

Fuel tanks must have breather pipes so that when they are filling the expelled air does not blow back through the filler orifice. They also allow the ingress of air as the engine draws fuel out of the tank. The breather should be vented to the outside of any coaming. This presents a real danger of allowing the ingress of water, rain or sea, back into the tank in bad conditions. A high swan neck may help. The end of the breather pipe should always be fitted with a gauze end to prevent fire or explosion. The gauze will pass fuel vapour, but not allow sufficient heat for ignition to pass into the pipework and back into the tank. The breather gauze should be cleaned regularly as the fine gauze can soon become blocked with dust. The minimum size for a breather pipe on most small craft tanks is ½ in (12 mm) but a larger size ¾ in (19 mm) or 1 in (25 mm) is far better for fast filling small tanks.

### PIPE RUNS AND MATERIALS

Although exceptions are made for fuel pipes to leave tanks other than at the top, this is by far the safest place for them to emerge. This also applies to diesel fuel return pipes, all breather and filler pipes and tank contents gauges.

Although copper is not a safe tank material, it is the most commonly used for fuel lines. Its small internal surface area, plus the fact that fuel is usually drawn through it rapidly, ensures that gum and chemical deposits are minute and can be dealt with easily by the pre-engine fuel filters and those on the engine itself. Steel Bundy tubing is used on some inland waterways boats; although its cost is lower it is more subject to corrosion. Pipes that are badly supported or clipped are vulnerable to fatigue – vibration and resultant work hardening being the things to look for.

When checking the fuel system at fitting-out time, see that clips and support brackets really are doing their job. Clips should be checked to ensure that the pressure they put on a pipe does not deform or constrict the bore. Clips should be placed at 8 in (200 mm) centres.

Compression joints are often used on pipe terminations. On assembly with new olives, they should be tightened just sufficiently to produce a tight leak-proof joint. Later they can be tightened, if this is necessary, without having to dismantle and renew the olive.

As pipes emerge from the tank, a shut-off valve should be fitted. These must be fully accessible if they are hand-operated – a difficult thing to achieve in the initial design, but if not they should be of the electrically operated solenoid valve type. Larger installations may incorporate an automatic fire valve which shuts off fuel from the tank immediately a dangerous temperature is reached. Hand or electric shut-off valves also prevent the syphoning of fuel into the bilges should part of the fuel system fail and have to be dismantled for repair. Check that fuel valves are closed before starting any dismantling work, and leave them closed when the boat is laid up. To prevent condensation water polluting the tank it should be either totally full or totally empty at this time. Petrol tanks are safest left empty and cleaned – perhaps asking too much for many owners.

## Flexible fuel lines

The worst horror to be found on a boat, presenting a major fire hazard, is a piece of plastic pipe connecting the solid metal fuel line to the engine. In a fire, this material will melt immediately and add fuel to the flames. All engines, whether flexibly or solidly mounted, produce some vibration that will fatigue a solid fuel line connection to them. The flexible line must be of the metal-armoured type that is both flexible and fire resistant. Armoured flexibles must still be installed correctly as they can fatigue. Always obtain technical installation details from the manufacturer.

## Tank contents gauges

The simpler these are the better – and they often give greater accuracy. The calibrated dip stick takes some beating for low cost and reliability. However, many tanks are positioned in boats where they cannot be readily 'dipped'. In these cases it is necessary to use a remote reading tank contents gauge. These are of the electric or pneumatic types. At best, even after they have been factory calibrated to suit a particular tank shape, they are seldom really accurate and contents registered should always be regarded as a guide only.

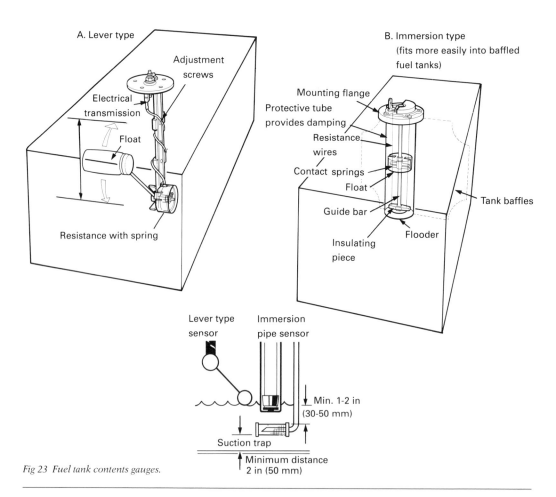

Fig 23 Fuel tank contents gauges.

*Electrical sensors* are of two basic types – lever and immersion pipe. Fig 23 A shows the lever type, which might be difficult to fit into tanks with baffles. In this case, the immersion type, shown in Fig 23 B, will be easier to install, take up less room and – dare I say it – usually lasts longer. It is important to check your own tanks at cleaning time to assess just how the immersion of the sender and fuel up-take pipes has been arranged. Neither fuel up-take nor the lowest fuel level registration should be at the base of the tank. You do not want the up-take pipe to suck in tank debris, neither should it suck in air on a diesel engine, which usually means the whole system must be bled of air after refilling. There should always be a safety margin on both items, and it is suggested that the up-take pipe should have a minimum level of fuel beneath it of 2 in (50 mm). This is regarded as unusable fuel where water and dirt will accumulate between cleanings. The lowest registration mark of either type of fuel gauge (L) should be another 1¼ in (30 mm) to 2 in (50 mm) above the lower end of the fuel pipe intake level. This gives a small safety margin when the gauge reads EMPTY.

The vertical shaft on the lever type gauge is adjustable so that the correct arc for the float to move from its lowest level to the full tank level (H) is accomplished. Things that occasionally go wrong and need simple cleaning and servicing are:

1. The float punctures and sinks; replace with a new float unit.
2. Debris prevents the arm swinging fully through the arc; clean.
3. Adjustment screws loosen or wires drop off; tighten.

## PNEUMATIC FUEL GAUGES

The pneumatic tank contents gauge, such as that made by Eurogauge, measures the hydrostatic liquid head pressure at the base of the fuel tank. Depending on the specific gravity of the fuel and the liquid head, this is variable. The liquid head usually starts about 20 mm above the bottom of the tank. The instrument, being non-electrical, is extremely safe with all fuels. When properly installed and calibrated it is fairly accurate. Calibration tables are supplied by the manufacturer, or the job can be carried out when ordering the instrument, provided tank dimensions and fuel are specified.

Since it is dependent on measuring the pressure head, it is vital to ensure that the capillary tubing and connections are not allowing air to leak into them. If a fault shows, check this first. A blocked capillary is indicated by the pointer moving past the 100% mark, and the blockage must be eliminated.

## Fuel consumption and power curves

Engine manufacturers publish graphs showing the power and specific fuel consumption curves of the engine plotted against engine revolutions per minute (r/min). These graphs are of interest to those who want to operate their engines at maximum economic level. Even for those with money to burn (literally), efficient operation should enable an engine to operate within parameters that allow it to be less noisy, smoother running and more pleasant to live with than an engine which is flogging itself to death. It may well be my imagination, but I have always found that when engines are operating at between about 78% and 85% of their maximum rated revolutions, specific fuel consumption is at its most economical for the power produced and the engine seems to run at its sweetest. Find out where your engine sounds good and then look at the r/min fuel graph to check this out.

From the point of view of safety, it is important for the skipper to know how many hours running time, or the range, he can achieve with full tank capacity. As a very rough and ready reckoning for old hands who are not used to the modern International System (SI) metric units of measurement, we used to say that imperial measure fuel consumption on a diesel engine would be approximately 0.4 pt per horse power per hour and a petrol engine about 0.6 pt/hp/h. Thus a diesel engine running at 70 of its 80 hp would be consuming roughly 70 × 0.4 pt per hour or 3.5 imperial gallons per hour.

The SI units give specific fuel consumption in grams per kilowatt/hour. Looking back at Fig 6 we see that the Perkins Prima M80T, which is a turbocharged engine, has an interesting specific fuel consumption curve. Usually the curve is a simple one dropping to a minimum in the region of 75–85% of maximum r/min. In this curve we see the interesting effect of the turbocharger efficiency where there is almost a flat mid-section between 2600 and 3300 r/min when its positive boost begins to contribute towards the efficiency of the engine.

The same graph gives a more precise idea of the fuel consumption of the Perkins Prima Curve, when at 3500 r/min the output is 50 kW and the engine is using approximately 248 g/kWh:

$$\text{Fuel consumption} = \frac{248 \times 50}{1000} \text{ l per hour} = 12.4 \text{ l per hour}$$

Specific fuel consumption of a four-stroke diesel engine varies between about 220 g/kWh and 300 g/kWh. While a four-stroke petrol engine will usually be in the 270 to 380 g/kWh. To convert g/kWh to lb/hp/h (pounds per horse power per hour) multiply by 0.0016439868. Past generations of engines used lb/hp/h for fuel consumption. An imp. gallon of petrol weighs between 7.15 lb (regular) and 7.5 lb (premium) per gallon, and diesel fuel between 8.3 and 8.8 lb per gallon.

## Fuel tank size

Once specific fuel consumption for a boat's cruising speed is known, and the total volume of the tank/s, then it is simple to calculate the cruising range. Always deduct the 'safety' volume left at the bottom of the tank or about 10% of total volume. Thus, if the total tank volume is 300 l, safe volume is 270 l. Looking back at the Prima M80T at full power 57 kW, the fuel consumption would be about 16.53 l per hour.

$$\text{Hours running} = \frac{270}{16.53} = 16.33 \text{ hours}$$

If the speed of the boat is 12 knots this gives a safe range of 16.33 × 12, or approximately 196 nautical miles.

A gallon of fuel occupies a volume of approximately 0.001 m³ (cubic metres) or 0.16 cubic feet. Thus 300 l (66 gallons) of fuel will fill a volume of

$$300 \times 0.001 \text{ m}^3 = 0.298 \text{ cubic metres}$$
$$\text{or} \quad 66 \times 0.16 = 10.56 \text{ cubic feet}$$

If for any reason you are adding tankage, or renewing to a better design, then the final dimensions are now easily calculated from the above figures. Fit the space available to the shape of the tank size you are working out: e.g. volume = length × height × width. For example, the approximate dimensions in feet for a tank of 10.56 cu ft might be 4 ft × 2 ft × 1.32 ft = 10.56 cu ft.

## Fuel tank positioning

The designer of a boat must take into account the positioning of fuel tanks within the hull to ensure that performance in both sailing craft and planing boats is maximised and not jeopardised. Weight of fuel is not generally important in a heavy displacement boat, but even there it can effect stability, roll and pitch. Weight should always be used to enhance stability characteristics, which make life aboard comfortable. When adding fuel tankage to increase range this must be kept in mind. A professional naval architect should be consulted if there are any doubts about how the extra weight will affect the safety and performance of the craft.

## Fuel filters

These play a vital role in the safety and service life of all types of engine installation, particularly so in diesel installations using fuel injection equipment where engineering tolerance is so small.

Over quite a short period of time, a diesel fuel injection pump can be wrecked internally by solid debris equivalent to just four or five peas. The critical areas inside the pump are the sharp-edged apertures that should close promptly as fuel passes through them. On inlet metered distributor pumps such as the CAV DPA the areas of the rotor in contact with the ports are the most sensitive.

Penny pinching on fuel filters may well cost hundreds of pounds in repairing damage. There are over 100 filter manufacturers around the world, and sad to say, there are spurious ones who turn out dangerously inferior products, often boxed to look like original spares. The simple way to avoid any problems is to buy only from the engine maker's approved dealer or one of the major filter manufacturers such as GM A-C Delco or Lucas CAV.

Contaminating particles in fuel or oil are measured in microns, but if a filter claims to filter down to so many of these minute measurements this does not say very much. Inferior products using paper as the filtering element often disintegrate under test, letting all debris pass. It is not, then, good practice to go on micron measurement alone. This offers only a guide to the particle size that can be stopped if all else is well. Lubricating oil filters might filter down to 20 microns, diesel fuel filters down to 5 to 7 microns and air filters to 8 microns. Far better if the filter you buy is tested to one of the following standards:

*Oil filter* Tested to BS4836 1972 which covers oil filtration life and efficiency.
*Fuel oil* Tested to ISO 4020
*Air filter* Tested to SAE J726 B

## FUEL AND LUBRICATING OIL FILTRATION

Most filter units today use a paper filter element, although felt elements are also found.

Two design approaches are made by different filter manufacturers. The first favours filtering the fuel in depth, the element being of felt or, more usually, thick paper similar to oil-filtering elements in common use. The pores are large, but because the fuel has so far to travel through the medium there is a good chance that it will come across a small pore and the debris will be left behind. The second approach is to use a very fine-pored paper whose construction will be a balance

between the finest filtering and one that will still provide a reasonable service life. Too fine a filter would soon, even with reasonably clean fuel or lubricant, become blocked. As already mentioned, the biggest danger is not from blockage but from the seams in the filter splitting and allowing unfiltered fuel through. It is therefore imperative that any type of filter should be properly manufactured and then replaced at, or before, the maker's recommended interval. I say 'before' since laying up time is an excellent one for replacing all filters found on or off the engine.

The second contaminant that needs to be removed from the fuel is water. This can be as damaging and disastrous as dirt. Extra wear, corrosion and even seizure can take place.

## TYPES OF FUEL FILTER (Fig 24)

All fuel should be filtered at least twice. The first pre-engine filter should remove any water present in the fuel. This is known as an AGGLOMERATOR. Generally speaking, unless an excessive amount of water is expected in the fuel, a combined filter agglomerator like the CAV 7111-296 type will be sufficient to mount between the tank and the engine. Larger tankage might be better equipped with a water separator before a pre-engine agglomerator/filter. On no account should a water stop type of filter be fitted in a system which automatically shuts down the propulsion engine when there is an excessive presence of water. If warning is necessary it should be either visual or aural so that the engineer can service the filter. Automatic types may be acceptable for generating equipment.

The type of unit to fit on the propulsion engine would be a CAV Waterscan which is a pre-filter that separates the water, and through an electronic probe, can be coupled to a warning device which will advise the operator when it requires drain down.

Classification societies usually insist on all filtration equipment using metal bowls because of the fire risk if a glass one is accidentally broken, or shatters in a fire. Personally, I believe that the glass bowl types where visual inspection is easy are safe enough provided they are installed in a position where possible damage is minimised. There are many more cases of boats getting into dangerous situations from fuel problems than from fire. Safety is greatly increased when fuel contamination is so easily spotted. I base my claim on RNLI statistics from a seven-year period when 1945 rescues were made to craft with engine failure, another 144 – a grand total 2089 – were out of fuel, and just 73 caught fire.

Still dealing with pre-filtration – for boats that make long sea-passages – the wisdom of fitting a twin fuel filter with changeover is a good choice.

By simple operation of a changeover tap, a suspect filter can be by-passed while the engine continues to run with fuel supplied by the second filter. Racor's valved manifold units allow one filter to be serviced while the other gives continuity of supply – an excellent safety feature for any seagoing craft. Even doing a simple job like changing a filter in a seaway can be difficult, especially in the confined space of most small craft engine spaces, but it is easier to do with some way on and rolling is at least minimised.

In marine applications it is not generally neces-

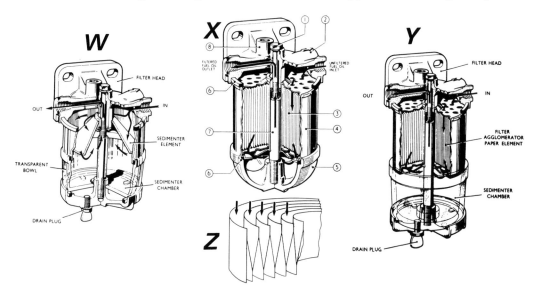

*Fig 24  Lucas CAV diesel fuel filters.*

W) Simple sedimenter Type SS, which is a pre-engine filter designed to separate larger dirt particles and water droplets. It requires inspection for water, drain down and occasional bowl cleaning. An electric 'waterscan' can be fitted for remote warning of water level.

X) Lucas CAV FS bowl-less filter fitted with the 296 element. These are usually found fitted on the engine itself. The flow is shown down through the paper filter element and this provides consistent protection for the injection equipment.

KEY

1. Centre fastening bolt.
2. Cast light alloy head with mountring flange.
3. Pleated paper filter element enclosed in metal canister.
4. Metal canister.
5. Cast light alloy base with centre stud.
6. Square section synthetic rubber sealing rings.
7. Centre stud.
8. Vent connection.

Y) The FAS filter/agglomerator-sedimenter carries out all three operations and should be built into the fuel line between the sedimenter and the main engine (FS) filter. The Type SS filter may be dispensed with if

little or no water is expected in the fuel as the agglomerator will collect water. This filter requires regular inspection and emptying of accumulated water and an annual change of the 296 filter element.

Z) The pleated filter element of the FS and FAS Filter Agglomerator. In cheap imitations there is always the danger of the pleated paper rupturing and allowing dirty fuel to pass. Many larger engines fit a twin version which ensures greater safety and which has the ability to fine filter fuel over a longer period or deal with a much greater volume of fuel.

sary to fit twin filters in series – that is, the first filter taking out the main debris and then the second ensuring cleanliness. Some engine manufacturers use this system and it does ensure that efficiency is improved and there is protection against an element failing.

Finally, the majority of engines will incorporate their own built-on fuel filter. All European filters should conform to Test Standard ISO 4020/1, which evaluates different filter materials, the nature and extent of particle retention as well as choking and bursting characteristics.

## CHANGING FILTERS (Applicable to both fuel and oil filters)

This is potentially the most messy part of boating, when the unskilled operator and his boat are covered in fuel and dirty oil. It need not be like this provided there is some forward planning.

First, arm yourself with plenty of newspaper, two or three large plastic bags and an old shallow roasting tin, or even an old plastic oil container with one side cut out. Place newspaper in the bilge with the container for oil on top if there is room. Alternatively, use a plastic bag (without holes!) to catch the dirty filter and oil.

Filter elements are of three basic types:

1. *Spin on or canister filters* (Fig 25) which need a filter strop tool to loosen them. As they spin off, drop them into the plastic bag. Oil or fuel will still be in them so try to maintain them in the position in which they are fitted, or turning them will spill the fuel out over the bilges.

To replace this type of filter, smear a little engine grease on the rubber sealing ring before replacing. Hand-tightening is all that is needed to give a perfect seal, but check this when you test start the engine. Remember that an empty filter needs filling, so it is necessary to do this after filter replacement. With oil filters, simply add a little extra oil until the dipstick level is correct after the engine has been run. For all fuel filters except those that are self-bleeding, bleeding the air out of the fuel system is vital and is dealt with under its own special heading.

2. *Filter element with central mounting bolt.* These may be sub-divided into two types:

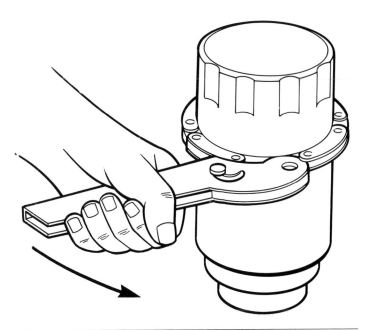

Fig 25 *Removing a canister oil filter with a filter strop tool. The one shown is the Turny Filter model.*

A The first type has the filter element already in its own canister. The mounting bolt simply connects the base casting through a central hole in the filter to the top casting.

B The second is where a separate filter element is contained in a canister, the central bolt holds and seals it to the top casting. Only the filter element is discarded and replaced.

When replacing all of these types, particular attention should be given to the special rubber seals supplied with the filter. It is as important to replace these in the correct place as to replace the filter. Failure to do so may result in leakage of contaminated fuel or oil past the filter element, so rendering it inoperative.

The sequence is as follows:

1. Undo the central securing bolt – this may be either on the top or bottom of the filter so look for the central hexagonal bolt head.

2. Use a fine pointed penknife blade to prise out the rubber sealing rings in the head and base casting of type 2A filters. Note that if a small rubber sealing ring is included in the pack this should be used in the head casting. Type 2B filters only have a single sealing ring in the head that the canister beds down onto, but you will find extra seals and maybe a compression spring on the central shaft. Before you pull the central shaft out, carefully note the sequence of these so that re-assembly will be correct.

Care is needed to ensure that any metal blade used to remove the seals does not damage the casting. Metal scrapings are not wanted floating around inside the engine. Also check that the large seal rings which are of square section do not get twisted in the casting groove. A twist and you will have fuel or oil pouring everywhere when the engine is started.

## Diesel fuel injection equipment

We have already seen the importance of clean, water free fuel for all diesel engines so that the fine tolerance engineering of the injection equipment

can be maintained to provide a satisfactory service life.

It is equally important to realise that there is nothing an amateur can do about faulty injection pumps and injectors except have them properly serviced by an accredited agency, or buy factory guaranteed rebuilt replacement parts. The servicing of all injection equipment calls for highly skilled technicians using specialised tools and calibration equipment for the job.

Having said this, it helps if an owner is able to recognise the injection systems being used on his engine and carry out the maintenance that the owner's handbook advises. Above all else, for all owners – other than those who have a modern self-bleeding fuel system – the ability to bleed the system of air is vital. This will be dealt with shortly.

## Diesel fuel systems

Figs 26A and B show typical diesel fuel systems: (A) is for an IN-LINE pump; and (B) for a DISTRIBUTOR TYPE pump. You will notice that both systems have parts in common:

A. The pre-filter/s, already discussed, should prevent water and contamination reaching the engine's own filter. Although filter renewal is not strictly necessary when considering the short engine hours run each season, I would suggest that for the small cost this is highly desirable.

B. FUEL LIFT PUMP. This type of low pressure pump is also found on petrol engines to pump fuel to the carburettor. On the Minimec in-line injection pump, the fuel pump is incorporated on the side of the injection pump.

A typical diaphragm lift pump is shown in more detail in Fig 27. The diaphragm (13) is actuated to and fro from the drive arm (27), which in turn is moved by a cam on the cam shaft of the engine itself. The downward stroke sucks fuel into the upper chamber via an inlet valve (10) and the upward stroke forces it out of another valve (10) into the pipe leading to the engine filter, and thence to the injection pump on a diesel engine or the carburettor on a petrol engine. On some modern units

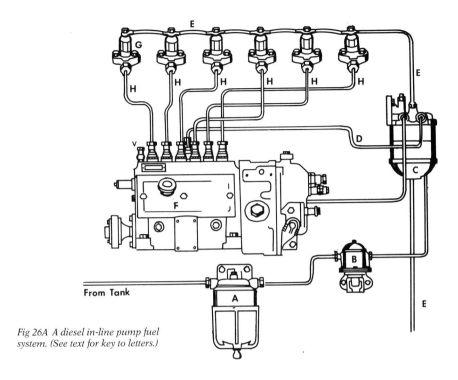

*Fig 26A A diesel in-line pump fuel system. (See text for key to letters.)*

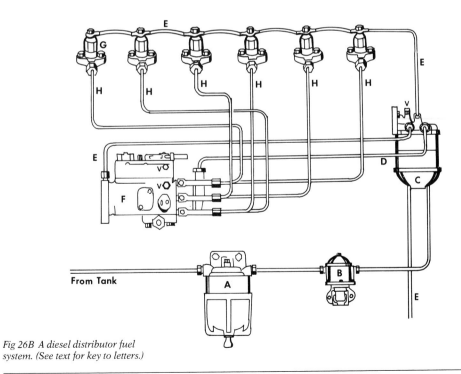

*Fig 26B A diesel distributor fuel system. (See text for key to letters.)*

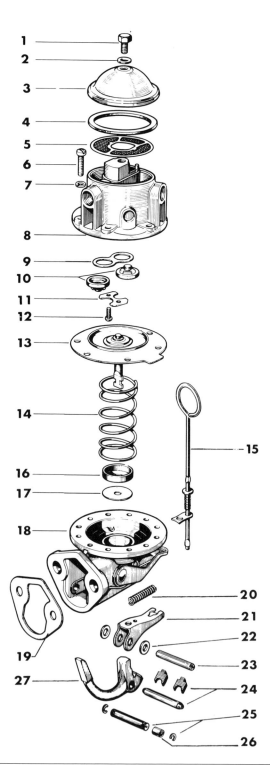

*Fig 27  Diaphragm fuel lift pump.*

KEY

1. Cap securing bolt.
2. Sealing washer.
3. Cap.
4. Sealing gasket.
5. Fuel filter gauze – should be regularly cleaned if one is fitted.
6. Body securing screw.
7. Washer.
8. Upper body casting.
9. Valve clip.
10. Inlet and outlet one-way valves.
11. Valve retaining clip.
12. Retaining clip screw.
13. Diaphragm – can rupture but in seaway can be difficult to replace. It is easier to carry a complete spare pump.
14. Diaphragm return spring.
15. Hand priming lever to actuate pump when filling fuel lines or bleeding air from diesel fuel lines.
16. Retaining cup.
17. Washer.
18. Lower body casting.
19. Heat isolating gasket. The pump might be prone to heating up and producing a vapour lock as a result. Very important on petrol engines.
20 to 26. Diaphragm actuating arm, retainers and spindles.
27. Pump actuating cam which is driven from engine camshaft and actuates the arm linked to the diaphragm.

a single two-way valve is used rather than the double one shown. Often a fuel filter gauze (5) is incorporated under the cover cap (3) but this is *not* sufficient to filter fuel properly, although it does give a little protection to the valves. The upper bowl and filter gauze should be cleaned each season.

Lift pumps are extremely reliable, but the diaphragm can rupture and valves jam. Although it is easy to carry spares, rebuilding a pump in a seaway would be a nightmare job and so it is recommended that deep-sea going boats should carry a complete replacement pump. Note that heat-proof gaskets are often used between the pump body and the engine itself. This is to isolate the fuel from the engine heat, which could initiate a vapour lock.

The gasket also maintains the correct cam movement. As we shall see, the hand priming lever (15) is needed for priming the low pressure side of the fuel system.

C. The modern engine fuel filter is usually of the bowl-less type (Fig 24X). I favour replacement of the engine fuel filter element when the engine is laid up and the fuel system preservative oils are passed through to give protection over winter.

D. The low pressure feed pipe to the diesel fuel injection pump. As with all parts that might be removed for servicing, it is important to clean it before disassembly to ensure no dirt gets in. A small paint brush can be used to get into crannies, a fluffless rag and a spot of preservative or fuel oil can be used for cleaning.

E. There are a number of low pressure back leakage pipes that return excess fuel from the pump or injectors back to the filter and thence back to the fuel tank. Some systems on high performance engines prefer to return the hot excess fuel directly back to the tank so that it will cool down, but for most small power units this is not necessary.

F. Fig 26A shows a system using an in-line fuel injection pump, easily recognised by the pumping elements along the top. Fig 26B shows a distributor type pump. There are many variations on each of these basic types and it is important to note any type of plate which details the precise specification. Small engines, especially single and twin cylinder units, often have flange-mounted pumps in which the pumping element is driven directly from the engine camshaft. General Motors Detroit

engines have a single unit mounted directly into the cylinder head which creates the high pressure, meters the correct amount of fuel and times the injection into the combustion chamber.

It is equally important to note that injection pumps are 'timed' devices which must be perfectly synchronised with the moment that the injectors spray fuel into the combustion space. Two scratches across engine and pump casting joint will aid a refit if the pump is removed for servicing, but as only the engine workshop manual details retiming procedures never upset the adjustment unless you intend having a mechanic restore it for you.

I will not detail what happens inside each type of pump, but Fig 28 gives some idea of the complexity of the working parts of the Lucas CAV Mechanically Governed DPA injection pump, which is a distributor type pump used on many marine diesel engines.

The Minimec fuel injection pump shown in Fig 29 looks inside an in-line pump, which is easily recognised by the line of high pressure pipe connections along the length of the top of the unit.

When the make and model of the pump on your engine is identified, I would advise (if you really want to become familiar with the working of the pump) that you write to the manufacturer (Appendix E) who is usually able to supply excellent detailed literature.

Occasionally, an owner's handbook will detail some basic maintenance which needs to be carried out on the injection pump. For example, a few in-line models require an oil gallery to have lubricating oil (generally the same grade oil used in the engine) drained and renewed at set intervals. This is because leakage from the pump elements dilutes the oil and must be drained and replaced with the correct grade. Other in-line pumps do not need this kind of attention as they are lubricated by the same oil the engine uses. Distributor type pumps are self-lubricating.

Another mysterious section of an injection pump is the GOVERNOR. The governor is necessary to maintain any particular engine speed as it controls the amount of fuel the pump elements are able to deliver to the injectors. There are three basic types of governor – mechanical, hydraulic

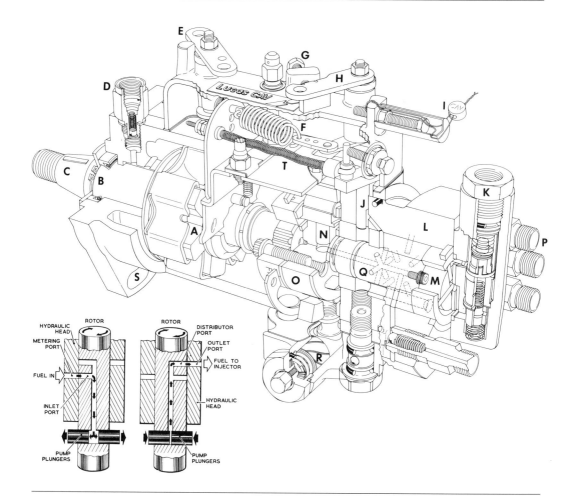

Fig 28 The Lucas/CAV mechanically governed DPA diesel injection pump.

KEY

A) Centrifugal governor weights provide sensitive speed control.
B) Front bearing oil seal and retaining circlip.
C) Tapered drive shaft.
D) Back leak connection feeds excess fuel which has also helped lubrication of the pump back to the fuel filter.
E) Shut off lever, hand operated by cable control.
F) Return spring to hold speed control lever against idle stop.
G) Idling speed control stop.
H) Speed control lever usually connected to helm position by cable control system.
I) Maximum speed stop and adjusting screw sealed to prevent tampering.
J) Fuel metering valve, governor controlled.
K) Low pressure fuel inlet with nylon filter below it.
L) The stationary hydraulic head which houses the transfer pump (M) and the distributor rotor (Q).
M) The transfer pump which transfers low pressure fuel from inlet (M) to high pressure plungers (N) via metering valve (J).
N) High pressure pump plungers are driven outwards by fuel pressure from (N) and pushed inward by the lobes on the cam ring (O).
O) Cam ring.
P) High pressure outlet pipe connections to injectors.
Q) The distributing part of the rotor contains a central axial passage (dotted) and two radially drilled ports. The distributing port aligns successively with each high pressure outlet port to P, there being one for each cylinder of the engine. A similar number of inlet ports in the rotor align successively with a single port in the head, called the metering port, and admits the fuel from (M) under the control of the governor. See inset.
R) Fully automatic advance device.
S) Pump fixing and locating bolt slot that allows rotation of pump about axis for timing. Score marks across engine and pump flange can help re-install pump to same timing position.
T) Governor spring.

and pneumatic. Lucas DPA pumps use either a mechanical or a hydraulic governor, but again the pump manufacturer's literature should give details of the mechanics involved. No basic maintenance is needed and, once again, they are the province of the professional service agent. There is often a seal on the maximum speed adjustment screw (Fig 28I) to prevent maladjustment which could over speed the engine to destruction.

Most injection pumps incorporate an EXCESS FUEL STARTING device. Many modern pumps automatically produce an excess amount of fuel to

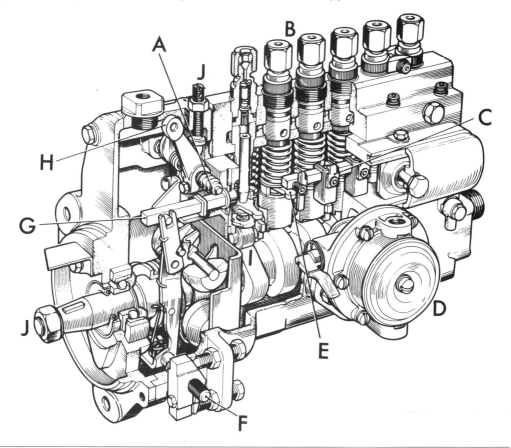

*Fig 29 The Minimec in-line fuel injection pump.*

KEY

A) Excess fuel button for cold starting.
B) High pressure fuel line connectors that feed the injectors. Six in this case for a 6-cylinder engine.
C) Control fork that moves levers on the plunger arm on each pump to control the quantity of fuel injected.
D) This model has the low pressure fuel pump built onto the side of the injection pump. This is a diaphragm type working exactly like the one shown in Fig 27, but in this case driven from the injection pump's camshaft rather than from the main engine camshaft.
E) The actuating arm that along with C moves the pump element to control the amount needed for injection at various engine speeds.
F) Control lever connected by cable to the helm position.
G) Control rod assembly which is moved by F and a combination of the excess fuel device, the engine governor and the stop control to provide exactly the right control of the pumping elements to suit the particular running or stopping conditions.
H) Stop lever.
I) Cam and roller cam follower which drive the pumping elements. This is a pump which requires the gallery to be topped up with engine oil for the internal lubrication of the moving parts.
J) Maximum fuel stop screw, usually has a seal placed through it to prevent tampering.

help the engine to start. Some older in-line pumps had a manually set excess fuel button which was pressed in for starting, but which automatically returned when the engine fired up. Corrosion can jam the button and this was not helped when rain water dripped into the pump from above. If you find one of these on an old installation, check that the button moves freely. Excess fuel may also be controlled by a temperature sensitive device or even operated remotely by cable. If starting is poor, therefore, check the excess fuel device.

Among a number of add-on modules that may be found on pumps used on turbocharged engines is a MANIFOLD PRESSURE COMPENSATOR. This device is used on Bosch pumps fitted to Perkins Prima M80T. In the lower engine speed range it reduces the full load delivery as a function of the boost pressure in order to reduce smoke emissions. Without it, smoke emissions can be a problem when the throttle is opened up rapidly, i.e. the fuel gets into the cylinder but there is insufficient air to burn it.

*The stop control* on the pump shuts down the fuel supply to stop the engine. This may be by means of a cable operated 'pull' or by an electrically operated solenoid which does the same job. The electrical type, switching through the key starter switch, is perhaps safer as the stop contact can be arranged so that the alternator diodes are not damaged, which can happen if the electrical circuit is switched off before the engine is stopped.

After the fuel emerges again from the injection pump (Fig 26H), it is contained in high pressure pipes that run to the injectors, one for each cylinder. Although it seldom happens, it is possible for one of these pipes to burst and spray fuel over a hot engine where it either explodes or causes a severe fire, especially if a hot turbocharger is nearby. It always pays to ensure that these pipes are not mechanically damaged when removed, or allowed to weaken through corrosion.

G. *Injectors*, one for each cylinder, meter a precise amount of the high-pressure fuel into the cylinder. They are high precision units which must always be taken to a service depot for cleaning and recalibration.

If an engine is running well, my instinct is to leave well alone, but if rough running and heavily polluted exhaust emissions persist the injectors must be suspect. They can be removed and reversed on their high pressure pipes to see if the spray pattern is correct, but while you are doing this it is probably quicker to take them directly to the service depot for cleaning and calibration. With both high-pressure lines and injectors the mechanic must never allow any part of his body, particularly the hands, to get in the way of the high-pressure spray which these units handle. The pressure is such that it can puncture the skin – and most humans don't run very well on diesel fuel!

Whenever part of any fuel system is dismantled all orifices should be covered to keep dirt out. Kitchen foil, cling film or plastic bags are excellent for this kind of job. On a seagoing boat, a full spare set of injectors should be carried.

## Bleeding air from diesel fuel systems

If your engine does not have one of the modern self-bleeding, or as some would say self-purging, fuel systems, knowing how to bleed it is something every owner must master. It is vital to know how to do this as the safety of a boat crew may depend on the skipper being able to operate quickly. Normally, bleeding air or venting a system is only necessary when part of the fuel system has been dismantled, when pipework or gaskets have allowed air to leak into the system, or the engine has run out of fuel and the tank has had to be refilled.

The fuel system should be divided into the two basic sections to bleed the air.

*The low-pressure side* from fuel tank supply pipe to the engine fuel filter is the first section to deal with. Always work from the tank towards the engine. The fuel pump hand priming rod (Fig 27 (15)) or the lever under the pump are worked up and down to suck fuel into the primary filter, but the air bleed screw – usually situated on the top of the engine filter Fig 26V – must be undone to allow air in the primary filter and lines to be pumped out. It is possible to undo the fuel line to filter union itself, but this is not recommended if the proper bleed nut can be found. The suction created by the pump will suck fuel into the primary filter and lines. When fuel, clear of air bubbles, is pumped out of the bleed screw hole on the engine filter, it is closed. The air is purged each time either, or both, of the filter elements are renewed, or any pipework undone. Incidentally, old copper pipe gets a deposit on its inner surface which normally does no harm, but if the pipe is rebent or knocked during servicing, this deposit can break off and clog a line. Although the filter will remove it before it can damage the engine, a high-pressure air line (or more usually, simple blowing) should remove this debris.

Each injection pump has a specific screw or screws (again marked 'V' on Fig 26B) which must be undone before the rest of the air in the low-pressure line and pump can be bled off. If you cannot remember which screws are the correct ones on your model pump, a spot of coloured paint below each will provide a quick reminder. Pump again until clear fuel emerges and then immediately close the bleed screw/s down.

It is possible to turn the engine over on the electric starter to actuate the pumping, but the mechanic must be aware of the danger of working on the engine if it accidentally starts. Normally if only the low-pressure side of has been disturbed to replace a filter, the high-pressure side will be intact and the engine will start. If the high-pressure side has been dismantled, the engine will not start until all air has been bled from the section between the pump and injectors.

## BLEEDING THE HIGH-PRESSURE SIDE

First slacken off any two high-pressure injection pipes (Fig 26 (H)) at the injector end. A fluffless clean rag is best placed over the pipes to prevent high-pressure fuel spraying all over the engine. Open the throttle fully and use the starter motor to turn the engine over until air-free fuel emerges from the pipes. Check that the stop control is in the 'run' position, because if it is in the 'stop position' no fuel will get through the pump. The loosened pipes are now tightened up and the engine should

start. The other high-pressure lines should self-bleed. If not, repeat the process on them.

## Petrol engine carburettors

If any petrol engine is to work properly and efficiently, each cylinder must be supplied with the right homogenous mixture of fuel and air to burn in the combustion space. The carburettor does this job.

There are two basic types of carburettor – the variable jet and the fixed jet types. Within these two basic types there are many variations, and again, the owner of a marine petrol motor may obtain additional tuning information not only from the basic handbook, but directly from the carburettor manufacturer. The precise year and model must be specified. Look for the type plate on both the engine and the carburettor if the exact type and specification are to be traced.

All carburettors have similar basic functions, but unless you have the proper service manual and a high degree of competence they are not an item that the amateur should tamper with. Otherwise, poor running and wasted fuel may be the result, or worse, you may cause damage to the engine, particularly the pistons and valves.

Over the years, when an engine has had a long production run there are usually many slight variations not only on the engine itself but also in the 'bolt on' items – and the carburettor in particular. These apparently small modifications can mean quite different tuning procedures must be used. As an aid to tracking down proper servicing needs, Appendix D lists the major carburettor manufacturers whose products may be found on marine engines.

There have been big changes among carburettor manufacturers in recent years, a number having gone out of production and their lines then split between other firms as they cease to trade. Very often it is possible to substitute another make of carburettor on a marine engine perfectly satisfactorily. In fact, many manufacturers of car as well as boat engines do offer power increases by chang-

58

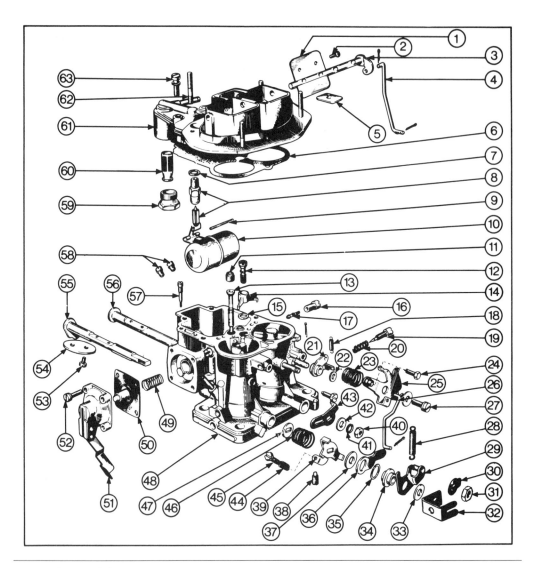

Fig 30 Weber twin choke
downdraught carburettor.

KEY

1. Choke plate.
2. Choke plate screw.
3. Choke shaft assembly.
4. Choke control rod.
5. Seal.
6. Gasket
7. Inlet valve washer.
8. Inlet valve assembly.
9. Float shaft.
10. Float assembly.
11. Air correction jet.
12. Pump discharge valve.
13. Starting jet.
14. Pump discharge nozzle.
15. Nozzle gasket.
16. Idler jet holder.

17. Idler jet.
18. Choke lever spring.
19. Mixture adjustment
    needle.
20. Spring.
21. Choke lever assembly.
22. Pivot washer.
23. Choke lever spring.
24. Pivot bolt.
25. Choke control lever.
26. Fast idler rod.
27. Choke lever retaining
    screw.
28. Throttle control spring-
    secondary.
29. Throttle control lever.
30. Tab washer.
31. Nut
32. Throttle control lever.
33. Washer.

34. Throttle shaft bush.
35. Washer.
36. Throttle control lever.
37. Washer.
38. Idler adjustment screw.
39. Fast idler adjustment lever.
40. Nut.
41. Throttle shaft spring.
42. Washer.
43. Throttle stop lever.
44. Throttle adjustment screw
    spring. .
45. Screw.
46. Throttle control spring-
    primary.
47. Washer.
48. Lower body.
49. Accelerator pump spring.
50. Accelerator pump
    diaphragm.

51. Accelerator pump cover.
52. Screw.
53. Throttle plate screw.
54. Throttle plate.
55. Throttle shaft-primary.
56. Throttle shaft-secondary.
57. Accelerator pump
    discharge needle.
58. Main metering jet.
59. Inlet strainer plug.
60. Inlet strainer.
61. Upper body.
62. Stud.
63. Bolt.

ing to a more efficient type of carburettor. Weber, for example, produce high-performance twin choke downdraft carburettors, shown in Fig 30. These allow the engine to 'breathe' better, allowing a larger amount of fuel/air mixture into the cylinders – particularly at high revolutions when the single choke carburettor is beginning to strangle the engine by restricting the air flow too much. In large American V-8s, four-choke carburettors which are able to produce and distribute the mixture over this number of cylinders more efficiently are found.

Tuning for power cannot be included in this book, but I am assured by some of the carburettor manufacturers that not only can they offer substitute carburettors, but they may well be less expensive than the same model offered through the marine engine manufacturer's spares list. Although I preach caution in case special marinising has been carried out, I am assured that perfectly suitable substitutes are available if an old, badly worn or damaged carburettor needs to be replaced.

Carburettors have many parts which carry out similar functions. For example, all carburettors have a float chamber which controls the level of fuel available to the carburettor itself. The chamber ensures that the fuel pump does not over feed (flood) or under feed (starve) it.

From the float chamber the liquid petrol is fed to a jet, or in a fixed jet model several jets, where it meets a stream of air flowing from the air cleaner into the engine through a venturi. As the air flows over the jet the liquid fuel is vaporised and the resultant fuel/air mixture should then be in the right proportion to burn properly in the cylinder.

## AIR LEAKS AND CABLE CONTROLS

Before taking more drastic measures, it is worth checking whether simpler things such as an air leak or improperly adjusted cable-choke or throttle are the source of a carburettor problem.

With any type of carburettor, the only air let into it should be through the air cleaner and venturi. Worn throttle spindles and poor joints will upset the fine tuning of the air/fuel mixture, causing

rough running and poor fuel consumption. A piece of hose used like a stethoscope can be used to listen for high-pitched whistling round the carburettor parts, but it takes some practice to dissociate this from the noise of the intake roar through the air cleaner.

Control cable to the carburettor must run freely and allow the total movement necessary for the correct operation of the throttle and choke.

## VARIABLE JET CARBURETTOR

The variable jet in Fig 31 shows a SU HS carburettor. Looking at this figure, the dome-headed section at the top (the suction chamber or dashpot) houses a close-fitting piston which slides up and down within it. The movement is dictated by the differential pressure between the air flowing across the venturi and that inside the suction chamber. When the engine is running at idling speed, the piston almost sits on the bridge (10) in the venturi, nearly blocking it and so reducing the air flow.

On the manifold side of the carburettor is a throttle butterfly valve (not shown) which is opened and closed through the throttle control cable to the helm position. This is closed when the engine is idling, but as the control cable opens it the venturi is exposed to greater air flow as the downward stroke of the engine pistons sucks in more air.

At this moment the carburettor piston is still blocking the full air flow, but air is pulled through two small holes in the bottom of the piston, creating a vacuum in the top side of the suction chamber. This pulls the piston up out of the way, allowing more air to flow over the venturi. As you see, the lift also means that the tapered needle (7) is lifted with the piston, increasing the available size of the jet hole, thus allowing a greater quantity of fuel to be ingested into the air stream. Hence this type of carburettor is known as a variable jet unit.

To prevent sudden movement of the piston as the throttle is opened, it is damped with a piston (17) working in a small quantity of oil which must be topped up at service time. There is also a piston return spring (3) to ensure it drops towards the bridge as the throttle is closed. The Stromberg CD series carburettor is also a variable jet carburettor, but in this model a flexible diaphragm moves in sympathy with the differential pressure between the interior of the dashpot and the venturi to actuate the piston. The other major difference is that the Strombergs have the float chamber beneath them.

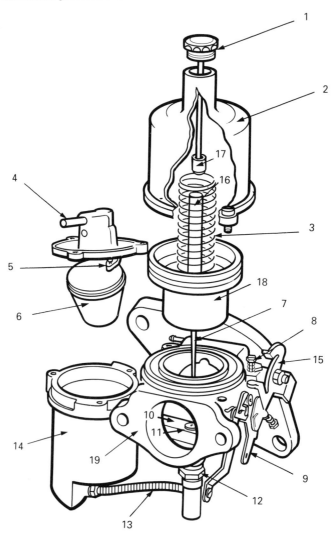

*Fig 31 SU Carburettor.*

KEY

1. Piston damper screw top.
2. Suction chamber or dash pot.
3. Piston spring.
4. Fuel inlet to float chamber.
5. Needle valve fuel inlet.
6. Float to control level of fuel in float chamber.
7. Fuel metering needle.
8. Idle speed screw.
9. Choke lever which moves fuel jet down in relation to piston to provide extra rich mixture for starting.
10. Bridge.
11. Jet hole, which must be perfectly concentric with fuel metering needle (7).
12. Jet assembly.
13. Fuel feed pipe to jet assembly.
14. Float chamber (clean to service).
15. Throttle linkage.
16. Piston damper tube (service by filling with correct grade oil).
17. Piston damper.
18. Piston. Must move freely up and down.
19. Flange to bolt on air cleaner.

# HINTS ON SERVICING VARIABLE JET CARBURETTORS

Full details will, of course, be found in the service manual, but here are some hints that may help. The kind of things that need servicing or which may go wrong are detailed below.

Mis-alignment of the fuel metering needle and jet hole. If these two are not perfectly concentric, some sticking may occur, creating uneven acceleration until the piston can rise properly. The needle should be fitted in the piston body (usually by a small grub screw) precisely as detailed in the service manual – too low or too high will not produce correct running. The needle can become worn and a careless mechanic may bend it. When replacing a needle always renew the jet at the same time so that both match perfectly, and check that the needle and jet coding are the same as the original.

For the needle/jet centring procedure Fig 32 shows the Stromberg CD, but the same principle can be used for the SU. Proceed as follows:

1. Lift the air valve (18) and tighten the jet assembly (12) up fully.
2. Screw up the orifice adjuster until the top of the orifice (19) is just above the bridge (28).
3. Slacken off the whole jet assembly (12) approximately half a turn to release the orifice bush (23).
4. Allow the air valve (18) to fall; the needle will then enter the orifice and should automatically centre itself. If necessary assist the air valve to drop fully by pushing it down gently with a rod via the damper access hole on top of the cover.
5. Tighten the assembly (12) slowly, checking frequently that the needle remains free in the orifice by raising the air valve about one quarter of an inch and then allowing it to fall back freely. The piston should then stop firmly on the bridge.

*Now set the idle*:
6. Two items need adjusting, the throttle stop screw (3) and the adjusting screw (13). Keep the air cleaner off the unit and damper removed. The air valve (18) is held down on the bridge of the throttle bore (28) while the

jet (19) is screwed up until it just comes into contact with the underside of the air valve. The jet adjuster (13) is then screwed back about three turns to establish an approximate running position.

7. Replace the flame trap/air cleaner. It is not only highly dangerous to run an engine without the flame trap, but a waste of time as perfect tuning is not possible without it in place. This is because even the best air cleaner produces some air flow resistance compared to the 'free flow' condition.
8. Start and run the engine until it is warm and then by means of the throttle stop screw (3) reach an idle speed of about 600–800 r/min. The engine beat should be smooth and regular and by gradual adjustment of the screw (13) a final position can be determined. This position should provide smooth acceleration over the whole speed range. If the engine speeds up appreciably when the throttle control is suddenly opened the mixture may be too rich. On the other hand if the engine stops, it may be too weak. A weak mixture can make an engine run hotter than it should.

In the Stromberg CD Series, the diaphragm can on rare occasions rupture. This, of course, prevents the correct movement of the piston. The dashpot on both types is easily removed with the screws on the rim, but it is worth putting two scratch marks on opposite sides of the body casting to make sure the dashpot and lower casting can be perfectly lined up on re-assembly. Dash pot dampers need an oil change at the same time that the engine oil is changed. They invariably use the same grade of oil, but do not overfill. Often high-performance engines use twin carburettors and their tuning is best left to a professional as it is quite difficult to get them perfectly synchronised.

# FIXED JET CARBURETTORS

This type of carburettor varies in complexity from a simple single choke model with a couple of fixed jets much like the one on your grass cutter's engine to the Pierburg Solex 4A1, for example, whose cost

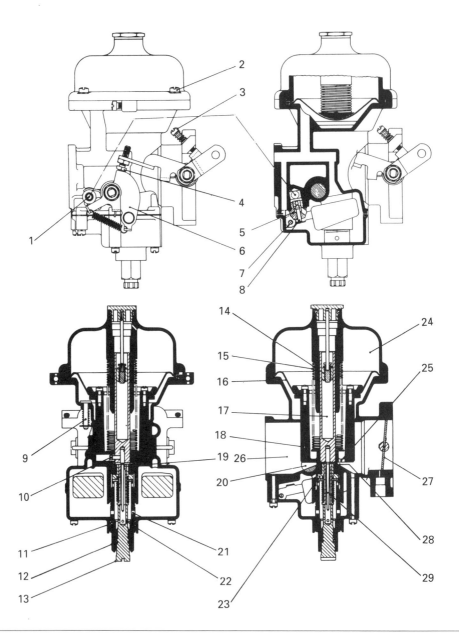

*Fig 32 The Stromberg CD Series variable jet carburettor.*

KEY

1. Petrol inlet.
2. Screw and spring washer for fixing cover.
3. Throttle stop screw.
4. Fast idle stop screw.
5. Fuel inlet valve seating.
6. Starter bar lever operated by cable from helm position.
7. Twin expanded rubber floats on a common arm.
8. Needle that controls fuel inlet

to float chamber.
9. Air valve lifting pin.
10. Screw holding tapered metering needle in place.
11. 'O' ring seal.
12. Bushing retaining screw.
13. Orifice adjusting screw.
14. Damper assembly.
15. Coil spring to assist downwards movement of air valve.
16. Diaphragm – check for rupturing.
17. Hollow guide rod housing the dash pot or hydraulic damper. Top up as directed with the correct grade of oil.

18. Air valve. Check for smooth up and down movement.
19. Jet orifice.
20. Starter bar.
21 and 22. Holes connecting float chamber with jet orifice.
23. Bushing for jet orifice.
24. Chamber.
25. Drilling in air valve to transfer manifold depression to chamber (24).
26. Bore.
27. Butterfly throttle.
28. Bridge of throttle bore.
29. Metering needle.

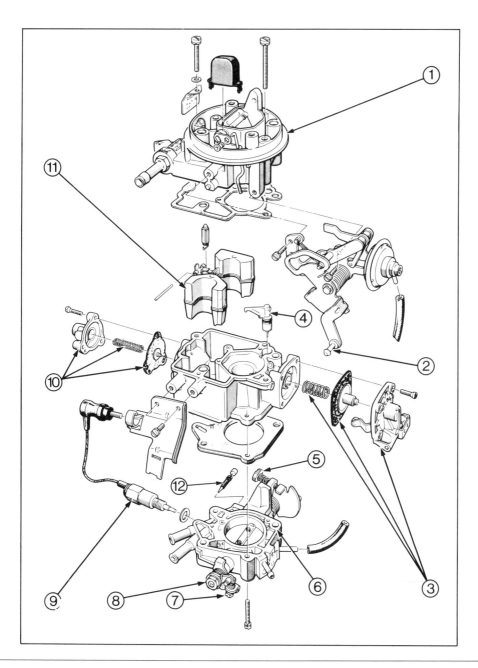

*Fig 33 Exploded view of a single choke fixed jet Ford IV carburettor.*

KEY

1. Upper body where air filter and flame trap (not shown) is fitted.
2. Manually operated choke mechanism which moves the choke plate into the closed position and a cam then partially opens the throttle plate when the choke control is fully pulled out.
3. Accelerator pump assembly enriches the mixture during acceleration.
4. Accelerator pump tube.
5. Fast idle adjuster.
6. Lower body housing the throttle plate.
7. Idling speed adjustment screw.
8. Throttle assembly.
9. Anti-dieselling solenoid operated valve which shuts off the supply of petrol to the carburettor when the ignition is turned off. Old IV carburettors did not have this device to prevent hot engines 'running on' like a diesel.
10. Power valve diaphragm assembly.
11. Float which controls the level of petrol able to enter the main float chamber through a needle valve. On a number of carburettors there is often a small filter on the main petrol inlet pipe immediately before a float chamber.
12. Mixture screw.

would buy several grass cutters complete. Thankfully, the 4A1 is so complex that models which appeared on the BMW six-cylinder marine engine were factory sealed and tamper proof. Automotive carburettors are often made tamper proof so that interference cannot put them out of adjustment, or outside anti-pollution laws presently manifesting themselves where car engines are concerned. We are almost bound to 'inherit' these laws and may find that either we need special tools to overcome the tamper proofing, or that we are not allowed to do this at all. In the meantime, there are many marine engine carburettors that can be properly cared for by the owner.

The Ford Motorcraft IV (Fig 33) is a fairly simple example of this type of single choke fixed jet carburettor. Many carburettors have needle valves (17) to adjust the mixture and these are often abused as shown in Fig 34. Wear is often caused by screwing them hard down onto the body casting and this immediately produces a shoulder on them and damages the orifice, which makes it impossible to achieve a finely tuned carburettor. If it is only the needle that is damaged this should be replaced, but often needle misuse damages the orifice itself and then both must be replaced.

## BASIC SERVICE NEEDS

I always suspect that there is a greater tendency for the fine drilling and jets to become blocked more easily than with the variable jet carburettors, but in all cases the bottom of the float chamber is where dirt will collect. This must be cleaned out at least once every season. Use a fluffless rag dampened with fuel – but take care! I prefer to use an aerosol electrical cleaning spray, which is safer and evaporates very quickly. Floats must operate the inlet valve at specific fuel levels and care is needed when disassembling to ensure any float pivot pin or spindle is not accidentally bent. Float height should be checked against the manual's specification.

Fixed jets usually have a screwdriver slot to aid removal. They are made from soft brass and care should be taken to see that the driver fits and no burrs are made. NEVER clean jets with a metal tool as the fine bores will usually be damaged. If they cannot be taken to a workshop where there is

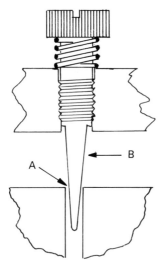
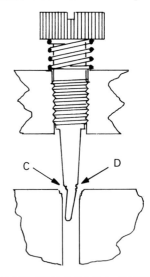

*Fig 34  Carburettor needle valve – use and abuse.*

KEY
A) The jet orifice must have a clean edge.
B) The needle must be perfectly straight with original taper.
C) Over-tightening or abuse with a

wire has damaged the orifice.
D) Over-tightening has damaged the needle taper and it is bent. Satisfactory operation is now impossible.

a compressed air line (which does the job best) use the pressurised aerosol mentioned previously. Old gaskets should have been removed with a gasket removal fluid. When removing them without this aid do ensure that the surface of the casting is not damaged.

New gaskets for mating parts of the carburettor are always needed and, as the accelerator pump diaphragm can occasionally fail, it is perhaps as well to renew this item every other season or so. The Ford Workshop Manuals are superb publications and perhaps an example for other manufacturers to follow as they make service and tuning jobs very straightforward.

## Manual and automatic chokes for starting

Although usually referred to as a choke, the device that allows a richer fuel/air mixture to be drawn into the cylinders is really a strangler on fixed jet carburettors. On variable jet carburettors, it is the piston that as it moves up the damper chamber draws the needle up from the jet on the bridge to produce a larger orifice and so take extra fuel into the intake air stream. However, for starting the choke lever actually moves the jet in the bridge downwards to produce the larger orifice and so obtaining a rich mixture into the cylinder.

Both strangler and choke can be operated by cable, but the user must ensure that as the engine warms up the strangler is returned to its proper running (open) position otherwise the engine will soon choke itself to death and probably stop.

I am not sure whether pulling a choke button in and out puts an undue strain on a driver, but skippers have again inherited automatic chokes from car engine makers. These are excellent for the lazy man as they do the job automatically using bimetallic strips heated by an electrical resistor or thermostatically from the state of the engine cool-ing water. They are perhaps unnecessarily complicated, when this is often the last thing wanted in a marine engine. However, if bad starting and high fuel consumption are in evidence they should be checked out by a professional mechanic.

## Carburettor drip trays

A serious fire or explosion hazard exists if fuel floods out of a damaged or badly adjusted carburettor. Most modern carburettors are of the downdraft type – Holley, Weber, Rochester etc – where the air and fuel streams are drawn down into the engine aided by gravity. If they accidentally flood the fuel should run harmlessly into the engine. US Coast Guard Rules are very specific about such dangers and state that each carburettor must not leak more than 5 cc of fuel in thirty seconds:

1. When the float is open.
2. When the carburettor is at half-throttle.
3. When the engine is cranked without starting.
4. When the fuel pump is delivering maximum pressure as specified by its manufacturer.

Every updraft or horizontal draft carburettor (SU and Stromberg) must be fitted with a device which:

1. Collects and holds fuel that flows out of the carburettor venturi section towards the air intake.
2. Prevents collected fuel from being carried out of the carburettor assembly by the shock wave of a backfire or by reverse air flow.
3. Safely returns any collected fuel to the engine's induction system after the engine starts.

Since this fuel is quite as good as dynamite if carelessly used, no leaks must be tolerated and engine spaces must be given ventilation, as specified later.

# 4  Oil and engine lubrication

Oil should be regarded as the lifeblood of an engine. In many ways it does some of the jobs that blood does in our bodies. Just as blood defends the body against invasion by microbes, so engine oil carries hostile materials – metal, carbon, gums, acids and varnishes to the engine oil filter. While the kidneys remove toxins and waste from the body, the engine oil filter removes destructive particles and neutralises the corrosive products which are produced in the combustion process. Oil also removes some of the heat from working parts.

The prime function of oil, though, is to keep apart metal surfaces which slide over one another within the engine. As anyone who has rubbed two boy scouts together knows, the friction caused produces fire! In an engine such high levels of friction first produce heat and expansion of the metals, then they seize solid – in some cases actually welding together. In recent years great progress has been made in producing lathes, drilling, milling and finishing machines and processes which make the working and faying parts of today's engines far superior to those in the past, when 'running in' an engine could take an owner many months of use on a small craft. The modern engine makes far greater demands on the lubricant than past engines did. Therefore we need to ensure that only the best lubricants suited to the engine are used.

## The oil circulation system

The good news is that engine lubricating oil systems are usually trouble free, and generally need little or no attention to unseen parts until a major overhaul takes place. The bad news is that if lubrication fails damage will be serious and very expensive to rectify, usually entailing a complete rebuild of the engine.

Fig 35 shows the system used on the Ford 2728T turbocharged diesel engine. Both petrol and diesel engines have many similar parts and functions in common with this one. I will draw readers attention to parts that may differ from the example as necessary.

The sump pan is sensitive to inclination and the boat builder is obliged to install the engine to the maker's specification so that oil levels will be maintained to feed the oil pump under all conditions. A coarse metal gauze filter prevents foreign bodies and large particles that would damage the pump from entering it. The pump itself will be one of two types:

1. A gear pump (Fig 36) where intermeshing gears, one being driven from the engine, force the oil round the close-fitting space between the gears and the chamber. As the gears mesh again, they force it out under pressure through a delivery port.
2. The double rotor pump (Fig 37) is sometimes referred to as a Hobourn–Eaton or epicycloidal pump. In this pump, a driven internal rotor with four teeth meshes with and drives an outer eccentric annular rotor with five teeth, both operating within the pump chamber. Larger pumps may have more teeth but the outer rotor always has one more tooth than the driven rotor. The displacement of oil from the suction port to the delivery port takes place in a similar manner to the gear pump, the intermeshing teeth of the rotors

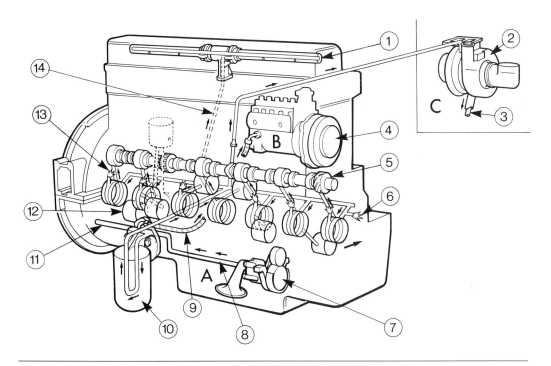

*Fig 35 The engine lubricating oil circuit.*

KEY

A The sump and coarse filter.
1. Rocker shaft.
2. Turbocharger (some petrol and diesel engines only (C)).
3. Oil drain to oil pan from turbocharger.
4. Lubrication for fuel injection pump (some 'in-line' diesel pumps only (B)).
5. Camshaft bearings.
6. Spray to timing gear.
7. Oil pump.
8. Feed pipe to filter and thence to main oil gallery.
9. Feed to diesel fuel in-line injection pump (see 4 above).
10. Oil filter.
11. Main oil gallery.
12. Big end bearings.
13. Main bearings and piston cooling nozzles.
14. Metered oil feed to rockers and rocker shaft.

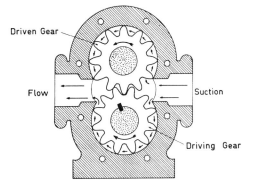

*Fig 36 A gear pump is sometimes used for pumping oil in either the main engine lubrication system or in the gearbox.*

alternately creating a chamber which carries the oil until the teeth close, forcing it out.

Eventually when there is excessive wear between the teeth, pump chamber walls and chamber end plates on either type of pump, pumping efficiency is lost and a rebuild or replacement will be necessary.

## OIL PRESSURE RELIEF VALVE

It is necessary to incorporate an oil pressure relief valve as oil pumps are designed to provide oil delivery slightly in excess of that normally needed for lubrication. The valve protects the pump, pipes, gaskets and oil seals from bursting, or the pump from absorbing too much power which might damage the gear drive or drive shaft.

The oil pressure relief valve is usually a spring-controlled ball or piston which operates at a set pressure. When this pressure is reached the oil drives the ball or piston back against its spring and this opens a port and allows the oil circuit to be bypassed. Under normal operating conditions pressure should remain steady. If pressure varies, it should be investigated immediately. Check the oil filter first to see that it is not damaged, loose or completely choked with contaminants, as this could be causing the trouble.

Pressure relief valves can stick, especially if filthy oil is constantly left in the system. Flushing oils should be tried before further drastic action is attempted. The seat of a ball valve may be eroded if acidic oil has attacked it. Springs can break or weaken so that working pressures are not reached.

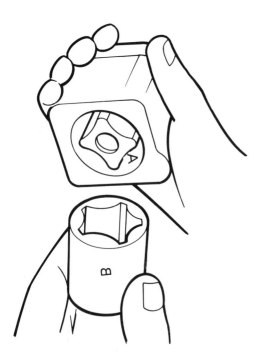

*Fig 37 A double rotor lubricating oil pump. A = driven rotor. B = free rotating rotor, which always has one segment more than the driven one.*

If the wear is in the pump itself, increasing the compression on the relief valve spring will still allow the engine to be starved of the oil it needs.

## OIL FILTERS

Oil is fed from the pump to the oil filter before it passes over the parts of engine to be lubricated. The different types of filter and methods of changing them are dealt with in Chapter 3, as oil filters are similar in basic concept to fuel filters. If an engine is winterized, the filter should be changed before winter when the oil is changed. Filters usually incorporate a ball relief valve similar in function to the one in the oil pump previously referred to.

## THE REST OF THE LUBRICATION SYSTEM

The clean oil is then fed under pressure by pipes, drillings, galleries or simple 'splash' or centrifugal 'slinging' onto the main bearings within the engine–crankshaft journals, connecting big and little rod ends, camshaft/s and rockers. All should receive their due share. On some diesels, as in Fig 35, part of the oil is diverted to lubricate the in-line fuel injection pump (b) and in turbocharged engines to lubricate the turbocharger (c). The oil drains down by gravity to the sump when the whole process is repeated.

## OIL COOLING

Normally, there is sufficient oil and a long enough cycling time to keep the oil temperature at safe levels. However, in high-performance engines it is often necessary to cool the oil using a heat exchanger, where the heat is extracted from the oil by the interface transfer of heat to the raw-water side of the engine cooling system. Normally the oil cooler needs little attention, but an owner should carefully monitor oil for water contamination that might be caused by the seals in the cooler failing.

The oil, of course, carries heat as well as dirt and contaminants away from all the internal surfaces of the engine. Often it is sprayed up into the underside cavity of pistons to cool them. Oil temperature is well worth monitoring with proper instrumentation.

Some gear-boxes also need their oil cooling and this might be done through simple heat transfer between raw-water passageways in the gear-box casting or through a heat exchanger.

## Running in an engine

If we could see the machined internal surface of the engine under a microscope we would notice that it looks like a landscape of mountains and valleys. The mountainous faying surfaces almost touch and create a great deal of friction. Running in should gradually reduce the landscape to a more consistent level so that even lubrication and even wear take place.

At one time the engine makers had to use prolonged periods on the factory test bench for the initial running in, and this was expensive both in time and labour. Better production methods have cut down factory running-in time to an absolute minimum – as little as 15 minutes for a normally aspirated engine and only 2 to 4 hours for a larger turbocharged diesel. Completion of running in is then left to the customer.

When a marine engine is received, it will normally have been despatched from the factory 'dry' with only sufficient preservative oils in it to give long-term (6 months +) storage to the internal parts, and perhaps a wax preservative sprayed on the outside. The outside can be wiped with towelling dampened with turpentine substitute to remove the coating. Once the engine is fully installed, the preservative oils are removed and the proper lubricating oils, water and fuel systems primed.

The manufacturer will give details of running-in procedures and times, but the first thing to check on starting up is that there are no leaks from oil, fuel or water pipes and filters. Idle at low speed while this is carried out, but speed and load are then *gradually* increased to hone down the faying surfaces. Diesels do not enjoy long periods of no-load idling. As the engine runs under load the

'mountains' should gradually be reduced, and the metal removed from them should end up in the oil filter. It is vital to replace oil and filter at the recommended time after this period as it carries much potentially harmful debris. Gearbox oil filters will also contain debris so these need equal attention. The first service may be anything between ten and fifty hours after the beginning of the running in period so the average yachtsman will need to be patient with the throttle.

The main problem that steady engine work and running-in avoids is scuffing between the top ring and the cylinder liner. This is where pressures are highest immediately after firing the charge, and lubrication at its poorest. In addition to the faying surfaces settling down, gaskets – especially the one on the cylinder head – settle and need retorquing down to the manufacturer's figures. In fact, all nuts and screw heads should be checked regularly during the running in period.

## General engine wear

Parts of the engine that wear are piston-bearing surfaces, cylinder bore, piston ring and grooves, valve train (rockers, push rods, tappets and cams) big and little end and other bearings. In pleasure craft engines we are fortunate that there is relatively little dust and grit that can enter the engine, especially if the air filters are kept clean. The big disadvantage is that for long periods, even during the season, the engine lies idle in the boat, especially over the winter lay-up period. I believe that more damage is done to an engine when it is not running than during its seasonal use.

The main source of wear is acidic attack on cylinder bores and liners, especially in diesel engines. This is produced by acids derived from the sulphur in diesel fuel and the combustion process. Generally the quality fuels we use are excellent, but it seems likely that as time goes on world shortages will force the use of lower grade diesel fuels with a higher sulphur content.

The acidic attack is related to the speed with which the engine warms up. The direct water cooled unit is the worst, the indirect much better and the air-cooled engine the best. The speedier the warm up, the quicker the acidic condensation (mainly sulphuric acid in the diesel) in the cylinder is eliminated. The dew point of the acids can be higher than the cylinder liner temperature at light loads and will increase with gas pressure so turbo-charged diesel engines suffer the most. This is one of the reasons why different types of engine need different types of oil. For each gallon of fuel burnt in the engine about a gallon of water is produced. Thankfully most is blown out in the exhaust gases, but some is dragged down in the piston stroke and contaminates the lower part of the engine. About 90% of the wear in the engine comes from this deadly combination of acid and water on the metal.

## Viscosity

The viscosity of an oil is a measure of its resistance to flow – thin oil has a low viscosity and is able to flow easily, while thick oil has high viscosity and low fluidity. The problem for the engine oil maker is to produce a viscosity which meets the varying conditions found in the engine and the climate it is operating in.

For example, when starting, much of the oil has drained off the faying surfaces before the oil pump and oilways can fully replace it. Fully oiled surfaces which slide over each other easily are necessary if there is to be only a minimum of power to start the firing cycle. As the engine temperature builds up, the same oil needs to have enough viscosity to lubricate under much harsher conditions of temperature and pressure. The USA Society of Automotive Engineers (SAE) classification of viscosity is now used almost universally.

SAE viscosity grades:

0W  5W  10W  15W  20W  25W  20  30  40  50

In 1980 the W grades were increased to the six above and the thicker grade oils, up to the thickest, 50SAE. Those without the 'W' remain the same as previously. If viscosity improvers are added,

engine oils can be formulated to fall into more than one of the above grades. These are the familiar 'multigrade' oils where a designation like 10W/30 means that the oil has a low temperature viscosity of the appropriate W grade, but as it warms its viscosity changes to that of the designated non-W grade. The viscosity index improvers are additives usually based on polymers. The importance of viscosity for the owner is not only of correctly lubricating the engine at its running temperature but to gain easy starting.

For any diesel engine, depending as it does on raising the temperature of the compressed air in the cylinder to the fuel ignition point, there are temperatures when it is impossible to start. The cold metal literally takes all the heat away and the thick viscous oil makes it too difficult for the starter motor to crank the engine at sufficient speed. True there are starting aids, but if the oil is thin enough at the starting temperature, then the unsticking torque will be that much lower for the starter to overcome. Although most of our boating is certainly not in freezing conditions, the basic principle of making it easy for the engine to start at the ambient temperatures in which a boat is operated is obviously important and it also has a direct effect on fuel consumption. Table 2 sets out the SAE grades which are generally suited to operating engines in various climatic temperatures. This is only a guide and the manufacturer's recommendations are best followed.

## AMERICAN PETROLEUM INSTITUTE SPECIFICATIONS

The engine manufacturer must not only guarantee his product for an initial period of use – usually one year (but Perkins now offer a 2 year warranty with their engines) – but also ensure that after that period the engine will still give a long trouble-free service life. The specification of engine lubricant given in the owner's handbook is made only after very careful testing and should be followed throughout the engine's life. Cheap and nasty reprocessed oil or an oil can that does not have a printed specification on it should be avoided at all costs.

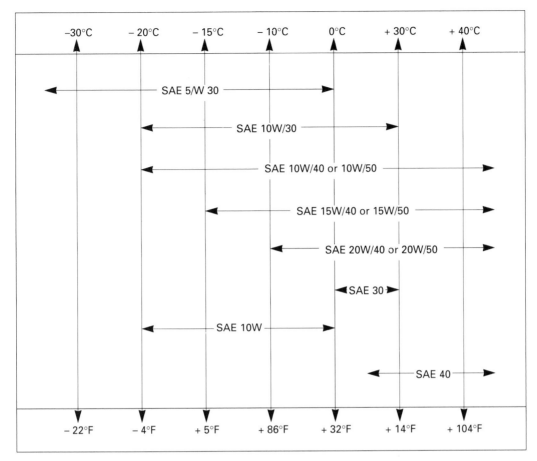

| −30°C | − 20°C | − 15°C | − 10°C | 0°C | + 30°C | + 40°C |
|---|---|---|---|---|---|---|

SAE 5/W 30

SAE 10W/30

SAE 10W/40 or 10W/50

SAE 15W/40 or 15W/50

SAE 20W/40 or 20W/50

SAE 30

SAE 10W

SAE 40

| − 22°F | − 4°F | + 5°F | + 86°F | + 32°F | + 14°F | + 104°F |
|---|---|---|---|---|---|---|

TABLE 2

As we have seen elsewhere, whenever committees meet to agree standards, they manage to produce so many that the layperson becomes bemused. Military defence boffins, engine manufacturers, standards bodies of one sort or another get in on the act, and instead of it being a simple job to select the correct oil the engine needs we end up reading a lot of confusing small print on the product label.

The American Petroleum Institute (API) has a simple classification of lubricating oils shown in Table 3, and this is now being more generally used alongside or to replace the many US Department of Defence 'MIL' specifications and those of a plethora of manufacturers. To add to the confusion, the Committee of Motor Manufacturers of the European Community (CCMC) has produced yet another set of specifications. While all this nonsense is going on, I would advise owners simply to determine the SAE viscosity index and the API service grade classification that the engine needs either from the owner's handbook, one of the major oil companies, or a specialist premium oil company such as Duckhams.

You should find the API and SAE specifications printed on the container in which the oil is sold. As engine performance is upgraded and puts greater demands on lubricating oils, performance classification will be extended from time to time. It is perfectly permissible for any engine to use a higher grade oil than the one normally specified.

## Oil additives

Additives are of two types. First there are those that are sold in beguiling packages which it is claimed will unbelievably enhance performance when added to the normal grade of oil. Then there are the additives which every quality oil already has blended into it. As far as I am concerned, the use of extra proprietary additives is a total waste of money. Not only do quality oils already contain the additives needed by the engine, but as the oil is generally changed every six months or so – at the end of the boating season – it is seldom that those present will have been 'used up'.

The two most important jobs additives do are to keep the engine clean and minimise wear. Some of the more important additives are listed below.

*Alkalines* are used to offset the acidity which gathers on the internal surfaces of the engine. After a time the alkaline content is used as it neutralises the acids. The oil may then be 'neutral' but it can no longer neutralise acid, which will then attack the engine – particularly the cylinder. Hence the need to remove dirty oil at the end of each season *before* winter storage so that the new, clean oil can give the proper protection. If, as I inferred earlier, we are forced to use inferior diesel fuels with a greater sulphur content, then these additives will play an increasingly important part in preserving our engines.

*Anti-oxidants* which slow down the natural rate of deterioration of oil. They help prevent high temperatures in certain parts of the engine, breaking down or oxidising the oil, possibly making it thicker, forming weak acids and breaking down into lacquers and other deposits. Thickening is not helped by addition of suspended solids such as carbon. As already mentioned as oil 'ages' the anti-oxidants are used up, hence the need to replace oil at the proper service interval or over winter.

*Dispersants.* The term 'detergent' is often used to describe oils, but it is one, I feel, that is best used only for washing powder. A detergent merely removes the dirt from a surface while a dispersant does not allow it to contaminate the surface in the first place. The dispersant continues by keeping the dirt in full suspension. The filter collects the larger particles, and the oil carrying the finest, harmless ones is fully suspended. This is why diesel engine oil sometimes looks filthy after being in the engine just a few minutes. There is nothing to worry about as it simply shows that the dispersant is doing a fine job, particularly in keep-ing the fine oil ways clean. It also prevents lacquer and other deposits forming on internal surfaces of the engine.

Sludge is often formed in direct, raw water cooled engines when the cooling system operates below its ideal temperature. It may deposit itself on cool surfaces such as the rocker cover where it does no harm, but it can block oil ways, oil drain holes and piston scraper grooves where it can jeopardise full lubrication or increase oil consumption. If this happens on your engine, change the make of oil to one that does its job better.

*Other additives* include ashless dispersants to rid the engine of soot and prevent lacquer and deposit formation. Extreme pressure additives prevent undue wear on cams and tappets or gears. Anti-corrosion and anti-foam suggest the functions they perform, and viscosity improvers reduce the loss of viscosity in the oil as temperature increases. At the other end of the scale, pour-point depressives improve the flow properties at cold temperatures. When it is extremely cold, oil can form wax particles in much the same way as diesel fuel can. The wax thickens the oil, making the starter motor work that much harder. At the same time the faying surfaces may be starved of proper lubrication. Finally, there are oil seal swell controllers which control the swell of oil seals as they wear to prevent oil leaks.

The cost of a good oil is minute compared to the cost of repair or replacement. Can any owner who takes pride in his engine and wants it to have a long life ignore this scientific alchemy?

## Engine oil analysis

Cummins Engines of Dallas own the worldwide Fleetguard Company which normally devotes its attentions to oil analysis for industrial and commercial carrier fleets to maximise usage and predict engine problems before they occur. General Motors Detroit Diesel Corporation also run a similar oil analysis programme.

Although these services are perhaps outside the

scope needed to maintain an ordinary pleasure boat engine, for the hire fleet owner or for long distance cruising they are worth consideration. Oil analysis can anticipate when a breakdown might occur and prevent loss of income and goodwill when applied to a hire fleet. The larger and more expensive your engine, the more oil analysis may appeal.

Normally, the analysis checks the quality of the oil sample sent to the laboratory. Over a period of time, with, say, a regular analysis every three months, the laboratory will advise of any increase in metal elements. Iron might be present from wear on rings and liners, the crankshaft or camshaft, while lead may be from crankshaft bearings or rocker arm bushings. Aluminium might be from pistons or the turbo-blower, and so the list goes on. The more sampling there is over a period of time, the better the laboratory are able to build up a picture of what is happening inside the engine and advise the owner on the analysis programme report.

For most of us, however, Eyeball Mk1 must suffice and we need to look for milky (water present) discoloration or 'silvery' looking oil which may indicate the unwelcome presence of metal. An engine will be in very poor mechanical condition if fuel is dragged down by pistons to dilute the lubricating oil and if this is suspected, an engine rebuild will probably be needed.

## Flushing and preservative oils

Some oil companies produce specialised oils that are of interest to boat owners. These are well worth investigation even if they only merit occasional use.

### FLUSHING OILS

Flushing oils are excellent when the interior condition of the oil ways, perhaps in a second-hand engine, is suspect. They are thin oils designed to dissolve surface deposits - carbon, gums, varnishes etc - and clean bearing surfaces and oil ways thoroughly. They are poor lubricants so

engines are generally run without load for a short time to circulate and allow them to work. They are then pumped out and ordinary oil used to replace them. It is not necessary to use them every season if the ordinary oil has been changed regularly, but every four or five seasons does keep things internally clean.

### PRESERVATIVE OILS

If an engine is to be laid up over a period of time exceeding six months, the engine oil should be changed to a fully preservative one. These contain a higher proportion of vapour phase and contact corrosion inhibitors. Most oil companies produce them, but for a normal winter lay up I find the ordinary grade oil quite adequate. I do, however, use engine manufacturer's 'special' laying up products such as Perkins Powerpart No 2 - an aerosol dispensed cylinder inhibiting oil that is used to douse the intake and preserve that part of the engine. To use it on my diesels I operate the fuel cut-off and turn the engine over on the starter while spraying the inhibitor into the manifold with the air cleaner removed. This type of product can be used on petrol engines, but on any engine do make sure that you do not fill the cylinder with oil and cause an hydraulic lock, which could bend the connecting rod when next you try to start up.

Diesel fuel system preservative oils such as Perkins Powerpart No 1 can be added to the fuel tank and run through to protect fuel line injection pump and injectors. Shell Calibration fluid 'A' or 'B' can be run into the fuel system from just before the engine fuel filter. This of course entails more work than just adding a preservative to the tank. Finally, although not strictly an oil, there are wax aerosol sprays, such as Perkins Powerpart No 3, which are sprayed over the exterior to give complete winter protection.

## Marine grease

It is usually the ancillary equipment, away from the main engine, which may require small amounts of grease for preservation and lubrication. Some stern glands have grease cups or remote greasers while a few old Jabsco type water impeller pumps use this type of lubrication for their drive shaft.

· A smear of grease is also useful when re-assembling gaskets and is often used on the sealing ring on the bottom of canister oil filters. A little can be placed on studs and smeared over machined surfaces which are exposed during winterisation.

Waterproof greases are available for skin fitting valves, but generally speaking an automotive grease suffices so long as it does not separate out

oil and base when it is under pressure in the greaser, or become hygroscopic to form an emulsion which then provides poor lubrication.

Although some condemn the use of greases with a high molybdenum content due to a possible interaction of this metal with the one it is coating, producing electrolytic action, I have not found this to be a problem. For many years, I have found molybdenum greases extremely useful when used to coat moving surfaces sparingly during a rebuild. They provide essential lubrication immediately the engine is turned over and before oil normally reaches these surfaces. Molybdenum oil additives

TABLE 3. API Service classifications

Petrol engine classes are prefixed with 'S', which stands for Service station, and diesel engine classes by 'C', which stands for Commercial. The second letter designates the severity of service, the lowest being 'A', with increasing severity in ascending order of the alphabet.

**Oils for petrol engines**

**SA** Service typical of engine operated under mild conditions. No performance requirements and may be only specified for very old obsolete engines where the makers can still advise this grade to be used.

**SB** Service typical of petrol engines operating in conditions such that only minimum protection afforded by the addition of additives is desired. These oils have been used since the 1930s and may still be suited to engines of this vintage. They provide only anti-scuff and resistance to oil oxidation and bearing corrosion.

**SC** Engines typically based on petrol engines derived from the car and truck base units in the 1964–67 era. They provide control of high and low temperature of deposits, wear, rust and corrosion.

**SD** Service typical of engines derived from base units in the period 1967–70, but may apply to some later models. These oils provide more protection than SC and may be used where SC is recommended.

**SE** Service typical of petrol engines derived for car and truck in the 1972–79 era. They give greater protection against oxidation, high temperature deposits, rust and corrosion. They may be used in place of either SC or SD.

**SF** Service typical of engine from 1980 onwards. They provide better oxidation stability and anti-wear performance than the SE oils and may be used to replace any of the three previous grades.

**SG** For 1989 petrol engines derived from car, van or light truck engines. There may be an overlap with diesel category here as some manufacturers of these engines have specified API Service CS or CD. These oils provide improved control of engine deposits, oil oxidation and engine wear than the previous categories and they may be used where SE or SF are recommended.

**Oils for diesel engines**

**CA** For light or moderate duty use with high quality fuels. Has been included for use in some light duty petrol engines. It provides protection against bearing corrosion and from piston ring belt deposits in naturally aspirated diesel engines. They were widely used in the 1940s and 1950s but should not be used unless specifically recommended by the engine manufacturer.

**CB** For diesel engines operated in mild to moderate duty but using lower quality fuels which necessitate more protection being given for wear and deposits. Again this has been specified for some heavy duty petrol engines. They cover naturally aspirated diesels where higher sulphur content fuels have to be used, and were first introduced in 1949.

**CC** These are for moderate duty diesel service and some heavy duty petrol engines. Service is typical of both normally aspirated and turbocharged diesel engines operated at moderate or severe duty. They were introduced in 1961 and service provides protection from high temperature deposits and bearing corrosion, and low temperature deposits on petrol engines.

**CD** This is for severe duty normally aspirated and turbocharged diesel engines where highly effective control of deposits and wear is vital, or when using fuels of varying quality – especially high sulphur content fuels. They were introduced in 1955.

**CE** For high performance diesel engine service, mainly turbocharged engines operated in both low speed, high load and high speed, low load conditions. These oils have been available since 1984 and provide control of oil consumption, oil thickening and piston assembly deposits.

are not necessary if a premium grade oil is being used, and should not be used when running an engine in. The use of graphite-based greases should, in the salt water marine environment, be avoided as they can produce electrolytic corrosion.

## Aerosol spray corrosion inhibitors

There are a great number of proprietary products on the market and most do an excellent job. However did we manage before WD-40 and similar products came onto the market? Nevertheless, it is essential for the yachtsman to be certain that he reads the small print to make sure that the product is totally compatible with the many materials on the engine with which it will come into contact. As well as metals, it will alight on many types of rubber and plastic. Most claim not to harm electrical wiring insulation, but there are materials that even the best will soften. Some types of red gasket material soften to the point of destruction. Read the small print before using, and try some out on waste materials just to make sure.

## Marine transmission and gearbox oils

The type of oil used in a marine gearbox is again specified by the manufacturer and this specific type must then always be used. Many simple marine gearboxes use the same oil as the engine – a very convenient situation as only one type has to be carried. However, when gears which are under high load, as with some hypoid gears, are employed in the train, extra anti-scuff, high pressure oils may be specified to reduce wear and prevent seizure.

Since any box that needs cooling is often served by raw water, one must guard against corrosion. When emptying the oil, check for water contamination.

# 5 Electrical systems on marine engines

If readers forgive my over simplification I might say that there are only two things that commonly go wrong with any marine engine. We have dealt with the first – fuel. We now deal with the other – electricity. Electrical installations and equipment are only troublesome because water conducts electricity as well as being corrosive, especially when loaded with salt. Fresh rain water, salt sea water and humid air condensing on cold surfaces all play a destructive part.

Just two things are needed to make electrical installations both safer and more reliable. They are a dry boat interior and proper ventilation. This latter item is sadly a recurring *bête noire* as far as I am concerned as the next chapter details.

There are a number of proprietary fire retarded plastic conduit systems available, such as 'Egatube', and marine wiring would be made safer and more reliable if they were used. In production boatbuilding their cost is the one disadvantage.

With the electrical wiring on marine engines, possible abrasion points should always be looked for. Provided extra wiring or loom length is allowed for it should be flexible enough for the movement imposed by a flexibly mounted engine. It must never be stretched to its limit or drawn across a sharp metal edge. Clips and conduit edges must not pinch it too hard to distort or break the outer insulation.

## Marinisation of electrical equipment

There is always the temptation for builders, and later owners, to use proprietary hardware from the automotive market. There is a disturbing grey area here. Although the important parts such as the generator may be made to a marine specification, there are often electrical components such as points sets sold at grossly inflated prices which, in fact, are precisely the same as lower priced automotive spares.

There are important differences in the major items. Automotive products have a ground (earth) return on their engine – marine engines and their electrics must have an insulated return to prevent dangerous electrolytic corrosion that may occur if there is current leakage. More than one propeller has simply dropped off its shaft when leaking current has electrolytically disintegrated the shaft end.

Plastic parts should be compatible with environmental conditions not only of engine oil, fuel and salt water, but of UV light. Metal items should be factory painted with a high performance paint finish to protect them from corrosion. Certain parts such as starter motor windings should be impregnated to maintain insulation levels, and electronic items fully encapsulated so that they are totally sealed from the environment. All this costs money but makes for greater reliability, safety and lower maintenance costs – all of which give us greater peace of mind.

We are not concerned in this book with the complete electrical system on the boat. However, as the engine is so dependent upon it for starting and since, on the vast majority of boats, it generates the current for the batteries, it must receive attention.

# Voltage drop

Most small craft electrical installations are 12 or 24 volt, or occasionally 32 DC (direct current). Large yachts carry their own 'shore' voltages of 110 or 240 AC (alternating current). We have inherited these low DC voltages from the automotive industry but the lower the voltage, the more problems are created for the design of the installation.

To carry the full current, a wire must have a definite cross-section of conductors (multi-strands of copper wire) for a given length. If the wire is too thin, then its resistance increases – it becomes warm and delivers less than full voltage to whichever appliance is demanding it. This may well be the petrol engine's ignition coil or the starter motor on either type of engine. This is bad news indeed, for it means that starting ability is jeopardised, and it can also mean that damage is caused to electrical motors and other equipment. Heating (a possible source of ignition in a fire) is kept strictly within safe limits – standards are laid down by the classification societies. In an international boatbuilding market, boats should be built so that the maximum temperature rise in electrical equipment and cable ratings are able to cope with the ambient temperatures prevailing in the area of operation. Good engine room ventilation which keeps machinery spaces cool makes a vital contribution.

Provided an owner is aware of the damage and danger from voltage drop in incorrectly sized cables, there is no need to go further into the technicalities. Any engine already installed should have the correct wiring, but further advice should be sought if wiring is being replaced, especially if the run is longer than the original, or if batteries are being moved further away from the starter.

# Diesel engine starting aids

Most marine engines use electrical starting motors now, but dual starting systems by either hand or electric power should be regarded as a real safety bonus.

Diesel starting depends on raising the temperature of the inlet air to a degree that will allow it to ignite the injected fuel. The problem is to prevent the cylinder head and piston crown surfaces taking away the heat generated by the compression stroke and to generate sufficient heat when the ambient air temperature is low to ignite the fuel in the cylinder.

Any engine that is in good mechanical order should have no problem at all during normal northern hemisphere summers, and in small engines right down to freezing point, provided that the battery and starter are able to produce full specification cranking speed. However, to take some load off the battery and help starting in extreme conditions, starting aids have been developed. Although the following are not all electric types, when used they take some off the load of the electric starter motor. I have therefore included them in this section.

## MANUAL PRIMING WITH DIESEL FUEL OIL

Small diesel engines can sometimes be helped simply by adding a few drops of fuel to the air intake manifold before cranking the engine. This improves the sealing of the piston rings and reduces the effective clearance volume of the cylinder to increase compression and produce a higher temperature in the compressed air, which will then ignite the fuel.

Great care is needed as excess fuel may cause a hydraulic lock – the engine will not be able to compress a cylinder full of liquid – and the result will be very expensive indeed to repair. The connecting rod may be bent, or even broken. However, with care it can be a last resort, and is particularly effective if an engine has been laid up for years and as a result compression rings are dry. In larger diesel engines the injectors are removed and a tablespoon of fuel is added to each cylinder. Place layers of cloth over the cylinder head and turn the engine by hand if possible to work the fuel into the rings and lubricate the cylinder walls. After a few minutes blow excess fuel out of the cylinders by fast cranking. Ensure that fuel from high pressure lines as well as the cylinder head is all caught, and that there is no danger from any nearby source that could ignite it. Now replace the injectors and piping and if everything else is working properly the engine should fire up.

## AEROSOL STARTING AIDS

These are the 'non-electric' items which I have allowed to creep into this chapter. Used sensibly, they can be a great help in starting a difficult engine. They are occasionally vital on some racing diesels where the compression ratio has been lowered to levels that would hardly allow the engine to start at all without them. The lowering of the compression ratio is to enable the engine to cope with very high boost and cylinder pressures at racing speed.

The products are manufactured to produce a fuel which has a lower ignition point than diesel oil. Most are based on ether. Some of the problems that ether creates are an undesirably high rate of pressure rise in the cylinder and total lack of lubricating properties. It is also a fire hazard and can be a human one, too. The aerosols include a lubricant and other additives to overcome some of the undesirable characteristics. However, I would say that in most cases it is better to spend money getting an engine in good mechanical order so that it will start normally rather than depend on these kind of products.

## HEATER PLUGS

There are two basic types of electrical heater plug that are designed to increase the temperature of the manifold air. They are made by Delco-Remy, Bosch and Lucas.

The first type is a purely electrical plug, something like a spark plug on a petrol engine. The difference is that the heating element attains a temperature of about 1000°C in 30 seconds or so, and the compressed air swirling over it is heated to ignition point. As they work best in cylinder heads which have rapid air movement at low cranking speeds, they are much used on engines with indirect injection, although they are found on small direct injection engines, too. The original type had exposed heating wire which in the high temperature corrosive atmosphere of the chamber limited their service life. More recent elements are sheathed, but still energy hungry, so it is important to have batteries in tip-top condition.

Lucas CAV have overcome some of these problems with their *Micronova* fast start system, which uses a sheathed heater plug in each cylinder that is temporarily overloaded with electricity so that it warms up quickly, but is then governed by an electronic controller which virtually eliminates the warm-up period and only energises the plug for a short time after combustion has commenced. This reduces the possibility of the engine stalling. If starting deteriorates, check the heater plugs are warming on the outside within a couple of seconds of switching them on. Take care not to overheat and then burn your fingers.

## COMBUSTION TYPE MANIFOLD HEATERS

The best known of these is the Lucas CAV 'Thermostart' which is found inserted in the air intake manifold (Fig 38A) of some diesel engines. It needs a diesel fuel supply line which can be taken from its own small tank, or a small tank supplied by the clean side of the engine's fuel filter which has a combined overflow/vent into the main fuel tank.

A thermostatically controlled valve (Fig 38B) is heated and expands the sleeve which allows the ball valve to open and admit fuel to the combustion chamber. The igniter coil is in series with the heater coil and sets the fuel alight. The burning fuel heats the incoming combustion air to achieve ignition temperature within the cylinders. Later we will look at the special sprung return starter switches used to actuate the heater/starter and run the electrical circuits involved. After the engine starts, the heater is shut down automatically as the electrical supply to the coil is cut off, which in turn cuts off the fuel supply as the incoming air rapidly cools the Thermostart body. Fault finding is illustrated in Fig 38C.

A

Cold air through air filter

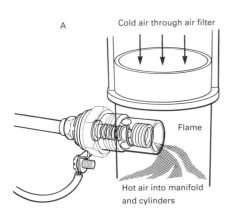

Flame

Hot air into manifold
and cylinders

B

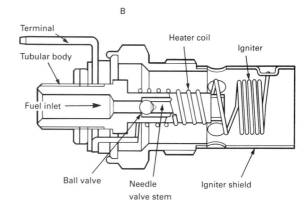

Terminal

Heater coil

Igniter

Tubular body

Fuel inlet →

Ball valve

Needle
valve stem

Igniter shield

C  Electrical check

1.  Check wiring connections.

2.  Start cold engine and shut
down immediately.  A warm
thermostart indicates the
electrical system is operating.
IF COLD REPLACE
THERMOSTART

Functional check
Operate Thermostart normally
but do not crank.  If fuel is
flowing a 'pop' will be heard in
the manifold.  IF THERE IS NO
POP REPLACE THE
THERMOSTART.

Leak check
1.  Check engine for black
exhaust smoke.
2.  Run engine for two minutes
and shut down.  Remove and
inspect.  IF DAMP WITH FUEL
REPLACE THERMOSTART.
Warning: Never operate the
Thermostart whilst it is
removed from the manifold.

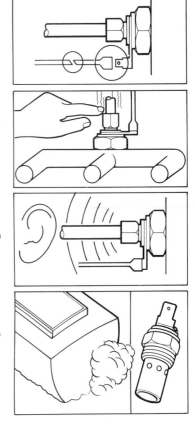

*Fig 38  Thermostart.* ®

## THE START PILOT (Fig 39)

This is an atomised fluid starting system mentioned as being fitted to the Sabre Marathon engines, but it finds its way as standard equipment onto many other diesel engines. Both manual and electric pumps are available which pressurise the starter fluid reservoir to mix the fluid with the air. This highly flammable vapour is then fed into the air intake manifold where it is drawn into the cylinders.

Like almost all starting fluids, Start Pilot fluid contains a proportion of sulphuric ether, but unlike them it is considerably modified to produce a more progressive burn and smooth spread of the flame front in the cylinder. This produces a more acceptable pressure rise within the cylinders rather than the often fierce detonation associated with aerosol/ether products.

## Petrol engine electrics

## THE BASIC IGNITION CIRCUIT

To ignite the petrol/air mixture in the cylinder of a petrol engine, a high intensity spark is required which jumps across the plug gap at a precise moment in the four- or two-stroke cycle. There are jobs that every skipper should be able to do which will keep the system in good working condition. You should still stick to the ones that are advised in the handbook, and even these may involve intermediate or even advanced skills and equipment.

The letters throughout refer to those in Fig 40 (basic petrol engine ignition system). There will be variations in a number of the components in most marine engines so it should be regarded only as a guide to what may be found, and the parts which will need some attention if the engine is to be serviced properly. Before starting any work make a note of the make and model of the distributor, spark plugs and coil so that you can order the exact

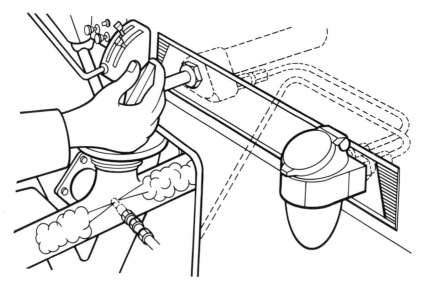

*Fig 39 The start pilot diesel starting aid.*

replacements needed. It is always handy to record information like this in the boat's log book, where the engine should be given a special section.

## DISTRIBUTOR BODY

The heart of the ignition system is contained in the DISTRIBUTOR BODY (A). A shaft, usually driven from the valve lift cam shaft, rotates inside the body which is held in position with a clamping device (H). The spark must be produced at a precise moment in the ignition cycle, so *timing* the spark in relation to the position of the piston as it moves over the top dead centre (TDC) of its stroke is vital.

Never undo the body fastening clamp unless you are capable of completely retiming the engine. It is always as well to put a scratch mark between the body and the casting where it enters so that timing can be set roughly back in place.

Clips (not on drawing) on either side of the distributor body are pressed outwards and the cap removed to gain access to the inside of the distributor. The rotor arm (F) must be removed, and sometimes a plastic cover, to gain access to the points.

The contact breaker points (B) open and close to make or break the low tension (12 V) electrical circuit, shown as thin wires in the diagram. The points suffer both mechanical wear as they move on the cam, and burning or pitting caused by the constant opening and closing and arcing that occurs. Points that are in bad condition cause poor starting and misfiring, especially at high speed.

The condenser (E) reduces arcing by soaking up the voltage surge as the points open. While it is a good plan to replace points at the beginning of each season when the motor is tuned up, a new condenser only needs replacing every other set of points. If you notice the engine misfiring and lurching into high r/min rather than cleanly accelerating, then suspect that the condenser has failed and replace it and the points immediately.

There are two contact points (Fig 41A), one fixed and one that is moved away from it by the cam on the drive shaft. The moving point has a steel spring which forces the cam follower to keep close contact to give a sharp 'make and break' at high revolutions. Designs vary but to remove the points the

first job is usually to undo the low tension wire and the fixed point securing screw (Fig 40C) and then gently lever off the moving point from its pivot post, making sure its spring does not flip the lot into the bilges. If you are new to the game, carry out this operation slowly and make a note of exactly how to put things back. Now fit the new points and set the gap. On some old designs, the pivot post and the cam lubricator (Fig 40D) may need a tiny spot of fine oil but do not overdo this.

On older designed engines, the points were always set using a feeler gauge and screwdriver to tighten up the fixed point. In fact, this is fine for all engines when the points are brand new and you may still use this method just to get an engine running so that the 'dwell angle' (Fig 41B) can be measured using a 'Dwell Meter'. This is an extremely accurate way of 'gapping' the points. Reasonably priced instruments, as outlined in Chapter 10, are available from car accessory dealers.

Fig 40G is an automatic ignition advance and retard vacuum assembly. We saw earlier how the spark needs to occur at a precise time; this varies with the engine speed from starting-up to full revolutions. Various devices are used to move the whole of the base plate on which the points are mounted back and forth around the cam to advance and retard the ignition. This particular vacuum device depends on the suction across the carburettor manifold. A tube connects a diaphragm in the unit to the manifold. As speed increases there is more suction and the diaphragm is moved to advance the timing of the spark. It is this movement which pulls on the base plate and pushes when the suction drops. To check the diaphragm simply attach a mouth tube – a small suck should allow you to see that the diaphragm is moving the base plate slightly.

## DISTRIBUTOR CAP

Now let us move on to the distributor cap (Fig 40I) which we removed earlier. This is made of high insulation materials as it must keep thousands of volts in their place. Keep the cap dry and totally free from moisture or the sparks will escape! It needs minute inspection for cracks as these, too,

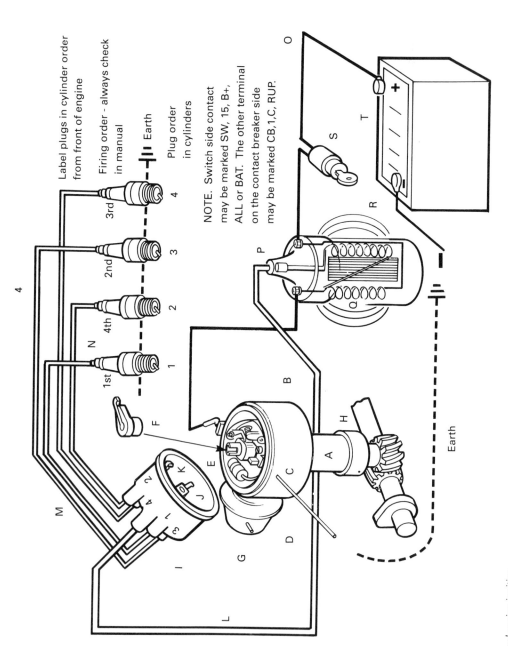

Label plugs in cylinder order from front of engine

Firing order - always check in manual

Plug order in cylinders

NOTE. Switch side contact may be marked SW, 15, B+, ALL or BAT. The other terminal on the contact breaker side may be marked CB, 1, C, RUP.

Earth

*Fig 40 Basic petrol engine ignition system (for key to letters see text).*

will allow the high tension lines to leak to earth. The cracks are sometimes so fine that a little white talcum powder wiped over the inside is needed to see them at all. Be sure to clean every trace of powder out afterwards unless you are renewing the cap. In darkness the sparks produced in a bad installation are clearly visible – you can see them leaping over the outside of the cover like the aurora borealis! Keep the inside clean and dust-free, too. Tracking, which I will discuss later, may occur between any of the electrodes – centre or side. If there are fine black lines of carbon deposited it is time to fit a new cap.

The central electrode (J) should have a sprung contact which holds firmly against the rotor (F) to transmit the high tension current through it and thence to the four outer HT contacts and leads (for a 4-cylinder engine) that send the spark to the spark plugs. Incidentally, when a boat is left, an excellent security measure is to remove the rotor since the engine will not start without it. Check that the spring is moving freely. Provided you remove the dust created, a piece of emery paper can be used to clean the outer contact and rotor but do not overdo it.

## HIGH TENSION LEADS

These pack a hefty electrical punch, and there is danger if you are foolish enough to work on them when the engine is running without using well insulated tools. There are two sets of high tension (HT) leads that must be serviced. The one that exits

from the central hole on the coil (P) and enters the same place on the distributor cap is often referred to as the *king lead* as it serves all the other four HT leads (M) that carry the current to the spark plugs.

In time, the insulation on the leads breaks down and allows the spark to 'track' to earth. Tracking may also play havoc with electronic navigation aids and the radio when its radio frequency emissions are picked up. On a boat, tracking may well be all that petrol fumes need to cause a mighty explosion. Always keep these leads clean. Damaged leads always need immediate replacement. It is best to buy a factory made set as perfect terminal ends are essential and it is not always guaranteed that the amateur will be able to make them up correctly. In any case, this is one of the spares along with plugs, points, rotor and condenser that all petrol engined boats should carry.

The king lead provides a quick test for a hefty spark when checking the HT circuit. After undoing it from the top of the distributor, hold it gently in insulated pliers about a quarter of an inch away from the block and well away from any petrol vapour that might emerge from the plug hole. Use an old clean plug to fill the hole temporarily. With the engine space well ventilated (no explosive fumes) switch on the ignition and turn the engine over. A fat blue spark should jump to earth if all is well. After replacing the king lead, each of the other HT leads (M) can be tested in exactly the same way, but remove the ones not being tested well away as you do not want the engine to start up.

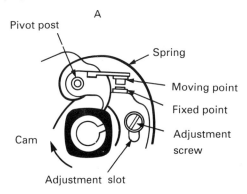

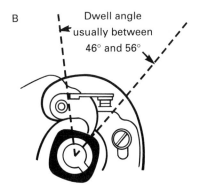

*Fig 41 The contact breaker assembly and dwell angle.*

## Ignition or starter switch (Fig 40S)

A key switch on the instrument panel is needed for both diesel and petrol engine starting. The only difference lies in the use made of the auxiliary contacts available for other switching functions. Basically, they switch a low amp current to the starter solenoid, which is then able to switch the high amp load to the starter itself.

### THE DIESEL SWITCH

The diesel starter switch has a spring-loaded return rotary action to use the auxiliary contacts. These perform the correct starting sequence which is dependent on the function needed. For example, when an engine is fitted with glow plug or Thermostart starting aids, these are first switched on to heat up and then, when they are ready, the next switch position brings the starter into action. The return spring action returns the switch to the 'run' position immediately it is released. Some also incorporate an engine 'stop' position which switches current to the fuel cut-off solenoid. Many small diesel engines do not use this method, and care is needed to see that the switches are NEVER cut before the stop cable controls are worked to shut down the engine. Ignoring this procedure could seriously damage the alternator.

### THE PETROL IGNITION SWITCH

This switch makes contact at one point for ignition/start and the return spring brings it to an ignition/accessories position very similar in function to those we are familiar with in a car – except it does not lock the steering wheel! As marine theft increases it may not be too early for manufacturers to be thinking of producing better key mechanisms to make it more difficult for thieves to start the engine. Automotive switches should never be used on marine applications as they usually give trouble through corrosion after a very short time.

Thankfully, proper marinised switches usually give little trouble, the most likely cause of trouble is a contact falling off the back.

## Batteries

Although these are shown in Fig 40T they are, of course, used for both petrol and diesel engine starting. This was not always the case.

In the past inboard petrol engines used magnetos – an electro-magnetic device which produced a spark at the plug without requiring a battery. Diesel engines, even quite hefty ones, had decompressors fitted which allowed them to be cranked up by hand to some speed before the compression was restored to fire the engine up. Indeed, most outboard engines use magneto ignition, usually modified by electronic circuitry to make it both more powerful and more reliable. There are still quite a few small diesels with hand starting. However, today, electric starting has become the norm for inboard engines and there is usually no back up starting system provided. In this situation, the starting battery plays a vital role in the pleasure and safety aspects of our boating.

### CRANKING REQUIREMENTS

All engines need to be cranked over at sufficient speed to either induce the air mixture into the cylinder in the case of a petrol engine or raise the compressed air to the ignition point of the injected fuel in the diesel engine. In fact, the petrol engine is far less demanding on the battery than the diesel since its lower compression ratio in the cylinder is usually about one third, and certainly less than about half, of that required in a diesel engine. A petrol engine may therefore compress its mixture to about 150 lb per square inch at a temperature of 400°F plus, while a diesel needs to raise the pressure within the cylinder to 500 lb per square inch at a temperature in excess of 900°F. As discussed in Chapter 4, the initial demand on the starter is to break the friction between the moving parts and lubricating oil film. We saw how this break-away torque is related to the ambient temperature. Assuming both types of engine to be in good mechanical order, the petrol engine should start in less than a third of the time that is needed for a similar capacity diesel. The reasons for the diesel engine being far more demanding may be summarised:

1. The friction that must be overcome in the diesel engine is much greater since it must have much closer fitting pistons to its cylinder walls in order to achieve the very high compression needed to heat up the combustion air. The 'break-away' draw on a 12 V battery may be in the region of 1,000 amps to 1,200 amps – almost double that needed for starting the equivalent capacity petrol engine. Fortunately, this figure drops off by about half when the already compressed air in the cylinders expands to offset the initial starting load.

2. The starter motor must turn sufficiently fast to achieve nearly adiabatic compression of the air. Initially there is some leakage of air past the best fitting piston, but as the engine is motored over on the starter the unburnt fuel gradually accumulates in the cylinder, temporarily increasing the effective compression ratio. Thus there is a cycle-to-cycle increase in the combustion air temperature. To maintain these conditions to the point where the engine fires and then goes on to self-motoring, the starter will demand about twice the rolling current and twice the cranking speed of the petrol engine.

From the foregoing, the importance of an adequate size starter battery will be obvious. Cranking speeds, usually in excess of 120 r/min must be capable of being sustained and only a battery in good condition will be able to do this. The higher the cranking speed, the better the cycle-to-cycle increase in combustion air temperature.

## SINGLE AND DOUBLE BATTERY INSTALLATIONS

For small craft, a single battery is the norm and it has two duties – starting the engine and supplying a few low power services such as navigation lights, a cabin light or two and little else. Generally speaking it is not a good system as it is all too easy to run the battery down with 'ship's services' and not be able to start the engine. A far safer mode of operation on a very small boat is to keep the engine battery exclusively for that job, but have a portable battery which can be taken home to recharge for supplying the services.

In larger craft, where more comprehensive 'ship's services' produce a heavy load, a double battery system is needed to separate the two functions. The double battery system does create a more complex electrical system as it needs both batteries to be charged at the same time, but automatically isolated from each other so that the starter battery is always kept fully charged, while the service battery can be discharged to a safe minimum voltage before it is again recharged. There are two methods of doing this:

1. Using a blocking diode which will allow the current from the generator to charge both batteries, but which prevents a return of current from one battery to the other thus isolating them when the engine stops. This is by far the most common method used where the propulsion engine also serves as prime generator for the boat. Diodes soak up quite a lot of current and the heat generated by them needs safe dissipation. They are, of course, provided with heat sinks for this purpose, but good ventilation and reasonable ambient temperatures are still necessary.

2. Using a solenoid switch connected through the ignition/starter switch. The solenoid switching automatically parallels the batteries as soon as the starter key switch is turned so that both receive a charge, but when the engine or engines are stopped and the key turned off, the batteries are automatically separated from each other. In a single engine installation this system has the danger that if the service battery has been heavily discharged, on turning the key the automatic paralleling may allow a heavy current to flow from the starter battery to the flat service battery and jeopardise starting. In a twin

installation there is less danger of this happening when one engine can be started before the switch contact linking the battery paralleling solenoid is used to start the second engine.

## BATTERIES IN SERIES AND PARALLEL

Fig 42 shows how batteries can be connected to produce a higher voltage or increase their amp/hour rating. The amp/hour rating gives the user an idea of the storage capacity of a battery. Thus a 200 AH battery should be able to give out 20 amps for 10 hours or 200 amps for one hour. It is as well to check that the hour rating is the same when making comparisons between batteries as ratings may differ, ten hour and twenty hour ratings often being used. What is significant is that the rating is related to the area of the plates inside the battery and hence its cost. There are many thousands of firms making cheap and cheerful batteries which may well be value for money in less demanding situations, but the yachtsman would be very foolish to put his trust in them. As always, you get what you pay for.

## TYPES OF BATTERY

You often see two main types discussed in boating publications. First, the expensive alkaline type which has a long service life and does not mind being left part or even fully discharged. These are comparatively rare on modern boats and seldom put into modest production line craft because of their high cost. The lead/acid battery reigns supreme for the majority of us.

As already mentioned, lead/acid batteries are not all exactly alike. If you choose the wrong type of battery for a particular application then it will not perform that function as efficiently as one designed especially for it. Neither will its service life be as extended.

Let us consider for a moment the different demands made on a starter battery and one that provides power for domestic (ship's services). The starter battery needs to produce a heavy current (amperage) for a very short time. It should seldom be deeply discharged since as soon as the engine starts it will be 'topped up' to full power, when it will sit happily waiting for its next short duty cycle.

Now, the poor old service battery, usually initially installed to power a few cabin lights and navigation instruments, is constantly under siege when new items are added to the electrical system. It regularly undergoes deep cycling when the dockside demands take it to the point where the skipper simply has to switch the generator on if the fridge motor is not to be damaged, or his bunkside light is to be anything brighter than a glow-worm. While it is not my intention in this book to go into the design of the whole electrical system, this observation indicates that a battery which is designed for starting rather than constant deep cycling is best for starting an engine.

SERIES

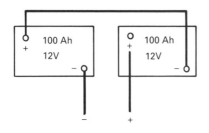

Amp hours remain the same
Voltage is doubled to 24V

PARALLEL

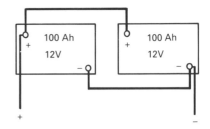

Amp hours doubled to 200 amp hours
Voltage remains the same at 12V

*Fig 42 Batteries in series and in parallel.*

# HOW THE LEAD ACID BATTERY WORKS

The battery consists of a number of cells which produce 2 volts, thus a 6 V battery has three cells, a 12 V battery six and a 24 V twelve cells. Each cell consists of a number of plates immersed in a solution of distilled water and sulphuric acid ($H_2SO_4$) called the electrolyte. In a fully charged battery in which the maximum amount of energy has been stored, some plates are pure spongy lead (Pb) carrying the negative charge and the others, lead peroxide ($PbO_2$), carrying the positive charge.

When a switch is closed a circuit from the negative plates through the boat's electrical system to the positive plates is completed. The electricity flows through the circuit and passes through the electrolyte. As the discharge current flows through the battery, the sulphuric acid breaks up into charged groups called ions – the hydrogen (H) group being positively charged, and the sulphate ($SO_4$) group negatively charged. The $SO_4$ ions combine with the lead from both negative and positive plates to form lead sulphate which remains on them until the battery receives another charge. The hydrogen ions combine with the oxygen released from the lead peroxide to form water. This transfer of negative and positive charges on the plates generates the flow of current through the electrolyte, but as discharge proceeds more and more sulphate ions are removed from the electrolyte to the plates and more water is added to the electrolyte solution to make it weaker.

This description is worth understanding as we can learn a great deal about how to anticipate problems with a lead/acid battery and, perhaps more important, learn how to look after it properly.

Since water is produced as the battery discharges it is apparent why the testing of the specific gravity with a hydrometer is used to determine the state of charge. This is clearly shown in the table showing the specific gravities of lead/acid batteries at varying temperatures. You therefore need an accurate thermometer as well as a hydrometer to carry out a regular check. The production of water should also remind us that in extreme low temperatures a fully discharged battery may freeze, damaging its plates and possibly bursting the case.

Temperature is important for other reasons. We have seen how the production of electrical energy is a chemical process in the battery and any chemical process is either slowed down by low temperatures or increased by higher ones. We find that a battery in a warm atmosphere accepts a charge more easily than a very cold one. More important, is the fact that as temperatures increase, so a battery is capable of discharging itself faster. At 18°C (65°F) the loss is about 1% per day, but at 38°C (100°F) this increases to 3%. A neglected battery, even if it starts out with a full charge in good condition, can discharge itself over a period when it is not in use. This is hardly likely if we get some good boating weather in the season, but highly likely for those that put the winter cover on the boat in November and don't charge the battery again until April. A battery should be recharged every month to six weeks – even during the European winter.

A final warning about temperature and lead/acid batteries is important, for although the temperature of a battery rises during charging it must never exceed 120°F. At this temperature the charging current can become unstable, rising out of control – to the detriment of both the battery and the charging equipment. A maximum temperature for charging should be 110°F.

As a battery ages, the plates begin to lose their

TABLE 4. Specific gravities for lead/acid batteries

| Condition of cell | Hydrometer reading at temperature | | | | | | |
|---|---|---|---|---|---|---|---|
| | 10°C | 16°C | 21°C | 27°C | 32°C | 38°C | 43°C |
| | 50°F | 60°F | 70°F | 80°F | 90°F | 100°F | 110°F |
| Fully charged | 1.288 | 1.284 | 1.280 | 1.276 | 1.272 | 1.268 | 1.264 |
| Half discharged | 1.208 | 1.204 | 1.200 | 1.196 | 1.192 | 1.188 | 1.184 |
| Fully discharged | 1.118 | 1.114 | 1.110 | 1.106 | 1.102 | 1.098 | 1.094 |

ability to reverse the deposition of sulphate. First they lose their ability to hold a full charge and then begin to deposit plate debris on the floor of the battery case. This eventually shorts the plates out and the battery is dead. Since the turn of the century there have been proprietary additives on the market which claim to give the 'kiss of life' to dying, or even dead, batteries but time and time again, research has shown that they are ineffective.

## SOURCES OF BATTERY TROUBLE

A battery will only achieve a full service life if it is properly maintained. Although the idea of 'fit and forget' may appeal to some owners, the sudden loss of the ability to start the engine can be a sharp reminder that no engineering system that is used in a boat is totally 'maintenance free' – it is only maintenance free until it fails!

The main problems that can occur are as follows:

1. *Under or overcharging.* Persistent undercharging results in the gradual running down of the cells, which produces a flat battery. Provided the condition has not been neglected for long this should be simple to remedy either by charging the battery up from the generator, shore side power, or by taking it home for a trickle charge. It is essential to check the charging circuit and generator – either to ascertain that the charging system is not doing its job or that there is some serious leakage to earth from the battery wiring. A good multimeter can be used to check for current leakage, which should always be dealt with immediately as galvanic corrosion in shafting, propellers or outdrives must be avoided.

Overcharging damages the plates (particularly the positive ones, which may deposit excessive material in the bottom of the cell) because it increases the temperature of the battery. This can be destructive to both plates and separators, and might in some cases even buckle them. If the battery case is not damaged or leaking, watch out for excessive gasing and loss of water. Unless you have a full workshop manual for the generator/regulator and a suitable multimeter for testing is available, a professional marine electrician should be

called in. Eventually, overcharging leads to a very common cause of battery failure – grid corrosion. This is simply oxidation of the positive grid structure which first decreases the cross section of the grid wires and then leads to collapse of the plate. In modern batteries the purity of plate materials and electrolyte has been a great improvement, but eventually – no matter how well we look after them – the lead acid battery has a finite life.

2. *Corroded terminals* can provide enough resistance to prevent a battery delivering sufficient current for starting even though charging has been carried out and small current draws have been passed satisfactorily. Corrosion is easily spotted on terminal posts and connections. It can be wiped away using a cloth wetted with a dilute solution of ammonia, which will neutralise any acid. Take care not to get the ammonia solution near the fillers. Cover the area where corrosion has taken place with petroleum jelly to prevent further damage.

3. *Cracked battery case and cells.* Marine batteries should be carried in a safety tray: lead lined or other corrosion resistant material for lead/acid batteries, and steel for alkaline. Although the battery should be strapped down into the tray to prevent it flying about in a sea way, care should always be taken to ensure that the pressure from the straps does not put undue strain on the battery case. Always check for hairline cracks if there has not been excessive charging yet there is still loss of electrolyte.

4. *Short circuits* may be suspected if the specific gravity readings remain low even though the battery has been receiving a good charge, or if there is a fairly rapid loss of capacity after a full charge, or low open-circuit voltage. Sometimes the internal problems can be remedied by taking the battery to a service station where the cells can be dismantled and washed to remove the accumulated sediment or 'treeing' – a shorting formation that sometimes occurs between the positive and negative plates. Today, most retailers will prefer to sell a new battery rather than repair an old one. They may well suspect that the failure is due simply to worn out plates and that it is necessary to fit a new battery or rebuild the old one. Usually, if a battery is unable to deliver more than 80% of its rated capacity, this is a

good indication that it has reached the end of its service life.

5. *Low electrolyte level below the top of the plates.* The electrolyte level in each cell should always be kept just above the top of the plates. If the job of topping up with distilled water has been neglected, the tops of the exposed plates suffer from abnormal sulphation and they slowly disintegrate. Provided the neglect has not been for too long, the cells can be topped up and they will recover sufficiently to give normal service.

6. *Sulphation* in the plates is a perfectly normal part of the chemical reaction of the battery. It forms as the battery discharges and is dissipated by the chemical reaction of recharging. However, this normal process must not be confused with the problems caused by excessive sulphation of the plates. This occurs when a battery stands in a severely discharged state, allowing large crystals of sulphate to grow. The charging current, when it is eventually supplied, will not dissipate them into the electrolyte. Again this is a chemical reaction which is directly affected by variations in the ambient temperature. In the temperature cycles between high and low the larger sulphate crystals grow and may push out active material and fracture the positive grids.

7. *Explosion* is a constant danger which, as we

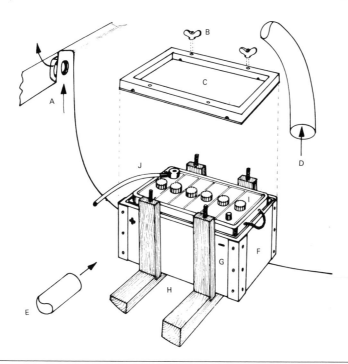

*Fig 43 Battery safety check.*

KEY

A) High level static ventilation should be provided.

B) Wing nuts and fastenings must be strong enough to hold battery in place in all weather conditions.

C) A lid should always be provided to stop falling cables/tools shorting the battery and starting a fire.

D) Mechanical extraction fans must be gas tight/spark proof to safely handle explosive hydrogen gas.

E) Low level cold input fan to keep battery cool should also be same type as above.

F) Battery box should have reinforced corners on seagoing craft to prevent battery breaking out.

G) Mark polarity on battery case to prevent wrong polarity connection.

H) The battery box must be well secured to hull and/or bulkhead to prevent breakaway.

I) Lead/acid battery vent plugs should be marine non-spill type.

J) Cables should be protected from mechanical damage and water, and must be of the correct cross-section conductor to handle the current carried.

shall see later, only proper ventilation of the battery space and care during servicing will prevent. The gases produced during the electrochemical reaction are oxygen and hydrogen. A single spark will cause these two to unite in a powerful explosion. In addition to proper ventilation the following safety points should be mandatory aboard any boat:

1.  Check wiring and battery terminals, in particular, to see that they are in good condition, tight and will not come adrift to cause a spark.
2.  Never smoke or use any naked light while servicing a battery.
3.  Static electricity can sometimes provide the necessary spark for an explosion. It may sound foolish, but some people when walking over certain types of carpeting, or handling certain furnishing materials – especially synthetics like nylon – can become sufficiently 'charged up' to generate a static spark. If you are one of them, it is worth 'earthing' yourself to the boat's ground plate bonding strip before working on the battery.
4.  Always use the battery master switch to isolate it before detaching the battery terminals that could otherwise spark as they are lifted off the posts. Note later the damage that may be done to the alternator by 'flashing' contacts like this. Fig 43 sets out some of the safety points that the owner should provide for the battery installation.

8.  *Loss of acid through vent plugs.* When purchasing a battery, check that its venting arrangements are suited to marine application. All batteries must vent off the gases produced during their normal cycle, but it is essential that the electrolyte does not escape with them. While it may be necessary for a lifeboat to have vent plugs that do not allow spillage even in the most violent capsize (the same common sense may equally be applied to sailing yachts that find themselves in violent seas), for most pleasure boats, normal marine vents are satisfactory. Although 'jelly' type electrolytes – mainly using water glass – have been developed to produce a non-spill battery, they do not last as well as the normal sulphuric acid/water electrolyte

batteries, and their electrical properties are not as good.

# The ignition coil

Returning to Fig 40, the next item to consider is the ignition coil (P). The coil uses a low tension 12 V current (R) to create a magnetic field (Q), which induces a high tension current – usually up to 30,000 V – that is used for the spark that jumps across the plug electrodes.

The coil is usually canister shaped and contains two circuits – the primary, or low tension one, fed from the battery through the ignition switch circuit; and the high tension one. If poor running and misfiring occurs, first check the other parts of the ignition circuit, especially the points and distributor, but if all is well there, the coil should be checked.

## TESTING THE LOW TENSION SIDE OF THE COIL (O)

The switch side (sometimes marked SW on the top of the coil) is first tested using a bulb (circuit voltage) in a holder. If you have a multimeter set to volts, use this for the tests as they are simple 'on' or 'off' readings of nil or 12 V. Contact the SW contact with one wire and the body of the engine (earth) with the other. When the battery master switch and ignition switch are on the bulb should light.

The contact/distributor side of the low tension circuit is tested in the same way, but now using the CB or contact breaker contact on the coil and earth. If the distributor cap is removed you will notice that as the contact points open the lamp shines, but as they close it is extinguished (multimeter on 12 V, or off nil volt).

If the multimeter has an ohm range setting this is useful for checking the coil windings. With the ignition switched off, remove both low tension leads (CB and SW) from the coil. Connect one lead from the meter to each contact and a reading of a few ohms should be seen. The exact reading is vital and this is usually found only in a workshop manual, but you can always ask your dealer for the figure. An excessively high or low reading, deviating from the specified one, means the windings have failed – either because it has broken or because the insulation has been burnt out. In either case a new coil is needed.

## BALLAST RESISTORS

Normally the voltage supplied to the coil is 12 V, but some ignition systems may use a ballast resistor in the low tension circuit to aid starting. It is used because when an engine is starting up the starter motor puts an enormous drain on the battery. The ignition circuit may be so starved of power that it can only produce a weak spark which is useless for igniting the relatively cold fuel/air mixture. This phenomenon is particularly problematical when cold weather puts an extra strain on the starter, as it tries to break the moving parts

away from an obstinate film of cold oil held between the static and moving surfaces.

Fig 44 shows that to overcome the problem and get a fat spark the ballast resistor is wired into the low tension side of the circuit between the ignition switch and the coil. This coil works on 7 V rather than the usual 12 V. During normal running the ballast resistor reduces the 12 V from the battery to feed the coil with the correct working voltage, but when starting the ballast resistor is bypassed to feed 12 V to the coil. The extra voltage more than compensates for the voltage drop caused by the starter motor drain. Once again the plugs can receive a nice fat spark.

Fig 44 shows a ballast resistor fitted to the side of the coil. However, there are several versions – sometimes mounted nearby, sometimes on top of the coil itself, or even in the wiring loom. The owner's handbook should detail the type and location of the ballast resistor, but if you are replacing a coil it is important to get one with the correct volt-

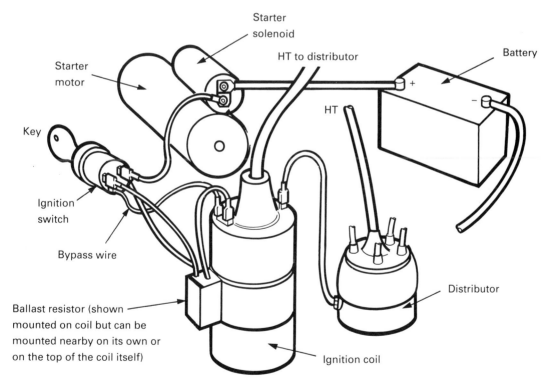

*Fig 44 Ballast resistor.*

age rating. Never accidentally connect the lower voltage coil into the circuit bypassing the ballast. This will result in a full 12 V being fed continuously to it. The engine will run, but the coil will quickly burn out.

## BALLAST RESISTOR FAILURE

Although the ballast resistor is fairly reliable, like any other part of an engine it can fail. Symptoms to watch out for are as follows:

1. Total failure of the ignition circuit when the resistor will not conduct any current.
2. The engine may fire up and start to run when the key is in the 'start' position, but immediately it returns to the normal running position the engine stops.

## BALLAST RESISTOR TESTING

A multimeter set to 'volts' is best for the job. Then proceed as follows:

1. Check the simple things first – that no terminal clips have dropped off, and that connecting wires are not broken.
2. Check the battery voltage with a meter to ascertain that there is full 12 V+ on a 12 V system.
3. Disconnect the HT king lead from the distributor cap and press the starter button. The voltage across the battery terminals should now drop to between 10 V and 11 V.
4. Connect the meter between the live (+) terminal of the coil and earth. If the resistor is working when the ignition is switched on the voltage reading should be between 6 V and 8 V. If the starter button is pressed now the reading should rise to about 9.5 V to 11 V.

If the readings are all correct, as indicated, the fault may be in other parts of the low tension circuit. If in (4) above the reading fails to rise, the bypass wire is probably disconnected or broken, or there is a fault in the starter solenoid itself.

## Crimp terminals

Electrical problems, especially those on the low tension side of circuits, are often caused by overzealous crimping of wires in crimp terminals. Squeezing the terminal clip too much usually severs some of the small conducting wires. The rest are immediately placed under extra fatigue, and they soon break away from the connector. On marine wiring, it is sensible to use a self-amalgamating rubber tape on the last inch or so of the wire and on the terminal itself to give a little extra support and protection where the wire enters the terminal. Bare conductor should never support the wire.

In marine electrical wiring, there is always a danger of water entering between the outer insulation material and the conductor to cause corrosion and failure well out of sight. The perfectionist can use an acid-free silicone rubber to seal the ends. Although this will not provide a perfect seal in multi-strand conductors, it will help to minimise the problem.

## Spark plugs

The spark plug (Fig 40N) is a deceptively simple device for producing the spark within the cylinder. It is both misunderstood and misused. The job it has to do seems simple enough, until we consider the working conditions of its environment. It must provide a very high pressure seal to prevent the gases within the cylinder escaping. It has to provide electrical insulation for perhaps 30,000+ volts. In addition it has to keep the heat generated within it at precise levels. This is exceedingly difficult when nearby burning gases are reaching temperatures of several hundred degrees. Overheating would allow it to glow like an electric fire and cause pre-detonation of the fuel mixture. Pre-detonation soon wrecks piston crowns and bearings. Running cold would allow the products of combustion to be deposited on it – mainly carbon which would soot it up. Soot may short out the central electrode or simply soot up the plug, creating a result that far too many owners of old fashioned outboards with their petrol/oil mixture are familiar with.

Let us take a closer look (Fig 45) at the parts of the spark plug and see what can go wrong and how we can look after it properly.

The buttress or top insulator is ceramic as this is normally an excellent electrical insulating material. It will fail to work properly if it is damp, or if there is an accumulation of dirt on its surface – the fat electric blue spark escapes down its outside. Water dispersant aerosols help, but good ventilation in an engine space and an occasional wipe with a clean dry cloth are valuable, too. Ceramics will break or crack. This is usually caused by the owner. Always use a proper sized hexagonal plug

spanner – *not* an ill-fitting one, or ordinary spanner that will slip off.

Replace any plug showing a crack in the ceramic, either inside or outside the plug. If possible, tighten down plugs with a torque wrench to the figures shown in Table 5 or as specified in the owner's manual. Always use new gasket seals. Even a common item like this has a technical function to seal gases and provide the essential heat path between the plug body and the engine block.

The central electrode reads like a book (Fig 46) to an experienced engineer. Sooty, burnt, eroded, covered in deposits of various kinds, the plug indicates much of what is happening within the engine. Even when all is well the central and side electrodes gradually burn away and a new set of plugs is necessary. The dirty deposits on the inside of the plug may be cleaned on a garage plug sand blasting machine, or a small 12 V plug cleaner as

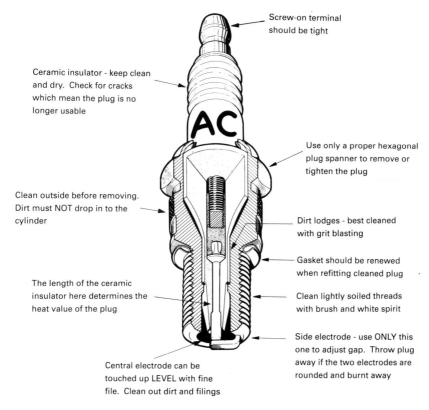

Screw-on terminal should be tight

Ceramic insulator - keep clean and dry.  Check for cracks which mean the plug is no longer usable

Use only a proper hexagonal plug spanner to remove or tighten the plug

Clean outside before removing. Dirt must NOT drop in to the cylinder

Dirt lodges - best cleaned with grit blasting

Gasket should be renewed when refitting cleaned plug

The length of the ceramic insulator here determines the heat value of the plug

Clean lightly soiled threads with brush and white spirit

Central electrode can be touched up LEVEL with fine file.  Clean out dirt and filings

Side electrode - use ONLY this one to adjust gap.  Throw plug away if the two electrodes are rounded and burnt away

*Fig 45 The spark plug.*

### NORMAL

IDENTIFIED BY LIGHT TAN OR GRAY DEPOSITS ON THE FIRING TIP.
CAN BE CLEANED.

### FUSED SPOT DEPOSIT

IDENTIFIED BY MELTED OR SPOTTY DEPOSITS RESEMBLING BUBBLES OR BLISTERS.
CAUSED BY SUDDEN ACCELERATION. CAN BE CLEANED.

### LEAD FOULED

IDENTIFIED BY DARK GRAY, BLACK, YELLOW OR TAN DEPOSITS OR A FUSED GLAZED COATING ON THE INSULATOR TIP.
CAUSED BY HIGHLY LEADED GASOLINE. CAN BE CLEANED.

### WORN

IDENTIFIED BY SEVERELY ERODED OR WORN ELECTRODES. CAUSED BY NORMAL WEAR. SHOULD BE REPLACED

### CARBON FOULED

IDENTIFIED BY BLACK, DRY FLUFFY CARBON DEPOSITS ON INSULATOR TIPS, EXPOSED SHELL SURFACES AND ELECTRODES.
CAUSED BY TOO COLD A PLUG, WEAK IGNITION, DIRTY AIR CLEANER, DEFECTIVE FUEL PUMP, TOO RICH A FUEL MIXTURE, IMPROPERLY OPERATING HEAT RISER OR EXCESSIVE IDLING.
CAN BE CLEANED.

### OIL FOULED

IDENTIFIED BY WET BLACK DEPOSITS ON THE INSULATOR SHELL BORE ELECTRODES CAUSED BY EXCESSIVE OIL ENTERING COMBUSTION CHAMBER THROUGH WORN RINGS AND PISTONS, EXCESSIVE CLEARANCE BETWEEN VALVE GUIDES AND STEMS, OR WORN OR LOOSE BEARINGS. CAN BE CLEANED IF ENGINE IS NOT REPAIRED, USE A HOTTER PLUG.

### OVERHEATING

IDENTIFIED BY A WHITE OR LIGHT GRAY INSULATOR WITH SMALL BLACK OR GRAY BROWN SPOTS AND WITH BLUISH-BURNT APPEARANCE OF ELECTRODES, CAUSED BY ENGINE OVERHEATING. WRONG TYPE OF FUEL, LOOSE SPARK PLUGS, TOO HOT A PLUG, LOW FUEL PUMP PRESSURE OR INCORRECT IGNITION TIMING. REPLACE THE PLUG.

### GAP BRIDGED

IDENTIFIED BY DEPOSIT BUILD-UP CLOSING GAP BETWEEN ELECTRODES.
CAUSED BY OIL OR CARBON FOULING. IF DEPOSITS ARE NOT EXCESSIVE, THE PLUG CAN BE CLEANED.

### PRE-IGNITION

IDENTIFIED BY MELTED ELECTRODES AND POSSIBLY BLISTERED INSULATOR. METALLIC DEPOSITS ON INSULATOR INDICATE ENGINE DAMAGE.
CAUSED BY WRONG TYPE OF FUEL, INCORRECT IGNITION TIMING OR ADVANCE, TOO HOT A PLUG, BURNT VALVES OR ENGINE OVERHEATING. REPLACE THE PLUG.

*Fig 46 Spark plug conditions.*

shown in the last chapter. With care, the amateur can remove some soft deposits with a small wire brush, but often the dirt is merely pushed up between the plug body and the central ceramic insulator – where it may either provide a path to short out the spark that should be at the gap, or heat up and glow to cause pre-detonation or running on.

## HEAT RANGE

Spark plugs have a heat range specification which will allow them to work at the correct temperature in a normal engine in good mechanical condition. Plug manufacturers make 'hot' or 'cold' plugs to cater for engines that are outside their normal operating parameters. The parameters are usually governed by wear, sometimes by unusual operating conditions, or a combination of both.

In Fig 47 the hot and cold refer to the heat transfer characteristics. A plug that is running excessively hot will burn the electrodes away and thus have a poor service life. It may produce pre-ignition and damage the piston head and bearings. A colder grade plug, provided timing and other mechanical aspects of the engine are alright, will solve this problem. An engine that is running too cold, perhaps because of an excessive amount of slow running, will soot up and cause other deposits to form on the interior. This will also shorten its life. A hotter grade plug may then help. It is unwise to experiment with the heat range, but an experi-

TABLE 5. Tightening torques for spark plugs. *Always* refer to owner's manual if available. The following torques may serve as a guide if manual is not available.

| Plug thread | Correct tightening torques | |
| --- | --- | --- |
| | Cast iron head | Aluminium head |
| 10 mm | 12 lb/ft | 10 lb/ft |
| 14 mm | 25 lb/ft | 22 lb/ft |
| 18 mm | 30 lb/ft | 25 lb/ft |

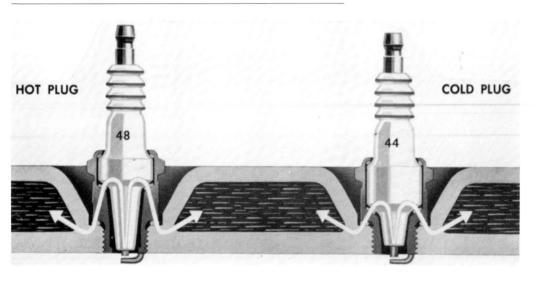

HOT PLUG                                    COLD PLUG

48                                          44

*Fig 47 The heat range of a spark plug is related to the length of the path that the heat generated at the tip of the ceramic insulator must* travel *before it can be dissipated to the cooling system. The hot plug has a long path while the cold plug has a short one. In AC plugs, the higher* the last digit the hotter the plug and vice versa for the cold one.

enced engineer should be able to advise and make a suitable new specification. Simply take your old plug along to him in the first instance.

## GAPPING A PLUG

The distance a spark will jump across from the central electrode to the side electrode is determined at the design stage of the engine. Usually it is anything between 0.018 in and 0.050 in. In an emergency try 0.025 in, which is a fairly common setting. Use a feeler gauge to measure the gap. The leaves of the gauge should be a smooth sliding fit between the electrodes. *Never* bend the central electrode as this will crack the ceramic insulator tip. There are unconventional plugs which some engine manufacturers specify, and for these the advice given in the handbook must be followed. Plugs should always be replaced in complete sets and the gap checked even when brand new. *Never* buy shorter or longer reach plugs than those specified. A shorter reach plug will change the combustion conditions and a longer reach one may well make a nasty and expensive contact with the top of the piston. Always carry on the boat a spare set of plugs, correctly gapped.

Over winter, the plugs should be removed from the engine for inspection, cleaning and regapping. Old plugs which are clean should be used to replace them in the engine. Special plugs containing a desiccant occasionally appear on the market, the silica gel in these removing moisture from the air trapped in the cylinder. However, the moisture is still retained within the cylinder, and unless the plug is removed and regenerated by heating to drive the moisture from the crystals, little or nothing is done to aid preservation.

## Electronic ignition systems

I suppose we are all a little frightened of little black boxes of one kind or another, including those black boxes associated with electronic ignition systems. The fear should be dispelled once we become familiar with what is going on inside.

There is no doubt that an electronic ignition system should be both cheaper and more reliable than the conventional system, which uses contact points to produce the triggering of the spark at the right time. We will soon become as used to the new electronic systems as we have to the conventional ones.

In electronic systems the triggering of the coil to produce sparks at the plug is done by a 'black box' (or even a red or yellow one). There are presently two basic systems being used – the capacitor discharge system being the one most commonly found on modern outboard engines, and the inductive discharge type on an ever increasing number of inboard petrol engines. We really have the car engine makers to thank for discovering that the electronic inductive ignition system is more reliable and – if mass produced – as cheap, if not cheaper, to make than points operated systems.

The reason it is more reliable is that, as we have seen, points pit and transfer metal (pile), which causes them to wear and go out of adjustment. Performance and fuel consumption suffer until they are either re-adjusted or replaced. As their heel is spring loaded, when a high performance engine is running at top speed the moving point may begin to bounce off the cam, timing becomes erratic and misfiring takes place. The spring has insufficient power to return the heel of the points between the high lobe points on the cam. It begins to 'skip', preventing the coil from receiving its full current. As the misfiring slows the engine down, the weak spring is once again able to come into full contact following the cam and the engine picks up – or stops altogether. The inductive electronic ignition system can be divided into two basic types.

## TRANSISTOR ASSISTED CONTACT (often referred to as a TAC system)

This system still uses conventional contact points, which have to be correctly adjusted. They should, however, need very much less adjustment, and replacement only when the heel wears down or the spring weakens. The engine should stay 'in tune' very much longer, be more reliable, and the system should produce a fatter spark.

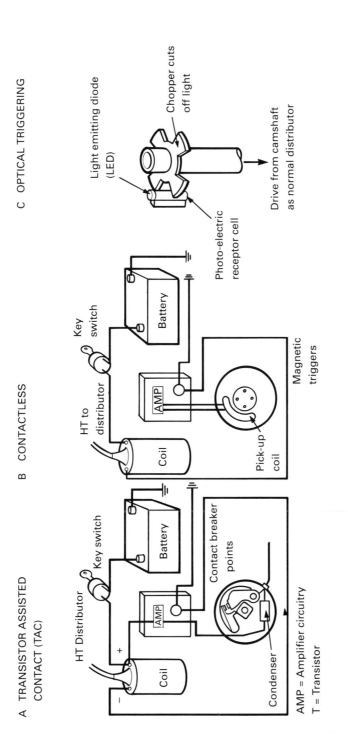

Fig 48 *Electronic inductive ignition systems.*

The reason for an extended service life is that in the TAC system shown in Fig 48A the points carry only a very small electric current (measured in micro-amps) which is used to trigger a transistor. A transistor is simply an electronic switch as opposed to a mechanical switch (which is what points are). The points make or break contact mechanically, the transistor does it electronically by using the small current that flows to it from the points. However, the transistor is able to handle a much higher current than points can. The transistor and the amplifier circuit are mounted inside the 'black box'. The box is wired into the low tension circuit so that when the points close the small current from the points triggers the transistor, which then switches a much larger current from the amplifier circuitry into the coil. As the points open, the transistor is again triggered to shut off the power supply to the coil, and the coil then produces the HT spark needed for distribution to the spark plugs in the normal way.

Previously, we saw how the conventional ignition system can be modified to produce a fatter spark during starting by using a ballast resistor and lower voltage coil that is overrun during starting. Since the transistor can easily handle a larger current than conventional systems, it is possible to use a higher power coil to produce a consistently fatter spark both for starting and running. Plug gaps are usually correspondingly larger and the spark is often longer in duration. Obviously, for the greatest gain from the system, the coil must be made to match. A standard coil would not provide the enhanced output and would probably overheat and burn out.

Electronic circuitry is often made so that it is totally sealed from the elements. This again contributes to reliability, but it does mean that if a fault develops inside the whole circuit may well have to be discarded and replaced by a new one. This can be more expensive than a new set of points, but don't forget that as nothing moves inside the box it will be cheaper in the long run since it should outlast several sets of points.

## CONTACTLESS INDUCTIVE ELECTRONIC IGNITION (Fig 48B)

This type of electronic ignition system does away with points altogether. One version is the well know Mercruiser Thunderbolt IV High Energy Ignition system, in which the distributor is modified, and instead of a lobed cam on the distributor shaft, either a magnetic or optical trigger is used to signal the transistor and amplifier circuits.

The magnetic rotor has as many magnets as there are cylinders. As each one passes a pick-up coil it generates a small electric pulse in the pick-up coil. As the pulse is so small, it is fed to an amplifier circuit which produces enough energy to switch the transistor off. As the LT to the coil is switched off, the HT current is released and fed to the spark plugs via the rotor and contacts in the distributor head. An alternative system uses a single magnet which is rotated past a number of pick-up coils corresponding to the number of cylinders.

Another alternative found inside the distributor uses optical triggering. The cam and rotor are again discarded, but a rotor (as shown in Fig 48C) 'chops' a beam of light which is produced by a light emitting diode (LED) that shines into a photo-electric cell. As the rotor turns, so the beam between the LED and photo-cell is alternately cut and restored. The photo-electric cell senses this and sends the small current signal to the amplifier and transistor box which, as before, initiates the spark from the coil.

While some electronic systems are sensitive to the gap between the magnet and the magnetic coil pick-up, others, like the Thunderbolt IV, are not. As with conventional ignition distributors, the whole distributor body is a 'timed' unit that rotates about the axis of its drive shaft. Bolts that keep it in the correct timed position must not be tampered with unless the whole ignition system is to be retimed. The conventional ignition advance system depending on vacuum and governor weights is often replaced by a non-mechanical electronic advance system. No doubt as time progresses we shall see variations in systems disappear as they become more standardised. In the meantime, I hope that I have dispelled at least a little of the mystery.

# Electrical generating

Some form of electrical generator is incorporated on all modern marine inboard engines to ensure that the starter battery can be kept in a fully charged state directly from the engine. I have mentioned the need for most cruising craft to have a double bank of batteries that need charging. This makes it essential for the generators to have sufficient capacity to charge both banks simultaneously. Money may be saved by having a smaller generator, and then depending on hand switching to charge first one bank or the other. But any system that relies on the skipper's memory is certainly not a 'fail safe' one! There is usually quite enough for him to think about.

Engine makers have noted the growing need for electrical power and, as well as increasing the output of the bolt-on generator, systems have tended to become fully automatic. If an older engine has an undersized generator, there is nothing to stop the owner either installing a larger capacity machine or using a power take off to drive a second one. However, like any other machine, this one also absorbs power. There usually comes a time when the electrical consumption of a yacht is such that it is more economic to run a special generating plant, rather than the main engine driving a relatively low output machine. Diesel engines, in particular, like to work hard and using one to drive a small generator is not cost effective.

Other alternatives which keep the batteries topped up are to use shore side connections to charge through battery charging equipment, or to use small portable generators that can supply either AC or DC voltages. However, I must restrict myself in this book to what you might find bolted on the engine itself. For many years dynamos reigned supreme, but their bulk, relatively low output, and servicing needs led to their demise. Alternators are lighter, more compact and need less servicing. They came into their own for mass production when electronic means of rectifying their AC current became possible. We have much for which to thank transistors and diodes. The dynamo rectified its AC output by means of its commutator and brushes, and unlike 'solid state' circuitry these wore and needed regular servicing to keep them in tip-top condition.

The other type of generator which served well on a small engine was a Dynastart. A machine with one part wound for generating like a dynamo and the other as an electric motor used for starting the engine, it was excellent for the job it had to do, but both starting and generating capacity were limited by the physical problem of having to contain two lots of windings into one small machine.

The modern alternator, if properly looked after, will seldom require servicing. However, it is an easily damaged machine so first of all we had better see what we should *not* do to it:

1. Douse it with cooling water as we drain or refill the cooling system. Always cover it with a plastic sheet or cling film during such operations.
2. Misalign the machine on its fixing bolts and place the rubber drive belt under excessive tension. If either of these is done, the machine bearings will be damaged. Misalignment will also shorten the service life of the drive belt.
3. Use excessively high voltage – this causes 'surge' or 'spike'. Surge is produced when, for example, the battery is accidentally disconnected from the alternator when the engine is running and the alternator charging. The very high voltage this creates will damage the regulator transistors and rectifying diodes. Spikes are short duration, high voltage peaks which are caused when a heavy inductive load is applied – for example, when an electric pump is switched off.
4. Another experience the voltage transistors in the control unit do not take kindly to is being 'meggered' with a high voltage insulation tester. This will destroy them.
5. Reversing polarity of the battery. If an accidental connection is made in this way, the diodes will be destroyed when an enormous current flows through them. Many circuits contain a fast fuse which will 'blow' very rapidly and which offers protection against reversed polarity damage. Always carry a

spare fuse – even though it is surprisingly expensive for its size, the protection it offers is much cheaper than a new alternator.

Keeping an alternator dry and clean, seeing it is driven properly, and keeping all the terminal connections to it tight are just about all the owner really needs to do.

## Starters

Marine engine starting systems are of the following types:

1. *By hand* using a crank handle. This system was fine for all types of engine, but diesels needed decompressors fitted to release their high compression. All that was then needed was for the operator to have enough breath and energy to produce flywheel momentum. On diesels the decompression lever was flipped down and, with luck, it fired up. Thumbs were best kept on the same side of the starting handle as the fingers – not wrapped round the starting handle, as a backfire could break a thumb. Space had to be found to swing the starting handle, but it was a great safety feature.

2. *Spring starters* (Fig 49) made by Simms to dimensions that allow them to be fixed directly to an engine in place of the electric starter. The operator winds up a very powerful spring and then, on moving a lever, the energy stored in it is released via a pinion to the flywheel. Spring starters are excellent for two reasons: in an emergency they can be wound up time and time again to get a start, and when tuning an engine, the handle allows it to be turned over slowly – particularly useful for adjusting the rockers.

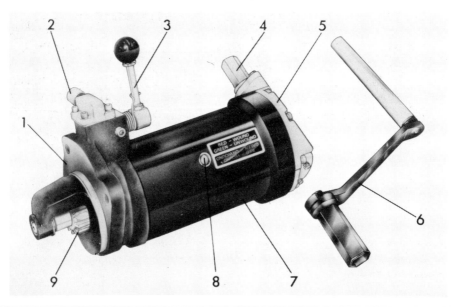

*Fig 49 CAV/Simms Spring Starter for diesel engines. The hand-wound spring starter is capable of starting diesel engines up to 1 l per cylinder. It can be carried as an emergency starter, quickly replacing the electric starter motor using three bolts on the flange. Design engine mountings so that there is room to wind the handle reasonably easily.*

KEY

1. Flange with holes to match conventional starting motor bolt holes.
2. Control box reset button pressed in before winding commences.
3. Starting control handle used after unit has been wound up.
4. Hexagon for winding up handle.
5. Housing for winding bevel gear that engages springs.
6. Hexagon socket cranked handle for putting twelve turns on the starter springs.
7. Starter body containing powerful springs should not be dismantled by the amateur.
8. Indicator window to show state of springs – red, wound; green, unwound.
9. Drive pinion.

3. *Hydraulic starters*, including Bosch (USA) and Bryce (UK). In the Bryce model, hand pumping produces great pressure (4,250 psi) in an hydraulic accumulator tank. Operating a starter lever then causes a two-stage valve to pass this pressure – first engaging the starter dogs and then releasing the full pressure to spin the engine over. An engine driven pump could allow the hand pumping to be replaced by mechanical energy, but this method left the system under full pressure. By using the pumping handle gently with the start lever open the engine could be turned over very slowly for adjustments to be made.

4. *Air starting* is used on larger marine engines, an air tank containing air under high pressure provid-

ing the driving force to an air motor starter. Ingersol Rand make one system, but its use is generally confined to larger marine engines.

5. *The electric starter motor* has now almost totally replaced any of the above systems on the pleasure boat market. Just as cars lost their starting handles, so boats have followed suit. As alternative methods of starting have departed, our sole reliance on the electric starter means that the battery and starter must never be less than 100% sound. The feeling of disappointment when you go down to the boat for the weekend only to find the battery is flat is bad enough. To find yourself at sea with an engine which will not start is much worse. While you yourself may overcome the panic and eventu-

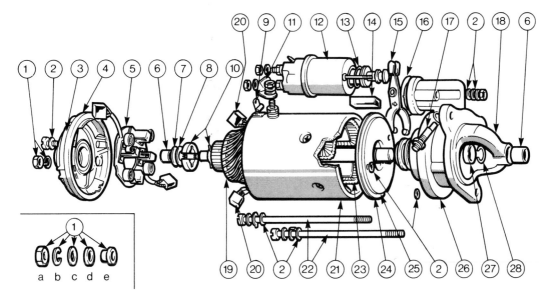

*Fig 50 The Lucas M50 starter. The marine version of the M50 is suitable for insulated return wiring systems, being fitted with an insulated main negative terminal and an additional solenoid negative terminal. It has marine finished components and casing paint system to give protection against corrosion but in all other respects it is similar in mechanical construction to the standard industrial product.*

KEY

1. Nut and spring washer.
2. Sealing washers.

3. Commutator end cover.
4. Sealing ring.
5. Brush gear assembly comprising earth brushes and springs. Marine version has insulated negative brushes.
6. Bearing bush.
7. Fibre washer.
8. Steel thrust washer.
9. Flexible link.
10. Brake shoe and cross peg.
11. Copper link.
12. Solenoid unit.
13. Return spring.
14. Sealing grommet which is deleted on the marine version.
15. Engagement lever.

16. Gasket.
17. Eccentric pivot pin.
18. Drive and fixing bracket.
19. Armature.
20. Insulated brushes – field coils.
21. Yoke.
22. Through bolts.
23. Field coils.
24. Sealing ring.
25. Intermediate bracket.
26. Drive assembly.
27. Thrust collar.
28. Jump ring.
*Inset* for marine version (a) Nut, (b) Plain washer, (c) Insulated washer for outside cover, (d) Insulated bush for inside cover.

ally get the engine started, the crew may well be put off boating for life.

## THE ELECTRIC STARTER

Fig 50 shows a Lucas M50 electric starter motor with an inset for the negative (insulated return) terminal components which are necessary on the marine version of this unit. This type of unit is known as a pre-engaged electric starter where the starter pinion is retained in position and continues to power the flywheel even when the engine first fires up.

The solenoid unit (12) is found on top of the motor. This one has two-stage switching – the first switch allows the pinion to engage gently with the flywheel ring-gear, the second allows full power to be supplied when all four field coils are connected

to the battery, producing full cranking torque.

The second family of starters may be classified as axial or co-axial, sometimes referred to as 'Bendix' starters. Instead of the pinion being engaged by a pivoted fork which is moved by the action of the solenoid, the solenoid and switching is mounted co-axially on the armature shaft. Only the pinion moves to take up engagement. On axial starters, which are designed for starting larger engines, the complete armature assembly moves longitudinally to engage the pinion. Instruction books giving full details are available from CAV/ Lucas. These describe all three designs in detail, but no doubt, other makers also provide this kind of technical literature to help owners become familiar with the hidden parts.

Thankfully, both solenoids and starter motors are extremely reliable and should not need atten-

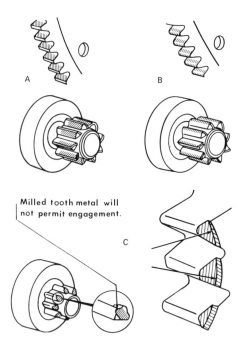

Milled tooth metal will not permit engagement.

*Fig 51 Starter pinion and ring gear damage.*

KEY

A) New and proper used gear teeth mesh smoothly as pinion slides into mesh on the flywheel ring gear.

B) Small wear pattern as top of pinion teeth and ring gear teeth become rounded.

C) Serious damage as pinion and ring gear teeth become milled.

Typical damage from pressing the starter button before the engine has fully returned to rest on first starting, or accidental use when the engine is actually running.

tion until they are due for a proper service depot overhaul, or replacement with a factory reconditioned unit. As usual there is still much the owner can do to ensure a trouble-free life:

1. Make certain the battery delivers full amperage at all times. Electric motors are damaged by under volting, which may be a result of a battery in poor condition or inadequate cross-section starter cables. Starter cable is expensive stuff and it is not unknown for penny-pinching to result in inadequate cross-section cables being used. To maintain voltage drop within safe limits the cables should be kept as short as possible. A compromise is often called for as some classification societies insist on batteries being outside the engine compartment for safety reasons. However, provided proper ventilation is built-in on small craft, it is acceptable for small battery banks to be placed within the compartment. This ensures that cable runs can be kept short. All batteries should have a top cover to prevent anything dropping on and shorting them.

2. Use the starter button sensibly. The pinion should engage smoothly with the flywheel ring-gear at all times. It slides along its drive shaft helped by a spring and a drive helix. If the lubrication has dried up, engagement, or occasionally disengagement, will be difficult. Some starters incorporate an 'overspeed' device that will prevent damage if the engine starts to drive them as it fires up. An unusual screaming protest from the starter signals you to cut the engine immediately. Generally speaking, on any make of starter this kind of situation will be avoided if, when there is the slightest suspicion that things are not working

or sounding right, boating is cancelled and the unit is taken off to a service depot.

Most damage is done when an owner does not allow the engine to come to rest completely before repressing the button. Fig 51 shows the kind of damage inflicted on the starter pinion and the flywheel ring-gear. Before working on or near a motor, *always* isolate the batteries with their master switch. If this is not done, the terminals and cables are able to carry sufficient current to cause severe burns if they are accidentally shorted. If damage is confined to the pinion, the starter can be taken to the service depot. If the ring-gear is badly milled then either a new flywheel or filing to recondition the teeth is needed. I have known people to file away in the confined access to the ring-gear to restore the teeth, but iron filings in the engine do not do a lot of good. It is possible to flush them out and use a magnet sump plug to gather them up, but I would not approve of this method. Although it means hard work, the best way is to remove the flywheel to regrind the teeth. This only works if the correct clearance can be maintained between the pinion and the new teeth. Once teeth begin to go missing on the ring-gear, the starter will 'scream' initially and then slam into engagement – a nasty noise which will probably mean that more of the remaining teeth are lost.

During winterisation provide a waterproof cover for the starter. Most are situated low down on the engine, precisely where cooling water that is being drained down will fall on them. I use clingfilm, but a plastic bag and sealing tape do just as well. Lubrication is generally not needed for most starters, but you may come across models which have drive end bearing with a wick lubrication system and a reservoir which needs topping up every couple of years or so.

# 6  Marine engine cooling, exhaust and ventilation systems

## Air-cooled engines

The advantages of an air-cooled diesel engine for marine pleasure boat applications are so numerous that one wonders why so few of them are used. Could it be that the vast research and development demanded by the car industry for high-speed, water-cooled units has eclipsed the development and marketing of air-cooled engines for use on pleasure craft? Several famous makes are still available and among these are Lister (Hawker Siddeley Marine UK), Deutz (Germany), Dorman (UK) and Ducati (Italy), to name but a few. Power range extends between 7.5 hp and 500 hp. The traditional narrow boat owner finds the air-cooled engine attractive as it avoids the cooling problems caused by silt and the plastic-laden water found in many of our canals and inland waterways.

### ADVANTAGES

1. The absence of cooling water avoids for both designer and owner the problems of damage associated with freezing, boiling, gasket failure, water associated corrosion and internal cavitation corrosion on cylinder liners. There is less to maintain – no water circulating pumps, hoses, header tank, sealing gaskets, thermostats or heat exchangers.
2. Reliability should therefore be better than in a water-cooled unit. Although it might be expected that the air-cooled engine would have a cost advantage, the fact is that cost is always related to the volume of production. The relatively low volume production of air-

cooled units means that they either have no initial cost advantage, or indeed, that they cost more than a water-cooled engine of similar power.
3. The air-cooled engine is almost indifferent to the climate in which it is operating. Since the heat transfer process is direct from engine to air, the difference between the ambient air temperature and the cylinders remains constant and the heat removed is almost independent of the ambient temperature. Thus, the air-cooled engine is well able to cope with extremes of climate.
4. Operating temperature is reached far more quickly than with a water-cooled engine. Thus, corrosion that normally takes place when an engine is warming up, but temperatures are below dew point, is greatly reduced. This is perhaps not an important advantage, but still one that will prolong service life. It also helps to reduce emissions of unburnt fuel.
5. Power-to-weight ratio can be very attractive as the cooling system must be totally integrated into the design from the start. Many water-cooled marine engine cooling systems are 'bolt on' adaptations to cater for the marine market. Although designs of integrated header tank/heat exchangers have improved in recent years, they still tend to take up more room compared with good air-cooled designs. When manufacturers give the engine weight for a water-cooled unit they do not include the weight of the cooling water, just the engine's 'dry' weight.
6. They offer a good designer an excellent opportunity to produce an installation with low noise levels. It is erroneously believed that

air-cooled engines are more noisy than water-cooled units of the same power, but the French organisation CIMAC (in 1970) and the Institute of Sound and Vibration, Southampton (in 1975) undertook extensive testing to show that the cooling system has no significant effect on engine noise levels.

However, since that time, many of the large volume engine makers have invested in acoustic engineering to satisfy the automotive market. Thus it is generally easier and less expensive to achieve a quiet water-cooled installation than it is a quiet air-cooled engine.

Early air-cooled engines had a bad

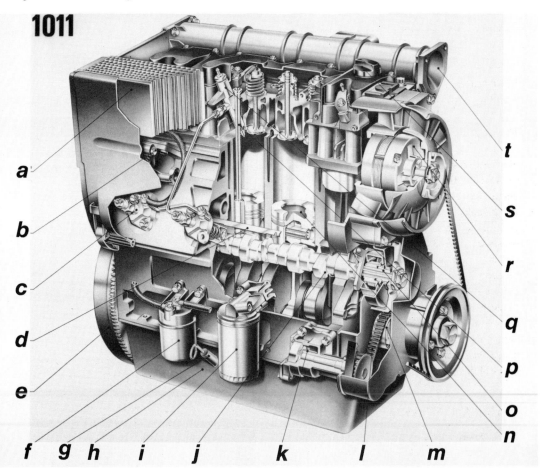

*Fig 52 Deutz F4 1011 Air-cooled engine.*

KEY

(a) Oil cooler.
(b) Oil thermostat.
(c) Unit injection pump for each cylinder worked off camshaft.
(d) Injector pump control rod.
(e) Flywheel.
(f) Fuel filter.
(g) Oil level dipstick.
(h) Sump pan for engine oil.
(i) Oil filter (canister type).
(j) Camshaft with lobes that work each unit injection pump.
(k) Oil pump for lubricating oil and oil cooling circuits.
(l) Toothed belt drive for engine control – quieter than timing chain and takes up less room than gear trains (which are usually used).
(m) Toothed belt tension pulley.
(n) Direct injection into piston with bowl.
(o) Speed governor.
(p) Valve push rod.
(q) Injector.
(r) Generator in air cooling fan hub (saves space).
(s) Oil filler cap.
(t) Air intake manifold for combustion air.

reputation for being noisy, mainly because the boat designer and builder did little or nothing in the installation to cater for noise attenuation. Nowadays most good boat builders must do this, and with greater understanding of noise attenuation it should be possible to produce a craft with acceptable

noise levels. It is still important to stress that careless installation would be sure to perpetrate the old image of air-cooled engines being noisy.

7. Modular design is an attractive proposition for both the engine manufacturer and the owner, as a single basic cylinder design can be

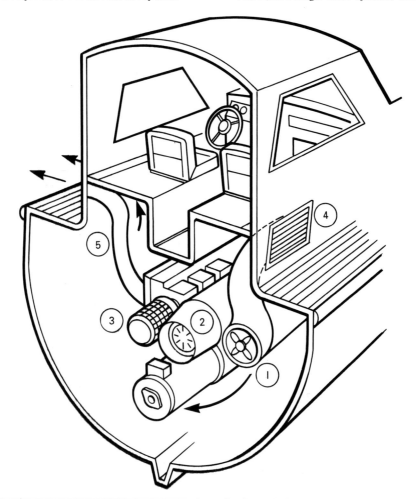

*Fig 53 Design considerations for an air-cooled engine compartment.*

KEY

1. Although the engine cooling fan will suck air into the compartment, blown air from an electric fan can contribute to a good cold air supply. Extra deck venting would ensure the

compartment does not become pressurised.

2. The engine's cooling air intake fan must never ingest hot air from the compartment or recirculated air from the outgoing hot air.

3. Combustion air must be as cold as ambient temperature outside the boat for efficient combustion and full power.

4. Calculations must be made allowing 25% extra area for louvred grills plus friction allowances for bends in ducting.

5. Hot air from the engine must be ejected from the opposite side of the boat to the incoming air and NEVER recirculated with it. Air or oil cooling (Deutz 1011) can be used for space or locker heating.

utilised for a whole range of engines, and components may be common to all. The Deutz engines can have upwards of 85% of parts common to the range. This has great attraction for the spare parts stockist and the owner wanting parts in a hurry. Fig 52 shows the latest 1011 Series which is available in 2-, 3- and 4-cylinder versions and a 4-cylinder turbocharged unit covering from 10 to 53 kW. To be fair, there are manufacturers of water-cooled engines who have also adopted modular design for a series of their power units.

Winterisation of the cooling system is simply a question of cleaning out all air passageways and cylinder finning. It is not a bad idea to remove the fan drive belt to relax it, but make certain that it is replaced after inspection, and perhaps renewal, in the spring. Name-tagging the different parts to jog the memory is an excellent idea.

## AIR REQUIREMENTS FOR AIR-COOLED ENGINES

The air used in the combustion process is as defined later for a four-stroke engine, but it is essential that this air is kept entirely separate from the air to be used for cooling.

Good installation design is necessary to achieve this, and the manufacturer specifies the minimum size air supply and extraction ducting necessary if the engine is not to overheat, lose power and waste fuel. Ducting specifications allow extra size to overcome the flow constraints caused by bends or restrictions such as louvres. Louvres, for example, often require a 25% increase in the cross-section of the inlet area. The flexibly mounted engine must have a flexible ducting section if it joins directly onto an inlet or cooling air exhaust outlet. It is possible to utilise surplus heat to warm accommodation space or a drying locker, but care must be taken to see that oily smells do not intrude, or that when heating is not wanted the full outlet volume remains available to the engine. The Deutz 1011 engine is able to use a secondary oil cooling circuit for heating cabin spaces. What must be avoided at all costs is the recirculation of hot air back to the engine. Fig 53 shows the ducting and cooling arrangements that would provide the essential elements needed to cool this type of engine.

## Raw water cooling (direct cooling)

Many small marine engines are raw water cooled – that is, the water in which the boat is floating (salt, fresh or polluted river, lake or canal) is pumped into and around the engine cooling system, before it is used to cool the exhaust gases and ejected overboard.

A typical system is shown in Fig 54, where the raw water is circulated by means of an impeller pump. Although the raw water cooled engine is simpler and therefore less costly both in initial and later maintenance costs, there are a number of disadvantages which should be heeded by any owner of a boat which will be kept for some time or one which is used very intensively. The disadvantages may still be acceptable to the owner who will only operate his boat engine in unpolluted fresh water areas.

## DISADVANTAGES OF RAW WATER COOLED ENGINES

1. The system is generally less efficient than either air or indirect cooling systems. This is because it is more difficult to control the engine temperature with a single water pump and thermostat. A very restricted and low operating temperature (55°C, 131°F) is necessary to preclude the precipitation of deposits and salts in particular, especially when an engine is operated in salt water that would otherwise solidify in the engine cooling water passageways. Precipitation from hard water reduces cooling efficiency.

   The result of these limitations of temperature control is increased cylinder and ring wear from the deposition of combustion acids. The oil grade specification needs to be such that the lower temperatures do not allow it to form oil films of excessive thickness which increase fuel consumption. Low oil temperatures, especially on diesel engines, can lead to sludging – special oils are often specified to cope with these conditions.

2. High rates of corrosion on cooling water passageways are found and may result in a shorter engine life than other forms of cooling. Proper winterisation is important so that corrosion is reduced to a minimum. There should be a complete drain down of the raw water from the engine and flushing by means of a hose pipe connected to the raw water intake. An emulsifying oil should be added to the last volume of flushing water to coat the interior passageways and inhibit corrosion. Volvo Penta and Ford produce their own brand, but Ciba–Geigy offer Inhibitor Type 71C, ESSO Cutwell, Rust Ban 392, Shell Dromus Oil B or BP Energol SB4, which are all suitable for this job when mixed as directed. Drain them down while the engine is still hot so that the interior is at least able to dry off a little.

Cathodic protection is sometimes incorporated into the system and an owner must be aware of where this is located and renew it as necessary.

3. In the past when marine engines were specially developed for raw water use, the

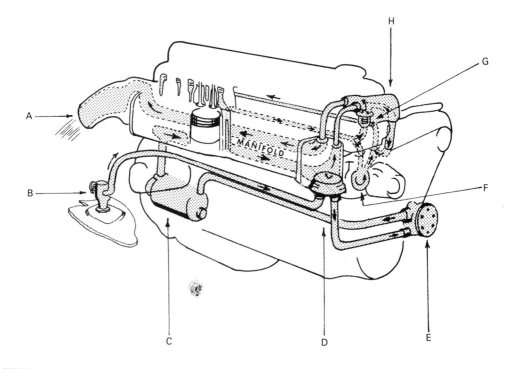

*Fig 54 Raw water cooled engine.*

KEY

A) Water injection bend – expect severe corrosion.
B) Raw water inlet. Here shown as skin fitting. May be a transom fitting combining inlet with exhaust or an intake via the out drive leg.
C) Oil cooler – heat exchange type. Often omitted on smaller engines.
D) Raw water filter.
E) Impeller type pump – often referred to as 'Jabsco' type but that is a trade name. Needs servicing – see text.
F) Circulation pump – often of centrifugal type. Large power units have this extra circulation to ensure even heat distribution. Smaller engines use only (E).
G) Thermostat (open for this diagram).
H) Distribution housing. The exhaust must always have water for cooling the manifold and exhaust when the thermostat is closed (engine cold).

castings were made enormously thick and would stand years of abuse and corrosion. The modern automotive block is designed to save weight and is therefore more vulnerable to the effects of corrosive attack.

## Indirect cooling (Fig 55)

Here, a closed water cooling system passes fresh water round the engine block, the cylinder head and the exhaust manifold, and the heat is extracted from it by a second raw water system using a heat exchanger. A header tank is used to accept expansion of the fresh water, and to save space the heat exchanger is sometimes incorporated in the header expansion tank.

The fresh water side uses an automotive centrifugal pump, usually rubber belt driven, to circulate the fresh water. A thermostat is used in the fresh water circuit to control circulation, restricting it to produce a quick warm up and then allowing full flow to cope with the higher operating temperatures. A water strainer inlet valve (Fig 56) allows the raw water to enter the raw water side of the system and this is circulated by an impeller pump – often referred to as a Jabsco pump – although there are a number of other manufacturers who make this kind of pump. This pumps water through the heat exchanger where the heat is extracted from the fresh water and the raw water is carried overboard after being injected into the exhaust gas stream to cool the hot gases.

The system is more expensive initially than raw water cooling, and costs more in both time and money to maintain. However, the advantages are such that it is by far the most favoured type of cooling system, especially when production boat builders must allow for their craft to be operated in both fresh and salt water areas all over the world.

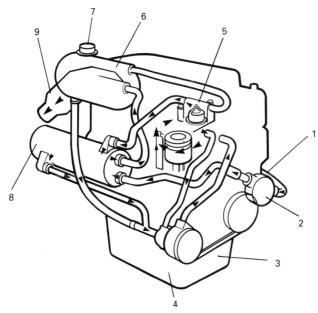

Fig 55 Indirect (fresh water) cooling system.

KEY

1. Raw water inlet pipe from seacock skin fitting.
2. Impeller pump, direct driven from camshaft.
3. Rubber drive belt.
4. Fresh water centrifugal pump.
5. Thermostat.
6. Header or expansion fresh water tank.
7. Pressure cap.
8. Heat exchanger – fresh water heat transferred to raw water.
9. Exhaust injection bend, where used raw water cools exhaust gases as it is ejected overboard.

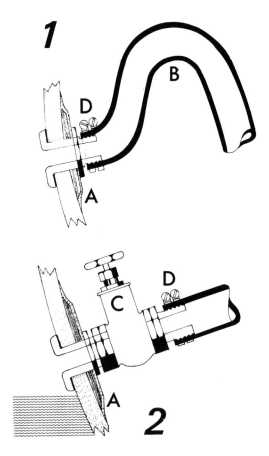

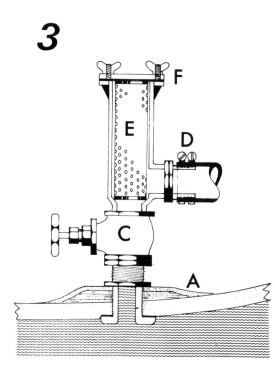

*Fig 56 Skin fittings.*

KEY

1. The *swan neck* is the least expensive to install and, provided the height (B) is sufficient, it will stop most water getting back down the exhaust line. It has the disadvantage that the bend adds to back pressure.
2. *Straight through valve* (C) causes no extra obstruction to exhaust gas/water flow and can shut down in an emergency. When the boat is left on a mooring it is always best left closed. Flap valves on the outside, which are less expensive, may stop some waves washing up the exhaust line but they are not fully watertight.
3. The raw water inlet, for engine cooling water/exhaust cooling, should always be through a full-flow valve (C).

A) All valves should be fitted on a pad which has been fully glassed in on GRP constructions. A suitable underwater rubber sealant is used on the valve itself so that it can be removed for inspection. The valve should be taken out every five years or so to check if the pad, usually made of wood, is rotting and that the concealed part of the valve is not corroded. This should always be done before purchasing a used boat.

D) Stainless steel hose clips used to secure rubber and plastic hose to skin fittings should always be doubled for safety.

E) The water inlet valve must always be fitted with a strainer which can easily be cleaned. Plastic bags and mud (from going aground) lodged in the intake are the usual cause of loss of engine cooling water.

F) The wing nuts and gasket should be kept in good condition. By making a new plate to fit over the studs, with a hose pipe stub welded into it, a hose connection is easily made. With the bottom valve closed, fresh water can be introduced via this top to flush the engine with fresh water during winterisation.

## ADVANTAGES OF AN INDIRECT COOLING SYSTEM

1. The problems of over cooling are overcome and mineral precipitation greatly reduced as fresh water can be safely circulated while working at a much higher temperature – usually around 80–85°C (176–185°F). By pressurising the system, the boiling point of the coolant is increased, but this means that gaskets, pipework, seals and the pressure cap must all work properly.

2. Lubrication is better, the readily available automotive oils operating within the parameters they were designed for. This reduces wear, prolongs service life and usually reduces both maintenance and depreciation costs in the long run.

3. The raw water side can sometimes be used for gearbox as well as engine oil cooling. In the former case, the inlet water is first taken through the gearbox casting and, if oil cooling is also incorporated, through a heat exchanger to cool the oil. It then proceeds through a second heat exchanger to cool the fresh water side of the system. It sounds complicated but is, in fact, simple once you trace the pipe and heat exchanger system around the engine to identify the parts.

## Cooling systems – maintenance and winterisation

## THE IMPELLER PUMP

This, as we have seen, is common to both direct and indirect cooled engines. Fig 57 shows the working parts. Most are driven directly from the engine, but fire, bilge and wash down pumps may be driven from the engine by means of a power take off belt drive. The pump has two great advantages. It is self-priming (it pumps without having to have the pump housing flooded) and it will cope with the pollution and small amounts of grit that are found in most water.

## IMPELLER PUMP SERVICING

Parts that will need an owner's attention are as follows:

A. The IMPELLER is made of a synthetic rubber, usually neoprene. It will soon disintegrate if you forget to turn the cooling water valve on and start the engine. Always carry at least one spare for each engine. Many owners treat the impeller very badly, by leaving it in the pump over winter, which distorts and damages blades. There is no excuse for this, all that needs to be done is to undo half a dozen screws to remove the end plate and to ease the impeller out with pump pliers. Eventually, the lobes that bear on the pump housing will wear. The rounded ends become flattened and this indicates that immediate replacement is required.

B. The END GASKET seals the end plate onto the body. Keep some in stock as a new one is needed each time the impeller is replaced. Rub a little grease on paper gaskets before fitting them.

C. The END PLATE often has verdigris forming on the edges, if not all over. Spray with an aerosol corrosion inhibitor. If the side that comes into contact with the impeller is showing signs of wear, it can sometimes be reversed. It is better, however, to replace it with a new one.

D. The SCREWS with slot heads are often damaged as the pump, usually situated near a bulkhead on small craft, is awkward to reach. Keep a replacement set handy because, even if they do not become damaged, they have a nasty habit of dropping into bilges.

E. The CAM PLATE SECURING SCREW.

F. The SEALS on the impeller drive shaft may begin to leak raw water back towards the engine. They can become rather chewed up when a stainless steel shaft succumbs to pitting corrosion (it pits beneath the seal where it is starved of oxygen). Stainless steel only remains corrosion free if its oxidised surface is maintained. When the film is rubbed off under the seal and there is insufficient oxygen to replace it, pitting takes place. If this happens, the whole shaft needs to be replaced. To replace seals, prise them out carefully and simply press new ones into the casting recesses.

G. The GREASE CUP may or may not be found on an impeller pump (some are self-lubricating). If a greaser is fitted, it needs a turn every day.

H. The SLINGER WASHER (not found on all pumps). Its job is to use centrifugal force to fling off any water to prevent it reaching the drive end and the engine. It is made of rubber and is easily replaced. Check that it is centralised in the slot so that water is thrown clear.

I. SET SCREW OR SPLINED SHAFT DRIVE. The impeller may be driven by a set screw across a slot in old pumps, or on modern ones the drive shaft is splined to fit a splined bush in the impeller. Use a little grease on either so that removal of the impeller is easy. Splines can be greased over winter when the impeller is out, but clean off before refitting.

J. The CAM should give no trouble, but if it is worn it may be replaced. Do ensure that the fixing screw is always tight.

K. The WEAR PLATE takes the friction wear from the back of the impeller and is easily replaced as necessary.

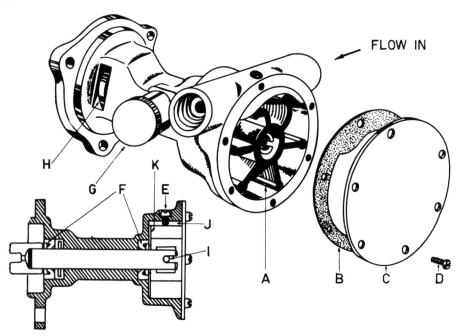

FLOW IN

*Fig 57 The working parts of an impeller pump.*

KEY

A) Neoprene rubber six-bladed impeller. Blade number varies but they should be inspected for wear at the tips and cracking at base. They fail rapidly if the water cock is forgotten and not turned on.

B) End plate gasket. Paper ones should have grease rubbed into them when replacing.

C) End plate – inspect for wear.

D) End plate screw – keep spares.

E) Cam plate securing screw.

F) Water and oil seals.

G) Greaser – not on all models but turn once a day if found on a pump.

H) Slinger washer to throw off droplets of water that might pass down the shaft.

I) Drive pin. Most modern pumps have a splined shaft to drive the impeller.

J) Cam plate.

K) Wear plate. Reverse for small amounts of wear, replace if badly worn.

## SERVICING OTHER PARTS OF THE COOLING SYSTEM

*Rubber hoses* are usually made of reinforced rubber and may be either specially moulded shapes or straight sections. It is advisable to keep spares of the moulded ones, but a single length of straight hose in the various diameters the engine uses is usually much less expensive than buying several short lengths from the spares catalogue.

Rubber hoses have a habit of bursting at the most inconvenient times, so have some tape handy to effect a quick, temporary repair. Rubber age hardens, especially when used on the hot parts of an engine. A full replacement programme should be undertaken if a hose has burst, or if it begins to feel hard and surface cracks begin to appear. Check that the hose bores have not become restricted, as it is not unknown for light alloys that have been removed by corrosion and carried in the cooling water to stick to rubber and build up over a period of time into a hard deposit. Restricted bores can cause or contribute to over heating.

*Hose clips* should always be of stainless steel so that they do not corrode and can be easily undone. Double clipping is always recommended on the pipe sections between the skin fitting inlet and the engine raw water pump. Check and tighten if necessary each season. Never allow a joint to weep, no matter how insignificant this might appear.

---

## Header tank and heat exchangers

---

These come in a variety of metals and may or may not be protected by anodes. If anodes are used in a system, they must be replaced before they are 50% corroded away. The header tank is a tank which allows excess coolant to expand into it. It is sometimes referred to as an expansion tank.

When winterising, the indirect system can be left either 'dry' – that is totally drained down as with a raw water cooled engine – or 'wet' where the system will be protected by a solution of antifreeze added to the cooling water. The engine manufac-turer may well specify how the engine should be treated. Some insist on a 'wet' lay-up, the reason being that antifreeze, as well as doing its normal job, gives some lubrication to the fresh water pump, inhibits corrosion and prevents gaskets and seals drying out. All these factors are particularly important in engines which have a high proportion of light alloy in them.

It is essential that antifreeze is added to the fresh water side of the system to give protection down to the extremes of temperature. Weather has a nasty habit of producing records, and winter temperatures are no exception. The manufacturers of antifreeze specify the correct dilution rate. All you need to know is the volume of the water that goes into the cooling system to work out how much is needed. Some antifreeze manufacturers offer a specific gravity tester to check that the solution is capable of giving the necessary protection. Antifreeze, provided it is not constantly diluted by topping up with fresh water, will last a couple of seasons – but, for the cost involved, I would say it is easier to flush it out at lay-up time and then circulate a fresh lot through the engine. This ensures it is really up to standard and saves messing about with a hydrometer. Antifreeze solution is excellent for finding out weaknesses in gaskets, piping and clips where it seeps through any weak spots.

Only buy top quality antifreeze to protect the engine. Engine manufacturers often make recommendations and these should be followed. The best antifreeze solution consists of pure ethylene glycol, and standards are often agreed between the engine makers, antifreeze manufacturers and standards institutions to fix quality. Cheap substitutes can be costly in the long term if they damage the engine or allow frost to damage the engine.

The raw water side of the engine is treated exactly the same as the raw water system previously mentioned.

*Heat exchangers* consist of a tube stack in an outer container. While cooling raw water is pumped through in one direction, the fluid to be cooled – fresh water or oil – is pumped through in the opposite direction. There is little that can go wrong, but like the small cooling water passageways in the engine, they can become clogged up by:

1. Running aground and letting silt, sand or mud enter them.
2. Forgetting to open the raw water inlet valve, which causes the impeller to disintegrate. The bits of rubber soon block the heat exchanger so dismantling is necessary.

With oil cooling heat exchangers, it is possible that the seals may fail and allow water to contaminate the oil. Whenever oil is emptied from the engine it is worth taking a close look to see that this has not happened. Any colour that is not 'normal' for the oil is a sure sign that something is wrong, but oil contaminated with water usually looks milky (emulsified) or has water droplets in it.

The tube stack seldom needs cleaning but a rebuild every five years is perhaps worthwhile, even when everything appears normal. Bad chemical deposits may be removed by boiling the tube stack in a solution of caustic soda, but this must not be overdone and a thorough rinse should be given before the rebuild. It is permissible to remove solid deposits with a knitting needle used in the opposite direction to the normal flow. Again, care is needed so that the tubes are not damaged. Finally, ensure that a set of end gaskets is carried aboard so that cleaning can be undertaken in an emergency.

## HEADER TANK PRESSURE CAP

I have already mentioned that the fresh water side of the indirect cooling system operates under pressure in order to raise the boiling point of the coolant and allow the engine to operate at its most efficient temperature. The pressure cap (Fig 58),

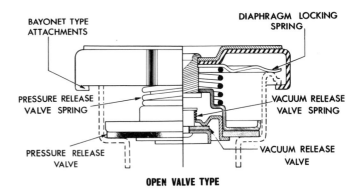

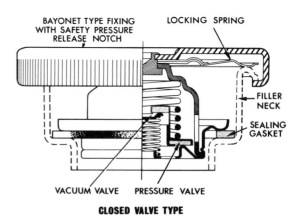

*Fig 58 Header tank pressure caps – open and closed types. The cap provides a two-way valve which produces a constant pressure for the coolant, with over pressurisation relief and an inlet valve for air to relieve the vacuum created when the coolant cools down.*

which is removed for topping up the fresh water, does much more than allow access. The spring under the cap controls operating pressure and serves as a relief valve which will allow some coolant to escape if the header tank has been over filled, or if the pressure rise is excessive. There is another valve working in the opposite direction to eliminate automatically a vacuum which develops as the engine cools. To guard against coolant spurting out when the engine is hot and you need to check the coolant level, a spring disc in the cap does not disengage until the main body of the cap is well clear of the sealing washer and the coolant is at atmospheric pressure. Ensure that the cap is only partly turned to release the pressure and avoid scalding.

Keep the pressure cap seating clean. If overheating problems occur check the pressure cap first. Even though the system is designed to be foolproof, it is as well to put a thick cloth over the cap when removing it from a hot engine. As you release the valve on the hot engine, listen for the hissing sound to see if pressure is present. Check that sealing rings and any fibre sealing washers are intact. Some fibre and rubber sealing washers on the cap are sensitive to oil and solvents – so their use, especially those contained in some aerosol corrosion inhibiting products, is not recommended. Water, mild soap and an old tooth brush can be used to clean the washers. If in doubt about their condition, replace.

The *thermostat* is found on both direct and indirect cooling systems. It is out of sight, but is usually at the forward end of the engine, either in its own housing on a direct cooled engine, or near or under the header tank on an indirect system.

Its job is to control automatically the rate of flow of the coolant around the engine block and cylinder head so that the engine is kept at its most efficient working temperature. On starting, the closed thermostat restricts the flow through the engine so that it warms up quickly. As working temperature is reached, the thermostat valve opens to allow the coolant to flow. In the raw water cooled engine the closed thermostat limits recirculation until the working temperature is reached. It is then fully opened to increase the flow rate. A bypass is arranged so hot exhaust gases are still cooled with some of the raw water, which is then ejected overboard.

In the indirect system, the initial circulation is again confined around the block and head until the thermostat opens to allow the heat exchanger to come into operation. Thus on either system the balance is kept to maintain the engine at its most efficient working temperature.

Most modern thermostats are of the wax type, but you may find a bellows type on older designs of engine such as the Bukh – more especially if they are conversions from older automotive units. The two types of thermostat are shown in Fig 59. The bellows thermostat works by the movement obtained from the expansion of a liquid contained in metal bellows. It fails if the metal becomes fatigued and cracks allow the liquid to escape. In the wax thermostat, the wax element begins to melt and increase its volume at perhaps 75°C. By 85°C it is fully melted and expanded. As the wax expands, it activates a plunger, in turn this opens and closes the valve to regulate the flow of coolant through the thermostat.

The owner's manual should declare the thermostat operating (opening) temperature, and this is usually stamped on a replacement thermostat. Replacement is needed if there is trouble with over heating or, more rarely, over cooling. The wax thermostat usually fails in the closed position, thus creating over heating, but it can jam with dirt or corrosion in the open position and produce over cooling in the system. The bellows thermostat fails in the open position. Although there are other causes for these problems, a failed thermostat is the easiest item to locate, test and, if necessary, renew.

Spare gaskets or jointing compound will be needed to hand before you start dismantling. The old thermostat is easily tested by holding it with pliers in a pan of water which is heated on a stove to see if it opens. A thermometer is needed for a proper test, but it is cheaper to buy a new thermostat than a thermometer!

## Indirect cooling system variations

Instead of using a heat exchanger to transfer heat from the engine's fresh water circuit to the raw water, keel cooling is sometimes used. Pipes are built on the outside of the hull – the hot fresh water is pumped into these and the heat is transferred. Because of the vulnerability of pipes on the outside of the hull and through hull fittings, keel cooling has not much to recommend it, in my opinion. Fouling and corrosion present extra problems of maintenance. Any hull protrusion is also vulnerable to damage when lifting out or slipping.

Not enough builders make the most of the waste heat from the engine's cooling water, and calorifiers (just another form of heat exchanger) are a great asset for supplying domestic hot water and central heating. The only snag is that alternative heat sources have to be found when the engine is not running. On large yachts carrying generators, electrical immersion heaters can be used, but on small craft it is often found that even a short daily run will provide enough hot water for evening ablutions and washing up.

## Exhaust systems

The importance of gas flow through the engine has already been stressed, but the last part of the system – getting rid of the exhaust gases – is more difficult than it first seems on boats.

Although directing exhaust straight into the atmosphere is a simple way to do the job, for the yachtsman, the noise and smell created are objectionable. The 'dry' exhaust system, though very popular on working boats and fishing craft, declines in use until the very largest motor yachts with tall funnels can again adopt a suitably designed system. Heat insulation is a vital part of the design as fire risk can be high. Both petrol and diesel engines can use a dry exhaust system but by far the larger number of pleasure craft use a 'wet' system.

### THE WET EXHAUST SYSTEM

The advantages are:

Bellows type thermostat

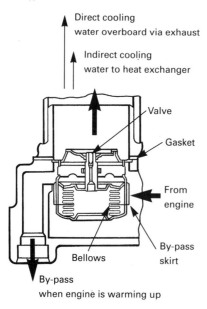

Direct cooling
water overboard via exhaust

Indirect cooling
water to heat exchanger

Valve

Gasket

From
engine

By-pass
skirt

Bellows

By-pass
when engine is warming up

Wax type thermostat

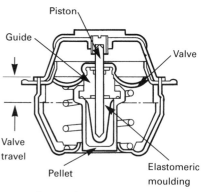

Piston

Guide

Valve

Valve
travel

Pellet

Elastomeric
moulding

*Fig 59 Bellows and wax thermostats.*

1. It is safer, as the sections of the exhaust which pass through bulkheads and compartments are relatively cool. Fire risk is reduced.
2. It is quieter, the water injected into the gases helps silence them.
3. When an engine is in good mechanical order it is cleaner, especially when discharge is made entirely under water.

The disadvantages are:

1. Systems usually create some back pressure, that is resistance to the easy passage of gases out to the atmosphere. If back pressure is high, this affects the efficient scavenging of all the exhaust gases from the engine's cylinders as the exhaust valves open. Underwater exhaust discharge may be quieter, but it creates greater back pressure in a system. The applications engineer must ensure that this is limited to the parameters laid down by the engine manufacturer.
2. Corrosion rate is high. Three factors contribute to this. First, the acidic content of exhaust gases, particularly from diesels, corrodes metal in the exhaust system. When any hydrocarbon fuel is burnt it produces water vapour, which condenses onto any cold surface. The internal combustion engine is no exception and this water plus pollutants will try to attack all metal surfaces as an engine cools.

Second, the high rate of flow of the water injection contributes to impingement attack on metal parts of the exhaust line. This form of attack occurs when the water constantly washes away the products of corrosion to expose new metal for renewed attack. Look particularly at the areas round a water injection bend immediately following the exhaust manifold on the engine, because in some designs the angle of impingement is less than perfect and serious attack takes place.

Third, engine and gearbox manufacturers will insist on mixing different metals in their power units; electrolytic corrosion can, unless guarded against by the use of the correct materials and cathodic protection, produce severe corrosion problems.

Although we have looked at the problems associated with the exhaust system, corrosion of one type or another manifests itself in many other parts of an engine. Fig 60 shows the damage that can be caused by mixed metals in an engine. Here, water-borne copper salts leached from copper piping by the raw water were carried to the light alloy connecting stubs used to join rubber piping to the marine gearbox. The stubs were developed by Perkins when their 4.108 engine was connected to the TMP 12,000 gearbox, and provided they are renewed when the indicator ring begins to disintegrate they give full cathodic protection.

This kind of corrosion is an example of ELECTROLYTIC corrosion. When two different metals are immersed in sea water a voltage potential is developed between them. The anode dissolves away by electrochemical reaction. If the potential is more than about 0.25 V, the less noble metal will be eaten away. Various orders of 'nobility' are published, with slight variations in the suggested voltage potential that is developed.

Table 6 shows a typical order applied to this problem. The trick is to see that the potential between any two metals that might be corroding have a potential that is the same or preferably less than the figure just given. Before I am accused of an over-simplification of a complex process, I would add that the relative areas of the two metals also have a direct bearing on the potential and rate of corrosion. For example, there is usually a large potential difference between stainless steels and light alloys of aluminium. Yet stainless steels are successfully used to fasten light alloys, as you will find if you look at most outdrive legs. As the area of the noble stainless steel is small compared to that of the light alloy, little or no corrosion takes place. Even so, some of the better manufacturers use special stainless steel inserts (see Chapter 10) so that the fastening bolt will not corrode the thread section of the light alloy into which it is inserted.

Magnesium and zinc are the least noble

TABLE 6. Galvanic series in seawater at 25°C, flowing at 13 ft/second

| Metal | Steady negative potential, volts |
|---|---|
| Type 316 stainless steel (Passive)* 18/10/3 | 0.05 |
| Monel 400 | 0.08 |
| Type 304 stainless steel (Passive)* 18/8 | 0.08 |
| Titanium | 0.15 |
| Type 316 stainless steel (Active)* | 0.18 |
| Silicon bronze | 0.18 |
| 70/80 copper-nickel (0.47% Fe) | 0.25 |
| Aluminium bronze | 0.26 |
| Copper | 0.36 |
| Type 304 stainless steel (Active) | 0.53 |
| Grey iron | 0.61 |
| Carbon steel | 0.61 |
| Cadmium plating | 0.80 |
| Aluminium 3003† | 0.94 |
| Zinc | 1.03 |
| Galvanised iron | 1.05 |
| Magnesium | 1.60 |

* Stainless steel is said to be passive when the self-protecting, oxidised surface protects the metal from further corrosion. If this surface is worn away by mechanical damage, friction or abrasion, then the underlying surface is presented for corrosion to take place and it is said to become active.
† There are many light alloys based on aluminium; this is but one of the many types.

Fig 60  Cathodic protection stubs on Perkins 4.108/TMP12000 gearbox. Left, *a new stub with safety indicator ring;* right, *used stub with indicator ring worn away ready for replacement before there is danger from the stub corroding through.*

metals. Alloys of these are used for protection in fresh water cathodic protection systems for the former metal and in sea water for the latter. The metals are made into sacrificial anodes, like the stubs discussed earlier. Zinc alloys are sometimes used inside engines as well as outside the boat on the hull or outdrive legs which come into contact with salt water.

Impressed current systems can utilise a DC current to alter the potential in a hull or outdrive unit, changing anodic areas to cathodic. While these are fine for large ships with constantly running generators, for small craft they impose an unwanted current drain on the battery. However, the Mercathode System has proved successful and popular.

3. FLOODING. When the engine is on or below the waterline, the design must ensure that water cannot get back into the engine either by syphoning or back flooding from the skin fitting.

These problems can be overcome by the use of good design and materials, but regular inspection of the whole length of the exhaust system is recommended each season.

Skin-fitting design features are shown in Fig 56. The installation of a full flow valve at the skin fitting outlet is recommended, as failure in the exhaust line apart from that at the skin fitting itself can produce flooding in an unattended boat. Even a hole apparently above the waterline can cause flooding when a boat bobs up and down on waves from passing craft or in bad weather. The movement forces just a few spots of water in at first but, as the boat fills, this turns into a flood. A valve also allows work to be carried out on the line safely while the boat is afloat, although it is not unknown for a packet of butter to be shoved up the exhaust line as a substitute!

Back pressure should always be limited by using pipe runs with an adequate diameter and as short and straight as possible. On acceptance trials, an applications engineer should measure these parameters before accepting the engines into guarantee.

## MATERIALS FOR EXHAUST LINES

While early marine engines often used copper pipe, this metal, as we have already seen, has a highly corrosive effect on light alloys. It is sometimes used on petrol engine exhaust lines, but should never be used on diesel lines. If a petrol engine has light alloy parts, copper must be avoided. In addition to electrolytic corrosion taking place there is always the danger when using copper pipe or fastenings that leaching of the zinc element will destroy their strength, causing them to disintegrate. Under the microscope copper pipe in this state can look like coral where the zinc has been removed. Stainless steels have proved excellent for sections of exhaust line, but some marine grade bronzes will stand up to the conditions found at the extreme end of exhaust outlets on both types of engine.

In water-cooled diesel exhausts, armoured rubber exhaust hose is now used extensively, which has the added bonus of helping to silence the exhaust gases. It should always be clipped with double stainless steel hose clips to ensure that joints are both watertight and gas tight. The integrity of exhaust lines is doubly important where they pass through accommodation spaces. Carbon monoxide gas in the exhaust will kill.

The least expensive exhaust pipe line can be fabricated out of steel pipe with flange joints. If the tube has sufficient thickness it will last some time before it corrodes through. However, the initial saving is not always as great as it may first seem when threads – which will not undo easily later – have to be made.

At one time, asbestos in various forms was used to isolate and insulate hot pipe runs and provide exhaust line sealing gaskets. Because of its links with cancer there are now forms of asbestos which are totally sealed in other materials to prevent the loss of fibre which is the cause of the trouble. However, there is still a risk when they are being sawn or worked during installation. Firms such as Turner Newall or James Walker and Co. Ltd can advise on the safe use of these materials. Although little emphasis has been put on it to date, my belief is that many of the asbestos substitutes must be

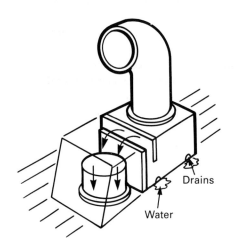

A Dorade ventilator

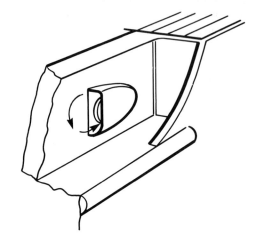

A Shell ventilator making use
of hollow GRP section

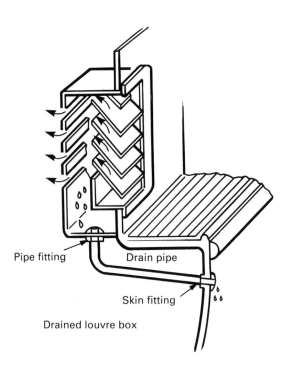

*Fig 61 Static ventilation systems for
an engine compartment.*

treated with the same safety precautions. Little research seems to have been done into the health hazards that might arise in the use of the many other mineral fibre materials that are coming onto the market as substitutes. All must be treated with caution, in my opinion. Specialist advice must be sought when amateurs are using, removing or replacing these materials. Protective clothing and masks should be worn.

Various types of plastic, usually polypropylene, are now being used for parts of marine exhaust systems – particularly mixer box (waterlock) silencers as shown in Fig 61J. Plastic has many attributes when used in the marine environment, but I am not at all convinced that it is the best one for use in exhaust line components. Although it is not subject to corrosion, plastic degrades in various ways. More importantly, it will melt, if not burn, in the high temperatures which will exist if the supply of exhaust line cooling water fails. Heavy cast iron has been a popular metal to use, but it *is* heavy as extra metal has to be used to give it a reasonable service life. Heavy gauge stainless steel is a better material for this application.

## TYPICAL WET EXHAUST LINE SYSTEMS

The design of the wet exhaust system is dictated by the height of the water injection bend at the manifold of the engine in relation to the waterline. Fig 61(1) is a constant drop system possible when the injection bend (P) is 12 in (305 mm) or more above the waterline, and a minimum fall of 3 in (76 mm) can be achieved between the bend and outlet. This, of course, limits the pipe run if the height is near to the minimum. A safe method of gaining height is to use one of the alternative methods shown at (2) or (3). The skin fitting valve (Q) is shown in all three diagrams as I do not like the alternative 'swan neck' bend (R) being used if it can be avoided, especially in motorboat installations – any bend in the exhaust system creates back pressure. For the builder, the swan neck is cheaper to produce than using a valve. However, my own view – perhaps a belt and braces one – is that it should still be protected by a skin fitting valve. A silencer (S) of the McMurdo type is not always needed when rubber

hose is used, but if used the positioning is critical and is dealt with under noise attenuation.

In (2), a riser (T) is made of cast iron and bolted directly onto the manifold. It does add one extra bend and must be heat insulated as it is not yet cooled. The normal water injection bend is bolted directly onto the new riser. An important aspect of many exhaust systems is the provision of stirrup supports (U) to take the weight off the engine manifold. Most modern engines are flexibly mounted and it is vital to allow the exhaust connection to flex with them. Sometimes stainless steel bellows are used immediately after the injection bend, but if the sweep of the exhaust line is made after the bend the rubber hose can be made to take up the engine's movement. Chafe protection should be given where a rubber hose rests on a stirrup or passes through a bulkhead.

In Fig 61(3) the injection bend is at or below the waterline, a situation commonly found in sailing craft. A waterlock system is used, but there are important design elements to make this both efficient and safe. It is best for the amateur to consult the engine maker's applications engineer.

For a waterlock system, the design parameters concern the height of the lift from the waterlock (J) to the swan neck. The total volume of water in pipes (E) and (F) must be able to be contained in the waterlock itself. There should be provision at the lowest point (G) to drain down all water during winterisation. Other critical dimensions are:

A. The bleed pipe of ¼ in (6 mm) bore should not be less than 14 in (355 mm) above the waterline. The other end must be slightly higher to produce a constant fall to its skin fitting.

B. The height of the swan neck must be sufficient to allow water to drain down to the skin fitting and stop waves entering when the boat is stationary and its engine shut down.

C. With exhaust lines up to 2 in (51 mm) diameter, a minimum distance of 3 in (76 mm) must be provided from the waterline to the centre of the skin fitting outlet and 2 in from the bottom of any outlet to the waterline.

D. An inverted 'U' pipe must be provided

between the raw water pump and injection bend with its apex at a minimum height of 12 in (300 mm) above the waterline. The bleed pipe (H) may be replaced with an anti-syphon vacuum relief valve (K) on top of the apex at the same height.

*Winterisation* of the exhaust line is seldom given the attention it needs. It is best to disconnect the line at the manifold so that the water-cooled manifold may be fully drained. The entry of damp air into the engine is blocked with a rag impregnated with a corrosion inhibitor. This is then sealed in, using cling film or plastic sheet held in place with a rubber band or cord. It is always worth draining the rest of the pipe completely and leaving valves open to provide some ventilation. Check lengths of rubber hose to see that the inside has not become delaminated to constrict the internal diameter. This can happen and may cause mysterious engine problems. The injection bend must be decoked each season and checked for corrosion damage. Use an aerosol inhibitor on valves and check the skin fitting for corrosion. If an air bleed valve is fitted, check that it is clean.

# Engine space cooling

Far too little attention is given to providing proper ventilation for marine engines, allowing them to develop their maximum power, ensuring that their service life is not jeopardised by elevated temperatures, and ensuring that they operate safely. It may well cost less to produce a boat without considering these matters, but it always creates problems for the owner. The problem at the design stage is to allow sufficient air into the compartment and to keep sea water out. It is a fallacy that, just because a boat has lots of fresh air around it, air actually gets into the engine compartment.

The penalty of poor engine space ventilation may be summarised as follows:

*1. POWER LOSS.* An engine will not develop its full power potential if it is ingesting hot air that is created from the radiation of heat from its own

surfaces. This is true of normally aspirated and turbocharged diesels as well as petrol engines. The reasons are more complex than those I give here, but basically much of what was discussed in the section on turbocharging is applicable to both petrol and normally aspirated diesel engines – i.e. the denser the air, and therefore its oxygen content, the more fuel can be burnt efficiently. In turn this creates a greater expansion of gas in the cylinder to produce increased power. An engine's efficiency is therefore directly related to the temperature of the air it ingests. The density of air decreases on heating. For this reason standard tests for horse power stipulate a set temperature or corrections in the testing specification. In the same way barometric pressure, which is also related to air density, is specified. Unless you are operating a boat on Lake Titicaca several thousand feet above sea level, the de-rating of power is not of interest, but density of air is part of the total picture in understanding why ventilation is so important. The overall effect of running an engine in a badly ventilated compartment is that exhaust pollution increases (from badly burnt fuel) and fuel economy decreases. Excessive temperatures also decrease the service life of many engine components and increase the risk of fire and explosion.

The picture is a little more complex with turbocharged engines. Although turbocharger efficiency is reduced by allowing it to ingest lower density hot air, its speed actually increases and to some extent will offset the loss in efficiency caused by the less dense air. The turbocharged diesel would not lose as much power on Lake Titicaca as a normally aspirated one would. However, there seems little point in putting a turbocharger on an engine if its efficiency is then limited by allowing it to operate in less than perfect conditions with a good supply of cold air. As the turbocharger warms up the air again as it passes through, we have seen how intercooling is often used to help restore and increase it before entering the cylinders. Why pay for increased power and efficiency only to throw it away in a badly ventilated engine compartment?.

*2. LOSS OF EFFICIENCY IN THE ELECTRICAL SYSTEMS.* Electrical generators and wiring are all sensitive to elevated temperatures. A fall off in alternator output is allowed for in the manufacturer's specification. Electrical wiring must take into account ambient temperatures when an installation is being made to a specification by a classification society such as Lloyds. Few small craft are built to such standards, but every owner should realise that all electrical systems work better and last longer in a cool atmosphere. The battery is a prime example.

3. *INCREASED CORROSION.* Condensation and the ingress of water vapour into the engine when it is standing idle lead to increased corrosion of metal both inside and outside the engine. Over winter, the engine can literally drip with condensation if there is no proper ventilation provided for it.

4. *INCREASED RISK OF FIRE AND EXPLOSION.* The engine space always has the greatest potential to produce a fire or explosion. The ingredients are all there – combustible fuel and gases under low pressure (hydrogen from batteries and petrol leaks) and sometimes gases under high pressure (broken high pressure lines to the injectors of diesel engines). There are also elevated temperatures to achieve the flash point of gas or fuel. Sparks from electrical motors, petrol engine ignition 'tracking', or accidental shorting of electrics are often present – ready to produce a fire, or worse, an explosion.

Although engine room ventilation is usually minimal on small craft, if it *is* installed then thought must be given to methods of stopping, or reducing, it in a fire. Fans must be switched off and static ventilation is best designed so that sliding shutters can be drawn across air inlets from an exterior position. The supply of air to the fire is reduced, while at the same time fire extinguishants are contained – particularly gases such as carbon dioxide, BTM (Bromotrifluoromethane) or BCF (Bromochlorodifluoromethane) – within the compartment.

Proper ventilation prevents the build up of explosive gases and keeps temperatures down to levels that reduce the chance of ignition. It amuses me when people buy a gas detector, but not a spark proof fan. A proper fan prevents explosive vapours from building up in the first place, and in addition it will safely rid a compartment of those that do build up. Will a gas detector do this when it is actu-

ated? Gas detectors are fine as a second line of defence, but a spark and gas proof fan must be the first. The use of small electric fans from the automotive industry is a dangerous practice if they are intended to ventilate compartments where combustible fuel or explosive gases might be present. They are neither spark nor gas proof.

## Designing engine room ventilation

There must be two systems, one for when the boat is static and engines closed down and the other for when the engines are operating.

*Static ventilation.* This consists of air inlets and outlets which provide a flow of air into the engine space via cowl, shell or mushroom ventilators, or specially designed coamings in the topsides. Topside ventilation should not be regarded as safe unless a unidirectional flow of air into the boat is achieved with a gravity arrangement which prevents quantities of water entering and allows that that does to drain safely back overboard. It is accepted that pleasure craft cannot reproduce the excellent arrangements that are made on RNLI lifeboats where gravity ball valves stop the entry of water in a capsize. However, pleasure craft should at least take note of the dangers and place ventilation ports as high up on the superstructure as possible. The more holes under, on, or slightly above the water, the greater the risk of flooding. Straight through ventilators are not good practice on sea going craft. The minimum that should be done (Fig 62) is to have a dorade box, fully baffled louvre, or shell ventilators on deck or above deck level.

## MECHANICAL VENTILATION

There are two distinct demands for air in the engine compartment which should be met:

1. COMBUSTION AIR which is used inside the engine

(A) For four-stroke engines

$$V\,\text{cu/ft min} = \frac{SW \times r/min \times 1.2}{28.316 \times 2}$$

where V = volume of air needed by engine
SW = swept volume of cylinders in litres
For two-stroke engines

$$V\,\text{cu/ft min} = \frac{SW \times r/min \times 1.2}{28.316}$$

(B) A rough approximation for combustion air consumption is

$$V \text{ cu/ft min} = 2.5 \times bhp$$

Thus, if we take a 2 litre four-stroke engine developing 50 bhp at 3,000 r/min formula (A) would give us a combustion air consumption of:

$$V\,\text{cu/ft min} = \frac{2 \times 3000 \times 1.2}{28.316 \times 2}$$

$$= \frac{7200}{56.632}$$

= approximately 127 cu/ft min or 7,620 cu/ft per hour
Formula (B) for the same engine using a rough approximation
V cu /ft min = 2.5 × 50 bhp = 125 cu/ft min or 7,500 cu/ft per hour.

2. ENGINE SPACE COOLING AIR which removes heat radiated from the surface of the engine and keeps ancillary equipment at reasonable temperatures for efficient working. In large engine rooms it allows a reasonable working atmosphere for the engineer.

I have come across designers who actually induce an atmospheric depression in the engine compartment solely to keep oily smells out of

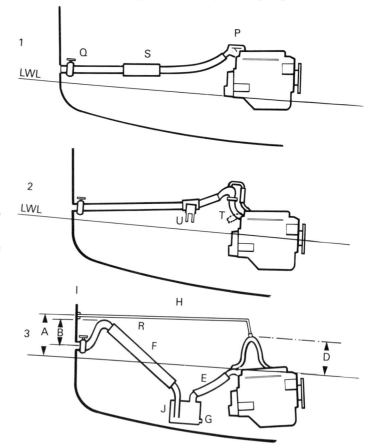

KEY

1. Constant fall with engine exhaust bend above waterline.
2. Engine too near waterline so raised injection bend is made to give it height for a constant fall as in (1).
3. Engine well below the waterline utilises mixer box. (See text for key to letters.)

*Fig 62 Engine exhaust systems.*

accommodation spaces. Atmospheric depression decreases the engine's performance so I do not condone this practice. It is quite easy to arrange for engine room vented air to be carried away when the boat is moving so that accommodation spaces are kept free of smells. When the boat is static, engine room extraction fans may be used to create an atmospheric depression so that smells do not reach accommodation spaces. In this way, neither engine nor crew suffer.

## LARGE ENGINE ROOMS

Where staff work in the engine room the volume of cooling air is based on the net volume of the engine room (total volume less volume occupied by machinery, ducting etc). In cooler climates such as northern Europe, 20 air changes per hour are acceptable, while this should be increased to 60 changes per hour in tropical climates. Marine applications engineers and heating engineers are able to advise on the most suitable figure, but in all installations, allowance should be made for frictional losses due to ducting.

## SMALL ENGINE COMPARTMENTS

Sadly, the smaller the compartment. the less attention is given to ventilation – that provided on the average sailing yacht is appalling. I have even known engines on prototype production boats that stopped because they created a complete vacuum in a compartment. The applications engineer who travelled 900 miles to sort out the problem was none too pleased when he realised what had happened!

## COMPARTMENT AIR SURROUNDING WATER-COOLED ENGINES

Formula (C). A rough estimate of the compartment cooling air required is:

At 20°C (68°F)      V cu/ft min = 5.5 × bhp
At 30°C (86°F)      V cu/ft min = 5.5 × bhp × 1.5
At 35°C+ (95°F+) V cu/ft min = 5.5 × bhp × 2

These temperatures roughly coincide with northern Europe, Mediterranean and tropical climates respectively.

TOTAL AIR CONSUMPTION. The total volume of air needed in the engine compartment is formula (A) *or* formulae (B) + (C).

If we take our earlier engine example to be operated in the Mediterranean we find:

| | |
|---|---|
| Combustion air | = 125 cu/ft min |
| Compartment air | = 412 cu/ft min |
| Total | = 537 cu/ft min |

This works out at 32,200 cu/ft per hour which should be supplied.

## AIR-COOLED ENGINE COMPARTMENTS

It is said that one third of the fuel consumed by an air-cooled engine is converted into heat, which must be dissipated by its air cooling system. In a 20 hp diesel engine burning one gallon of fuel per hour, provision needs to be made to dissipate hot air having the equivalent heat of 15 1-kilowatt electric fires burning continuously!

It is obvious that in this type of engine installation the combustion air, which should at least have a temperature as low as the air temperature outside the boat, is best kept totally separate from the cooling fan air so that both can provide optimum conditions for the engine. The air cooled engine manufacturers provide tables for their engines which give details of engine air requirements. If you are thinking of this type of power unit, ensure that there is consultation between the boat designer, builder and engine manufacturer to ensure compliance with all design parameters.

# 7 Engine monitoring and noise reduction

On any boat with an engine aboard, comprehensive, top-quality instrumentation should have a high priority. The reasons are:

1. *Safety*. We depend heavily on the functional reliability of the highly technical systems aboard a modern yacht. Proper instrumentation will ensure that ample warning is given as faults develop – before they turn into a disaster for engine, boat or crew.

2. *Financial*. Boat engines and gearboxes are expensive items. Proper monitoring ensures that audible warning systems and visual instrumentation give notice that all is not well. Problems can then be nipped in the bud before they become too severe.

Saving in fuel costs can occasionally be made by installing an electronic fuel consumption monitoring device, but in practice, since pleasure craft engines are used for so few hours by the average owner, their cost in the medium term is more likely to be in excess of the saving.

The best warning and monitoring systems in the world are less than useless if the skipper pays no heed to them, or is unable to interpret them correctly. Space in this book is limited so I would refer readers to Hans Donat's book *Engine Monitoring on Yachts*, a textbook published by VDO Marine of Frankfurt – available in English through VDO agents.

## Indirect monitoring systems

There are two basic methods adopted for engine monitoring – direct and indirect. The majority use the indirect method. In this type of system, a measuring device (sensor) is fitted to the engine, gearbox or any item that needs monitoring. This is electrically connected with a receiving display which then needs to be interpreted. Direct systems use measurements which are displayed immediately at the spot where they are being taken, without any intermediate connection.

Using an indirect system, we may be made aware of what is happening by a warning light, an audible warning from a small loudspeaker, or by visual means – an analogue or digital display. There might well be combinations of these, for it is possible to produce a cockpit so full of instruments that it would make a space shuttle pilot envious. Some will even go so far as to nag you by means of a synthesised human voice.

A skipper has to divide his attention between several disciplines in any type of boating, but you should take care not to have too few or too many instruments. An excessive number will not be monitored properly, while too few instruments may leave a major fault in the engine system undetected. We can perhaps learn a lesson from the instrumentation of the latest 'jumbo jet', which has managed to reduce the number of switches and instruments in the cockpit from 900 or so to around 300.

## TYPES OF SENSOR AND GAUGE

There are two basic types of sensor – those that simply transmit directly to an instrument head and those that transmit and have secondary contact to actuate both the instrument head and a warning device (light or sound). Frank Murphy of Oklahoma makes a quality range of *Switchgages* which operate with a standard sender, but electrical limiting contacts are fitted on the instrument display. The switching can actuate either abnormally high or low readings depending on the application. The range of products is extremely comprehensive. The VDO range is popular in Europe.

## SINGLE AND TWIN WIRE INSTRUMENTATION CIRCUITS

Modern craft should certainly have a negative return system for the main electrical wiring for ship's services and starting. Opinions differ as regards adapting this excellent practice for the whole of the electrical instrumentation, as many small craft still use a single wire system for the engine side of things. The justification for this is that, since all alarm circuits are 'closed circuits', where there is no current flow in normal conditions of operation there is unlikely to be any leakage of current that will cause electrolytic corrosion. My own preference for any size boat is to have a twin wire system. Leakage currents are all too ready to find a path to earth, a fact I noted when perfectly made electrical systems on a fleet of craft forced propellers to drop off at regular intervals. The wiring was fine, but a new plastic being used to isolate the generators happened to be hygroscopic – it took up water like a sponge after a time and allowed a stray current to find its way down the propeller.

## ERGONOMIC DESIGN OF INSTRUMENT PANELS

Because two out of the three monitoring systems depend on visual contact between the skipper and instrument head/warning light, the design of the instrument panel should be given early priority in the overall design of the boat. If this has not been done properly, the opportunity for redesign only presents itself when a major refit takes place. When buying a new boat, look carefully to see if the designer has paid enough attention to an ergonomic design that contributes to easy control and engine instrument monitoring. Just as important

is to ensure that the instrument panels have good access for later service work and replacement. A full lift-out instrument panel, or one combined with rear access doors, is ideal.

Although most 'marine' instruments should be made for use on boats and be adequately 'marinised' to make them waterproof, they still need some protection, as suggested later. Condensation can often be seen inside supposedly sealed instruments and it quickly ruins them.

The angle of a panel in relation to reflecting surfaces such as the forward windows is important. Daylight reflections make instruments difficult to read – especially the digital ones – and the reflection of instrument lights on the window at night can destroy night vision. It is all very well saying that the instrument light can be switched off, but what is the point since this makes them impossible to read? A dimmer should be wired into the instrument illumination circuit so that white light can be suitably dimmed. Perhaps red bulbs, which would aid night vision, should be made available?

From the skipper's position, the most important instruments should be arranged directly in front and just below eye level at an angle which allows the sight line to be at 90 degrees (or as close to this as possible) to the instrument face glass. Tachometer, oil pressure (gearbox oil pressure, too, if fitted) and engine coolant water temperature should have priority of place. The charging light should be near the ignition switch so that the light is noticed immediately the key is turned. When designing instrument layouts for twin engine installations, two schools of thought emerge. The first is that instruments should be arranged in pairs – the left instrument reading for the port engine and the right for the starboard. The short distance eye scan makes for quick comparison of the single common function. To my mind, this is not as easy as grouping all the instruments for each engine in a distinct asymmetrical layout either side of the steering wheel centre line, or perhaps separated by the rudder position indicator. Each grouping is then scanned in the natural reading way – left to right, and a quick overall picture assimilated.

Twin installations which put one set of instruments above the other are confusing to read. As regards analogue instrument heads, although it may look untidy, we should perhaps follow the lead of aircraft instrumentation and arrange for the pointers of all normally reading heads to be in the vertical position on the dial. This makes monitoring much faster, although not quite as tidy.

There are a few instruments which do not need to be so consistently monitored, such as fuel gauges and engine hours meters. These may be moved away from the main panel to a secondary position above or below the main panel sighting line. A pet hate of mine are yachts with instrument panels out of sight where they are next to useless to anyone in the cockpit. Instead they are sited perfectly for a crew member to kick the glass faces below the companionway steps. Recessing them simply makes them more difficult to read.

In craft with a wheelhouse steering position, warning lights are best fitted high up above the steering position where they are better seen even in the strongest sunlight. It also allows others in the vicinity to see them clearly. Although digital and LED displays have become very popular, they need to be carefully positioned so that the reading is not obscured by sunlight.

Boats with a flying bridge obviously need duplicated instrumentation. Even the best marinised instruments sited in an exposed position, such as the sailing boat cockpit or flying bridge, need some form of protection. Sunlight, with UV light content, can be as degrading as salt water and rain. The panels should provide some sealed covering. Plastics are available which contain a UV inhibitor, providing a longer service life to both them and the instruments.

Let us now take a more detailed look at the instrumentation to see how it works and what can go wrong. Although it is tempting to save cost by purchasing automotive instruments, they are definitely NOT designed for the marine environment.

## INSTRUMENT WIRING LOOMS

In large installations where really comprehensive monitoring is to be installed, the wiring is completed on an individual basis. This is best kept to its own conduit system away from ship's services wiring. This will aid fault tracing and repair.

For most high volume production marine engines, the makers supply ready assembled instrument panels with basic instruments fitted and wiring looms available in varying lengths to suit the customer's boat. These have the great advantage that they are very easy to fit by either a production boat builder or an amateur. The looms are often made in two halves which simply plug together. The first part at the engine is connected on to the sender heads and the other half onto the instrument heads. A single plug joins them all together. Better looms have a plug/socket at both ends.

Like all wiring, looms need to be properly installed so that their weight does not hang and fatigue the wires within them. It is not unknown for wires to break and it is then very difficult to trace them. A fault within the loom cover usually means the whole loom must be replaced. I have come across a shoddy loom manufacturer who joined odd lengths of wire inside the loom, which produced an intermittent fault before it finally broke. With any wiring onto the engine, and this includes a loom, ensure that it is kept well out of the way of rotating parts. The wires around the forward end and generator can easily be chafed or cut by the drive belt or cooling pump/pulley. Keep them away from hot exhaust lines and, if fitted, the turbocharger. When instruments give abnormal readings or none at all the first place to look is to see that a wire had not come adrift at either the sensor or display ends.

## OIL PRESSURE GAUGE

This is an important instrument which monitors the oil pressure that the main oil pump is developing. When an hydraulic gearbox is fitted, a second gauge to monitor the oil pressure generated by its pump is usually fitted. Since failure to lubricate either engine or gearbox will result in major failure, which is very expensive indeed to repair, a constant watch should be kept to ensure that readings are normal. The normal working pressure is usually found in the owner's handbook.

As you see in Fig 63, the oil pressure generated by the oil pump produces a movement in a flexible membrane or diaphragm. This movement is transmitted to a pusher unit which changes the motion to move a lever along a variable electrical resistance. The change in resistance is transmitted electrically to the instrument head to give the appropriate pressure reading. Things that can go wrong with the sender are:

1. The choke bore can become blocked with dirt. It is a simple matter to clean any prechamber and choke chamber with an electrical cleaning aerosol. Prechambers are often used to stabilise the pulsations of oil pressure caused by the pump itself.

2. The membrane ruptures and a new sender head is then needed.

3. The lever/spring or resistance wires break – this also entails a new sender head.

With a twin engine installation, the simplest way to test the sender is by swapping it over with the one on the other engine after checking and cleaning the pre-chamber and choke bore.

Apparent oil pressure failure may also be due to a sticking oil pressure relief valve which remains open rather than allowing pressure to build up and be maintained at the correct level. Again, this is a simple cleaning job, but occasionally a broken spring in the valve may need replacing. If oil pressure suddenly falls you should always stop immediately if it is safe to do so, and then little harm should result. Often it will be minor things that have gone wrong – like forgetting to check the dipstick level and top up either engine or gearbox to the correct level. Forgetting to replace a filler cap or dipstick allows oil to be ejected into the bilges. Look out for the air breathers on the engine and/or gearbox, for although the oil is under pressure the spaces around the engine are at normal atmospheric pressure. If a breather gets blocked these can become pressurised and blow the oil out. Clean the breathers and make sure that the plastic pipe which is often used for the oil vapour breather linking the rocker box to the air intake (which ensures oily fumes are ingested back into the engine) is clean and not kinked.

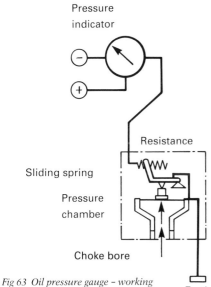

*Fig 63 Oil pressure gauge – working principle. The flexible diaphragm is actuated by oil pressure, pump pulsations being smoothed out by the choke bore. This type can be used for engine oil, gearbox oil and coolant pressure measurements. It can be fitted with a warning contact to provide visual or audible warnings.*

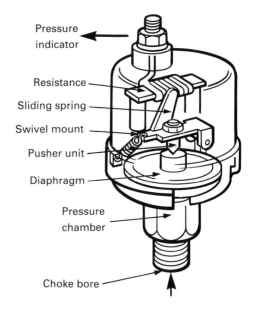

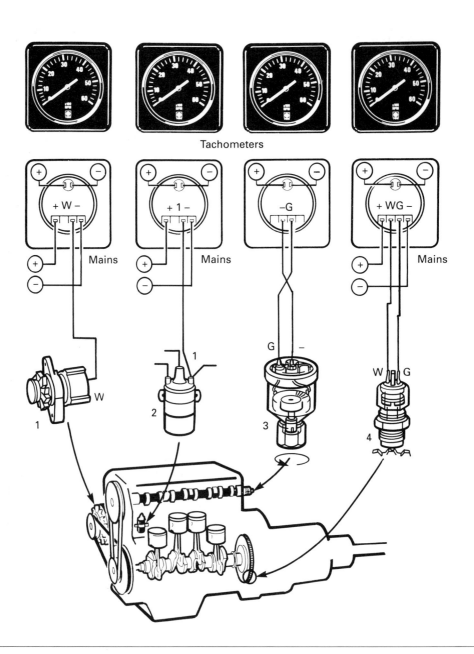

Tachometers

Fig 64 Different types of tachometer sensing for petrol and diesel engines. (1) The W terminal on the generator is a satisfactory way of measuring the speed at normal belt tension. The slip is negligible, but makes itself felt quickly if the belt is too slack. (2) In four-stroke petrol engines, the tachometer is usually connected to terminal 1 of the ignition coil and no special sensor is needed. (3) The generator sensor is arranged with its shaft connected to the injector pump or the camshaft of the engine. A generator in the sensor produces a voltage corresponding to the speed, which is then 'visualised' on the display device. (4) The inductive sensor receives 'mechanical' pulses from the ring gear of the driven plate, which it converts into electrical pulses for the tachometer.

# ENGINE COOLANT TEMPERATURE

This may be sensed with either a direct reading copper capillary tube carrying a fluid which expands and transmits the pressure to the instrument head, or an indirect electric unit. The capillary sensor suffers from engine vibration work hardening the copper tube. Expansion coils must be arranged in it between the engine and the bulkhead to help reduce this problem. If the capillary tube breaks or cracks, the whole instrument needs replacing. Where the capillary tube passes through a bulkhead or panel, it should have a grommet to protect it from chafe.

The electric sensor uses a thermistor in the sender. This is a device which changes its resistance in proportion to temperature change. It has high resistance at low temperature and low resistance at high temperature. The device is extremely reliable. An excessively high coolant temperature might indicate:

1. The cooling water seacock/s is/are not open.
2. The raw water impeller pump has ripped off its impeller blades (usually as a result of 1).
3. Plastic sheet, or other debris, is blocking the raw water cooling inlet. On large craft it is common to fit a coolant water flow monitoring system.
4. Blocked raw water filter. A grounded boat soon blocks the inlet, if not the whole of the engine cooling water passageways, with mud or sand. If flushing with fresh water can be arranged, this must be done as soon as possible. Reversing the flow of flushing water through the cooling system also helps.
5. In indirect cooled engines, the fresh water circulation pump has broken (not common). It is much more likely that the rubber drive belt which drives it has broken.
6. The thermostat has failed.

It is advisable to have a warning device fitted as well as visual monitoring for this important function.

Oil temperature is much more important than it used to be on older design marine engines. A much heavier duty is placed on oil to aid cooling in today's high-speed engines, especially the turbocharged diesel engines. Oil temperature monitoring is highly advisable for both engine and gearbox oil in these applications.

# THE TACHOMETER

Commonly called a 'rev counter', it measures the revolutions per minute that the engine can achieve at any given throttle setting, assuming the propeller is properly matched to the craft. Heaven knows why, but some technical quangos want to force revolutions per second on us – a nice round 2,000 r/min cruising speed will become a cumbersome frequency of 33.3333. Fig 64 shows four different methods used by VDO for sensing r/min on petrol and diesel engines.

The engine manufacturer decides what the appropriate r/min for his engine should be to give it a safe service life. The propeller should be matched to this to give the boat its proper performance. We saw in Chapter 3 how specific fuel consumption curves are related to r/min, and the sensible skipper will use the tachometer to achieve the best performance for his particular boat and situation.

The tachometer is also a guide to engine performance. A 'hunting' display needle indicates misfiring, 'flat spots' on carburettor tuning, or ignition faults when revolutions do not pick up smoothly through the speed range of a petrol engine. When the tachometer is used in conjunction with fuel curves, the best r/min for economic fuel consumption can be achieved. In twin installations they are used to synchronise the motors, although special tachometers are made which are specifically designed to do this. If you have an ordinary tachometer and a well-tuned ear, you can usually hear when engines are properly synchronised.

Few yachtsmen bother to take advantage of the tachometer which is a first-class aid to navigation when it has been properly calibrated over a measured mile. A table of r/min plotted against distance is an excellent back up for more sophisticated electronic navigation aids.

## AMMETER

The ammeter measures the current being generated by a dynamo or, more likely in modern engines, an alternator. It also measures the current being taken from the battery. The needle on the display is usually made to move to the right from its central position to indicate a positive charge and to the left when power in excess of that generated is being used by the engine and services. Normally it would handle very heavy currents, but most circuits adopt a 'shunt' – a resistance built into the current carrying line. Thus instead of hefty cables and problems with voltage drop, the remote ammeter connected through a shunt can have normal instrumentation cross-section wiring.

The information it should impart is the state of the generating equipment and a balance between what is being put into the batteries and what is taken out. If the generator warning light glows under normal conditions it might be something as simple as a broken generator drive belt. The ammeter will immediately confirm something is wrong when it shows a negative charge. However, in some systems a degree of feedback to the warning light is possible when twin generators are charging paralleled starting and service batteries. A diode can be wired into the bulb to prevent this, but it is quite normal as current from paralleled generators brings them up to full charge for one of the regulators to allow one generator to idle, while the other supplies what little current is needed to maintain a full charge.

## THE VOLTMETER

The voltmeter indicates battery voltage. When charging it should be showing something in the region of 14.4 V and should always stand at or slightly above the nominal voltage, i.e. 12 V on a 12 volt system and 24 V on a 24 volt system. The voltmeter is a vital instrument to monitor the ship's service battery bank to check that the ship's load is not draining it down excessively. On a small craft, when the weather is hot, fans and refrigerators will soon manage to do this. A voltmeter will indicate when voltage is falling below normal and a recharge is necessary.

## TURBOCHARGER BOOST GAUGE

As we have seen in Chapter 2, the diesel turbocharger works to produce a positive boost to air pressure entering the cylinders. It works towards the extreme limits of temperature, lubrication and engineering parameters that will allow it to attain a reasonable and safe working life. The turbocharger pressure gauge or 'boost gauge', as it is often called, allows the user to monitor the pressure being generated and to see that this is within the normal limits. The sensor is usually placed between the air intake filter and the air inlet manifold. Low pressure may indicate a blocked air intake filter. Since the engine oil pressure is usually employed to lubricate the turbocharger, this is perhaps a more vital instrument to keep an eye on as lubrication failure at these enormous rates of r/min can cause some very dangerous and expensive problems. At the extremely elevated temperatures at which they run, fire is a possible danger.

## OPERATING HOUR COUNTER

Although some yachtsmen would suspect that these are not needed for the few engine hours the average yacht runs its engines each season (both motor and sailing), this really is a worthwhile instrument to keep a check on total engine hours. A skipper seldom bothers to write his log to record accurately the hours the engine/s has run. Accuracy is needed to ensure that major service intervals are adhered to and so enable the engine to reach safely each goal in its designed life span. It is an advantage when selling a yacht to be able to assure a prospective owner that the engine hours are reasonable, but like 'clocking' car odometers the hour meter is no sure guarantee that the figure is genuine. However, it is interesting to see just how many hours the engine has been used each season. When small twin-engined craft use one of the main engines for topping up the batteries (not really to be recommended but often done), the hour meter allows the owner to balance out the work between them.

# EXHAUST GAS TEMPERATURE

Though seldom fitted on the more modest marine petrol and diesel engines, this device is an electrically self-contained pyrometer head which is connected to its instrument head to indicate the temperature of the exhaust gases emerging from the cylinder down the manifold. It is fitted before the water injection bend so it will tell you nothing about the exhaust line cooling water. It is normal for any increase in temperature to indicate a heavier load being placed on the engine. You need to know what the normal running temperature is likely to be, but when it is known and the temperature is rising you might suspect that:

1. You are flogging the engine by excessive use of the throttle.
2. You have incorrect trim on a planing boat needing excess power.
3. The air intakes, air filters or lines are blocked, so that the engine is starved of air.
4. Injectors are faulty, producing poor ignition and combustion although this can also be related to injection timing.

For high-performance, turbocharged engines, this instrument is particularly useful.

# FAULT FINDING ON DISPLAY AND SENSOR HEADS

Electrical instruments for reading or sensing temperature (other than a pyrometer), fuel and water tank contents, and pressure are all easily tested when they appear not to be working correctly. Two basic methods are shown in Fig 65 using the onboard current and an inexpensive multimeter with a measuring range of 10 to 200 ohms. If you are unsure where to replace wires, mark them with a short piece of masking tape and a ballpoint pen.

# TEST 1 FOR DISPLAY HEAD

Use a multimeter set to systems voltage (12 V or 24 V) from positive to ground (single wire), or from positive to negative terminal on twin wire systems, to first check that power is there. If there is no power check through the ignition/starting circuit wiring from the key switch onwards. Key switches seldom go wrong but it is not unknown and terminals can be vibrated off them. Then use the following procedure:

1. Remove sensor lead from its terminal (often marked 'G' on VDO instruments) when the current is 'off'.
2. With the current switched on the display pointer should be as shown in Fig 65A.
3. Now make a small bridge to join sensor terminal (G) to NEGATIVE (−) wire terminal and connect with current off. When the current is switched back on the pointer positions should be reversed to (B), those on the first part of the test. If the values are not reached then either the calibration has slipped or the display head is unserviceable. Expert attention or replacement is called for.

# TEST 2 FOR SENSOR UNIT

Set the multimeter for ohms (resistance) measurement on the 10 to 200 ohm scale. It is best to remove the sensor from the engine block so that proper contact can be made with the multimeter probes on the terminal and the threaded part of the body on single wire sensors, or with the two contacts on twin wire sensors. If the sensor is in proper working order values on the meter should be:

| Type of sensor | Starting value | Final value |
|---|---|---|
| Temperature | 700 ohms | 22 ohms |
| Fuel tank | 10 ohms | 180 ohms |
| Pressure | 10 ohms | 180 ohms |

Starting value is when the sensor is cold. The resistance of the temperature sensor falls as it become hotter.

| Display head type | Pointer should be in: | |
|---|---|---|
| Temperature reading | Left-hand position | lowest reading |
| Fuel tank reading | Right-hand position | lowest reading |
| Pressure reading | Right-hand position | highest reading |

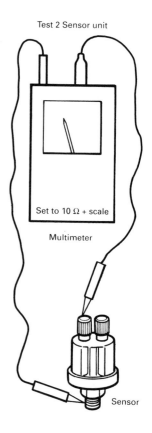

Test 2 Sensor unit

A  Test 1  Display head

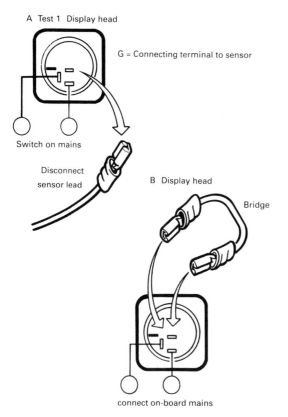

G = Connecting terminal to sensor

Switch on mains

Disconnect sensor lead

B  Display head

Bridge

Set to 10 Ω + scale

Multimeter

Sensor

connect on-board mains

| Display head | Pointer should be in: | |
|---|---|---|
| Temperature reading | Right-hand position | highest reading |
| Fuel tank reading | Left-hand position | highest reading |
| Pressure reading | Left-hand position | lowest reading |

Test the resistance in the sensor unit (best removed from engine) by setting Multimeter on to Ω (0hm scale). Readings should be approximately as follows:

| | Starting value | Final value |
|---|---|---|
| Temperature sensor | 700 0hms | 22 0hms |
| Fuel tank sensor | 10 0hms | 180 0hms |
| Pressure sensor | 10 0hms | 180 0hms |
| Rudder position sensor | 10 0hms | 180 0hms |

*Fig 65  Testing instrument display heads and sensors.*

## Noise reduction

In recent years, environmental demands and the need to produce quieter vehicle engines – especially those for cars – has ensured that much money and research has been spent on acoustic research. Analysis of engine noise is a science in itself, but generally speaking the major noise emissions on a diesel engine may be summarised roughly as follows:

1. Cylinder head and crankcase walls. The noise is picked up from the combustion process and reciprocating parts. Much computer modelling work has been done to stiffen the walls to change the frequency of sound and deaden it. Water passages in the block of water-cooled engines help a great deal compared to the direct sound path found in air-cooled engines.
2. The air inlet manifold. Air cleaners do much to deaden the sound of the air rushing into the engine, but frequently on marine engines this aspect could be very much improved. Some air cleaners offer little or no silencing.
3. Injection pump and alternator drive.
4. The cam and rocker cover both pick up sound from the moving parts under them.
5. Exhaust pipe. As we shall see soon, much can be done in a boat installation to see that noise emission is at least reduced by the way in which this is installed.
6. Gearbox clatter and rattle, especially at low speed.

### NOISE TRANSMISSION THROUGH THE BOAT STRUCTURE

The primary aim is to isolate the engine and shafting from the boat's structure. Flexible mountings, flexible couplings and flexible inboard propeller shaft glands are the first line of attack. A good applications engineer should be able to advise on these aspects.

Although the engine is the prime producer of noise, the structure of the boat transmits, modifies and amplifies it. Some sound frequencies are not so disturbing to the ear as others, but it is not surprising that most sailing yachtsmen enjoy turning off the engine because sufficient attention has not always been given to making it quiet.

Fig 66 illustrates that it is not sufficient just to have the right acoustic materials, but that they need to be used correctly to achieve the best results. The major obstacle is that, ideally, the sound attenuating module around the engine needs to be airtight so that sound cannot escape – it will do so through the smallest hole or gap. However, as we have seen, the engine needs to ingest enormous quantities of air for its combustion and cooling processes. This conflict can be overcome if – at the design stage – forced ventilation and extraction is arranged through acoustic baffles, which trap sound but not the air passing through them. Bulkheads are usually covered with the engine ancillary equipment – electrical wiring, pipes, filters and the like. This makes it impossible to present a soft sound attenuating bulkhead to face the engine.

Better GRP design to allow strong engine beds with transverse strengthening incorporated should mean that free panel areas which act as sounding boards are reduced or eliminated. Flexibly mounted engines which either need flexible couplings, constant velocity joints or flexible inboard stern glands are now almost standard. It is still worthwhile keeping a close watch on the fitting of such complementary systems as cost cutting can sometimes take place during building. The lucky individual who has a boat built to his specification, and indeed the owner wanting to upgrade his boat, would do well to look at the better quality products readily available and seek some impartial advice if problems are experienced.

### EXHAUST SILENCING

Typical exhaust systems, which were discussed earlier, should have a silencer placed at an anti-nodal point of the standing wave generated, but which is almost independent of the exhaust gases. The waves are directly related to the length of the exhaust line. The anti-nodal points occur as in Fig 67.

A   As far as possible, bulkheads should totally encase the engine area. They should also be free of clutter bolted on, forcing areas of bulkhead to be left without insulation.

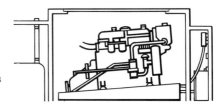

B   Insulation material should be fitted over the total surface of the engine room bulkheads, not merely between deckhead joists and in convenient clear areas.

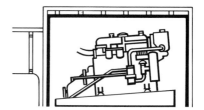

C   With engine boxes, remember that noise will flow under the general deck area. Bulkheads should continue right down to the hull, leaving limber holes for bilge water if necessary.  Insulate down to, but not into, bilge water.

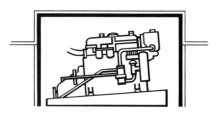

D   With sound insulation all round the engine, further improvements can be achieved by adding density to the bulkheads.  With powered craft, Aquadrive's high density 2mm barrier layer can be fitted between mats or carpeting and the actual deck.

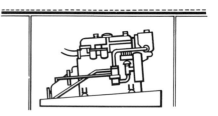

*Fig 66  Engine compartment design to attenuate noise.*

E Hatches and companionways must fit neatly, and should have a noise tight cushion such as Aquadrive's noise sealing tape.

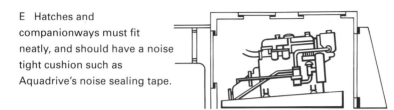

F Powered craft, particularly with twin engines, will benefit enormously from 'double decking' insulation, with a 6-inch gap between layers.

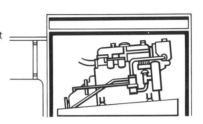

G Avoid leaving noise caverns on either side of the engine. Drop a removable bulkhead beside the engine and insulate this. Remember, fuel tanks collect and amplify noise.

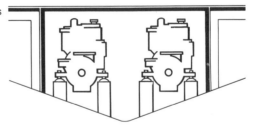

H With twin engines in a new vessel, try to put each engine in a separate compartment with a removable bulkhead between.

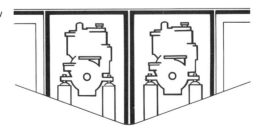

The water-jacketed manifold is usually the most inoffensive noise-producing unit on the engine. In fact, it is able to absorb some from the engine itself. It would be ideal to fit the silencer immediately adjacent to it, but this is not possible as water injection to cool the hot gases must take priority. The second best position is on the anti-node, two-fifths of the total distance between the manifold and the exhaust outlet skin fitting. Thus, assuming the length of the line is 21 ft, and the length of the muffler or silencer is 3 ft, the calculation for the anti-node position would be:

$$2/5 \times 21 \text{ ft} = 8.4 \text{ ft}$$

Subtract half the length of the muffler

$$8.4 \text{ ft} - 1.5 \text{ ft} = 6.9 \text{ ft}$$

Thus, the pipe from the manifold to the muffler will be 6.9 ft, the muffler the next 3 ft and the pipe from the end of that to the skin fitting 11.1 ft – total 21 feet. The next best position will be at the 4/5ths anti-node.

It is encouraging to know that as time goes on we will have quieter engines, but in the meantime there is a great deal we can do to prevent boats behaving like sounding boards.

In recent years we have seen the development of acoustic sheet materials and foam tapes (single and double-sided adhesive) which absorb sound waves when they are fitted into engine compartment walls and on the underside of hatches. Specifications of acoustic lining materials have to ensure that:

1. They are flame retarded to BS 4735. A better specification can provide totally fireproof materials, but these do cost more. There are a number of safe materials which are fire zero rated to BS 476 and these, despite their cost, should be used if at all possible.
2. They must be of closed cell construction so that they cannot absorb liquid. An open cell foam material will soak up both bilge water and fuel; in a fire it could act like a wick and produce a wall of flame.
3. Any fire-retarded material should not produce toxic fumes in a fire.

## FIXING ACOUSTIC PANELLING

Three basic methods are used:

1. Double-sided sticky tapes. It is essential to use marine grades that will take the weight of the panels without sag or environmental deterioaration.
2. Contact adhesives. Thixotropic adhesives which do not drip onto the unsuspecting installer are best, Dunlop 'Thix-o-fix' being popular, but check with the acoustic material manufacturer for the correct product specification.
3. Pinning and studding is needed for mineral wool products which should not be glued. Take note of any user health warnings if they are supplied with these products.

A = Anti-nodes
N = Nodes
S = Standing waves

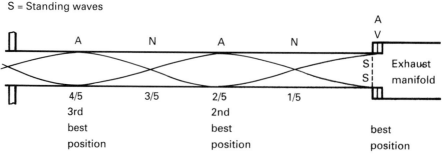

*Fig 67 Exhaust muffler location.*

# 8  Used engines – surveying, buying and converting

In Chapter 1 we discussed the main considerations an owner should give to an engine when he is buying new, and many of these still apply when:

1. Purchasing a second-hand craft with an engine or engines already installed.
2. Re-engining a boat with a second-hand, previously used marine engine.
3. Buying automotive engines to convert to marine use.

Among the important considerations to be taken into account we should ensure that there is easy access to spare parts and that they will continue to be available for the foreseeable future. There is a growing interest in vintage engines, but costs begin to soar when parts have to be hand-made. We must also still look at the engine to see what the access is like for servicing or rebuilding. This is particularly important when buying a second-hand craft as many, especially old wooden boats, have poor access to the engine space. Wooden beams and built-in furniture may sometimes mean that much destruction of interior woodwork must take place before access can be gained.

Engines often gain a reputation, sometimes good but more often bad – bad news seems to travel faster in club bars! It is always worth talking to people about engines as their experience can be valuable.

A most difficult decision must be made when an engine is purchased which has ceased, or is about to cease, production. Such an engine can have a value anywhere between that of scrap metal and a reasonable second-hand price. The larger manufacturers usually keep spares for engines for ten years or so after a model goes out of production. If the engine has only recently ceased production it should still have a reasonable life expectancy and a continuing supply of spares. Small firms may go out of business entirely, and few, if any, spares will be available. Stuart Turner made their robust two-stroke engine for many years, but fortunately for owners, when they lost interest in their marine engines, they allowed Fairways Marine Engineers to look after customers. Rolls Royce now look after the Foden engines. Interestingly, this is because the Royal Navy still have many in service. It is worth considering what the armed services use, for you can be sure that spares will be kept in stock by someone for a much longer period than normal after an engine goes out of production.

I am sure that Fairways and Rolls are not unique in this matter of looking after old engines, but it was revealing to find that even a complete rebuild of a Stuart to factory standards was less than half the price of replacing it with a similar engine. There are plenty of small engineering firms specialising in 'one off' engineering which can make special parts. Vintage car enthusiasts manage to find them and there is no reason why the keen boating enthusiast should not do the same. However, this kind of engineering is very expensive and only justified if you happen to have a really 'classic' engine to restore.

## Sources of information on old engines

In addition to information from club mates and owners, it makes sense to gather as much written information as possible. Previous owners often do not retain the owner's manual, especially if the boat has already changed hands several times. If the engine maker is still in business it is easy to write to him. Addresses can be found in old marine trade directories, from editorial departments of boating magazines, or even from the growing archives of the many boating museums which are springing up around the world. Trade directories such as *Sell's Marine Market* has an engine section 'Engines (old and obsolete – spares and advice)', which can be a starting point for research. Other possible sources of information are vintage boat clubs. Larger local libraries may keep copies of boating magazines in their archives and old engine reviews in them can be useful. There have been many marine engine books published in the past. Nigel Warren's *Marine Conversions* (published by Adlard Coles) provides excellent technical information as well as a list of parts suppliers. Other useful bits of information may be gleaned from the automotive section of a library. Remember that many of our engines started out as either car or lorry power units; more than one marine engine has been saved from melt down by a trip to the auto-breaker's yard.

## PROFESSIONAL SURVEY OF A USED ENGINE

If a yacht is on Lloyd's Register of Shipping (Yacht and Small Craft Department, 69 Oxford Street, Southampton, UK) or similar classification society then the business of having an engine survey is much easier either for the owner to keep the boat in classification, or for a buyer to have a condition survey. Lloyd's undertake three categories of machinery classification:

A. Machinery Class + LMC. This class is assigned to machinery which has been constructed under the Society's Special Survey at the maker's works and which has been satisfactorily installed in accordance with the relevant Rules for yachts or full powered yachts classified or intended for classification with the Society.

B. Machinery Class * LMC is for machinery which is of standard mass production and which is not surveyed at the maker's works,

but is satisfactorily installed in accordance with the relevant Rules, classed or intended for classification with Lloyd's.

C. Machinery Class LMC is without the two distinguishing marks and is assigned to machinery of yachts submitted for classification, although not built or installed under survey, if it is found or placed in accordance with the Society's requirements.

Machinery usually undergoes a survey every two years unless a special survey is called for, for example by a new owner.

## ITEMS INSPECTED IN A LLOYD'S MACHINERY SURVEY

Although the average yacht is unlikely to be classified at Lloyd's or a similar society, the following list is a guide to the items usually covered at some stage in either the biennial or special surveys in a Lloyd's Machinery Survey.

1. Starting with the boat on the slip, or dry docked, attention is first given outside the hull to the propulsion gear – to the stern tube, brackets and propellers, or on smaller craft it may be the outdrive, jet or saildrive. On small craft with conventional shafting, lift the shaft where it emerges from the stern tube bearing, or aft of the 'P' or 'A' bracket, to see if there is excessive upward movement. The bearing is usually a 'cutless' water-lubricated rubber bearing, but it may well be plastic 'Tufnol'. There needs to be a little free movement, especially in a Tufnol bearing, as this material swells in water and equally contracts as it dries out. Expect excessive shaft noise and shaft wear if there is a lot of movement. The cutless bearing will need replacing.

   It is often worth extracting the shaft to examine it for wear in both inboard and outboard bearing areas. Stainless steel is probably the most common material used for pleasure boat shafting now and it can pit badly in areas where bearings starve it of oxygen. Oxidation is needed to maintain the vital film on the surface of this metal to keep it 'stainless' or free from corrosion.

2. The sea connections – skin fittings and valves – are opened up and examined. As this is a most likely place for corrosion, and the place where water can enter to sink the boat. All owners should do this at least every other year for the easily removable parts, and the body of the valve itself should be taken out every five years or so to check the fastening bolts. It is shocking what sea water can do to skin fitting fastenings, especially if they have been subject to electrolytic action, shielding corrosion or, in wooden boats, the effects of chemical decomposition in the wood surrounding a fastening.

3. Fuel tanks and all ancillary fittings including valves, fuel pumps, drip trays and piping. Even Lloyd's says that fuel tanks need not be examined internally if they appear to be in satisfactory condition on the outside. I am probably keen to a fault, but if you examine the bottom of the average fuel tank – especially after a few years' use – even if it is made of the correct material, you will be surprised at the debris, rust, sludge and water that are commonly present.

When purchasing a second-hand boat you will probably not want the bother of opening up the tank. An alternative is to ask the owner's permission, and buy a spare fuel filter so that the old one can be taken away for examination. Provided the filter has not been recently renewed (owners seldom like wasting money when they know they are going to sell) the filter is easy to take apart in the workshop to see its condition. In sedimenter filters, take a clean piece of paper and wipe out the muddy deposit. Even if the filter is in reasonable condition, you will get some idea of the state of the tank from this kind of examination.

4. Lubricating, water cooling and bilge pumps are examined and tested under working conditions. It is surprising that boats are often bought 'as found' laid up ashore where these things cannot be properly tested.

5. The electrical equipment on small engines, where the system uses less than 32 V, is given a low voltage – 1.5 V test. Few of us are trained electricians and you should be aware that reverse polarity, or putting a megger on electrical circuits to do with the engine can wreck some electronic items. However, in the relevant chapters concerned with petrol engine electrics in particular, a few simple tests and test equipment (Chapter 10) are outlined.

6. Thankfully Lloyd's does not generally insist on opening up an engine fully until after twelve years service if the surveyor is satisfied that running tests are satisfactory. I can well imagine the annoyance of an owner with a perfectly good engine that is running well if someone insists he takes it out of the boat for a complete strip down and rebuild! The survey is supposed to include an examination of the following: cylinders, liners, cylinder covers, valves, valve gear, scavenging arrangements and blowers, piston rods, crankshafts, clutches, gearing, thrust and intermediate shafting, holding down bolts and chocks. In fact, if an engine needs this attention I believe it would be far more realistic simply to have the engine maker do the job, or buy a factory reconditioned engine. The fact is that with modern running test gear, computer analysis of instrumentation data extracted directly in a test cell, plus laboratory analysis of oil, most serious problems in an engine can be foreseen. True, you still need to take the engine out of the boat, but while you are doing this the engineering survey might as well be done in a thoroughly modern, scientific way. Firms such as Volvo Penta keep a computer record of every engine produced and run on their test facility; one day it might be possible for these kind of records to be made available to other Volvo bases round the world so that an engine survey could compare the present condition with the 'as new' condition. Perhaps this is looking a little too far into the future!

7. The surveyor must ensure that items like fuel pumps on diesel engines and ignition systems on petrol engines are overhauled and adjusted by a competent repairer. I must emphasise

that there are some items, especially injection pumps that should NEVER be tampered with by an owner, so it seems rather foolish to pay a surveyor and at the same time employ a certified service depot to do the job. Firms like Bosch and Lucas CAV are experts in their field and any owner should be able to have complete confidence in them.

8. Starting arrangements are examined and tested. This is another area any owner can look at, and most makes have excellent service depots to hand. A starter, for example, is usually very easy to remove from an engine in order to be taken to the nearest service depot. Often exchange schemes mean that you can walk right out of the depot with a factory 'good as new' machine and simply bolt it back in place.

## YACHT BROKERS, DESIGNERS AND SURVEYORS ASSOCIATION (GB)

Not all members of the Association are qualified to carry out condition surveys of engines but of those who are, most have a lifetime of practical experience on which to draw. Normally, when a qualified surveyor is employed to do a full survey on the condition of a second-hand boat, this excludes the engine and machinery. It is incredible that when surveys are called for, owners or prospective owners are more than reluctant to pay for an engine survey. When the cost of rebuilding or replacing engines for a power cruiser is considered, this attitude seems rather short-sighted. As the length of boats gets smaller, the proportion of the cost of the engines in relation to the total cost increases.

At the time of writing, a friend of mine is having one of his boat's twin engines rebuilt at a cost of £5,000 ($9,000). The cost of a survey for both engines would be about £150 ($270) – a small price to pay if you were actually buying the boat. Surveys save cash, both by saving the owner from buying a pig-in-a-poke and by allowing bargaining to take place where the cost of putting the engines into good order is deducted from the price paid for the boat.

A good marine mechanical engineer should be familiar with all the foibles of an engine and almost be able to pinpoint where to expect trouble without even seeing an engine. There are parts of some engines which, once they have reached a certain age, if you gently prod them with a marlin spike you can almost guarantee that the spike will enter corroded metal. Care and diplomacy are called for since, needless to say, the boat owner does not relish this treatment of his engine, especially if the surveyor is proved right and the sale does not go through. Sadly, it is the buyer who must reinstate an engine that has succumbed in this way during a survey. Fear not, the professional is skilled at not overstepping the mark!

If the boat surveyor is not qualified to cover the engine, then a prospective owner can often engage the services of the engine manufacturer's local dealer, or for perhaps a slightly larger fee the Marine Applications Engineer from the firm which made the engine. Good local engineers who have spent a lifetime repairing and servicing marine engines often have excellent knowledge. The one which has the dealership for the motor you are interested in is worth consulting.

## Surveying by yourself (Fig 68)

While it is often true that a little knowledge is a dangerous thing, a keen amateur can often survey an engine sufficiently well by himself before he spends money on a second professional opinion. Items to look for are:

1. On opening the engine hatch, get a general overall picture of what state the compartment is in. Do the bilges contain filthy, oily water? Is the engine covered in oily fluff and surface corrosion? An air of neglect is an ominous sign. Ask how long the boat has been left standing around unused – but do not use the words 'like this'. Being bored with boating, pressure of business, illness, or even death – these are just some of the human conditions that will be offered as genuine (and, sadly, sometimes ingenuine) excuses.

2. Static engine observations can now be more detailed. Have a list to check off each item. (a) *Oil.* Remove the dipstick and check if the oil is contaminated with water (emulsified or actual water globules). Sniff the dipstick to see if the oil has been diluted with fuel. It is possible to detect only heavily diluted fuel in this way, but a laboratory will test it properly with a gas chromatograph.

Check all around the rocker cover to see if oil has been leaking from its gasket.

Run your hand under the gearbox and sump to check how much oil the engine is losing to the bilges. You will probably become covered in filth, but you may be able to observe if major oil seals at the front and rear of the engine are intact.

Check terminations of oil cooler pipes for leaks, and in flexible ones check for chafe on exterior coverings.

*Fig 68 The Watermota Sea Wolf petrol motor. Simple engineering like the Watermota Sea Wolf is fairly straightforward to survey when buying second hand. It has good access to the main parts that need to be looked at. For the potential owner-mechanic this kind of engine is excellent to work on. This is an example from a small company that has been marinising Ford for a very long time and used to close customer relations.*

*The Sea Wolf is based on a Ford 2261 or 2271 4-cylinder OHV cross-flow design of 1098 cc producing 30 hp @ 2700 r/min. Parts are easily available from the mariniser but* many could be bought straight off the shelf of any Ford dealer.

KEY

A) Dipstick well placed for that daily check.
B) Flame arrester on top of downdraft carburettor.
C) Oil filler in rocker box.
D) Distributor high up away from water and giving good access for cleaning and adjusting points.
E) Gear lever. Out of date? No, as this allows excellent shifting in an open launch or fishing boat, although most of us are used to remote cable throttle and gear shifts. This engine can be supplied with a hydraulic box.
F) Gearbox oil dipstick.
G) Sump with larger volume of oil well aft to collect oil when engine is normally tilted for installation.
H) Alternator Lucas 15ACR.
I) Alternator drive belt.
J) Impeller raw water pump.
K) Thermostat housing.
L) Water cooled exhaust manifold showing core plugs and block core plug immediately below.
M) Brass drain cock for draining down the cylinder block.

Remove the air filter on a turbocharger to look inside the unit. If a turbocharger can be reasonably easily inspected, check the state of the contamination on the turbo blades. Worn oil seals usually result in severe contamination, and replacements are expensive. At the same time feel if there is end play in the turbine shaft. Marine turbochargers should have little or no end play.

(b) *Water*. First look all around the engine for any rusty weeping leaks.

Check the edges of the engine block core plugs. On old engines which used plain steel plugs, expect that replacements will be needed. A prod with a spike may puncture them, but do ask the owner's permission first! The core plugs themselves are cheap enough, but removing ancillary equipment to get at them can be very expensive. Both direct and indirect cooled engines need to have the impeller pump checked. A little verdigris round the edges of the front cover plate is normal, but it should be removed so that you can see the inside of the pump to check the condition of the impeller (easily replaced), and whether water has been travelling down the drive shaft back into the engine. Rubber hoses (easily replaced) age – they crack and harden. If they have been contaminated with oil for a long time, delamination between the plies shows up. Cost cutting may be indicated when ordinary steel clips are used instead of marine grade stainless steel ones. When copper piping is joined to other parts of the engine such as a heat exchanger, see if verdigris is forming around the joint on the copper section. This indicates some weeping is taking place.

(c) *Air*. Remove the air cleaner and examine the state of cleanliness. On diesel engines, run a finger round the inlet to the manifold and see how clean it is. It should be clean after the filter, although a well manifold heater starting device like the Thermostart may make a little black soot around it.

(d) *Rubber drive belts*. Are easily replaced, but a slack worn belt may indicate general neglect. Feel castings or auxiliary items directly under the belt to see how much rubber dust has been deposited there. Grossly overtight belts may have ruined the bearings on a water pump or generator.

(e) *Fuel system*. Look for weeping joints in pipework. In copper pipe, check that bends have not distorted to reduce the internal diameter, and that the pipe is supported and clipped properly. Are canister filters rusty, indicating that they may not have been replaced for some time? Feel under the filter for leaking fuel.

(f) *Exhaust line and skin fittings*. Do all valves turn freely? Are they stiff with signs of corrosion?

Does rubber exhaust hose look in good condition on the outside? Try to undo the end nearest the engine manifold and see if delamination of the plies is in evidence. Delamination might have been partially blocking the free run of exhaust gases and this type of line is not inexpensive to replace. If it feels very hard it may well have been 'cooked' when the owner forgot to turn on the inlet seacock. Check the state of corrosion on metal exhaust pipes and water injection bends.

(g) *Engine controls*. Mechanical systems should have a minimum of backlash. Check flexible cable systems for corrosion at the terminal ends and for chafe on the outer cables where they fay on other surfaces, particularly if they have been resting on hot areas of the engine. Two people are often needed to check that when the bridge control is moved full angular movement is given to the throttle and/or gearbox levers.

Cable controls should not be bent in a diameter that is less than that specified by the manufacturer – usually about 12 in radius.

(h) *Electrical wiring*. You do not need to be an expert to see poor wiring terminations, or badly clipped cable runs. In addition, look for poor installation practices such as running cables in bilges, or cables exposed to rain water. Look out for a dirty battery top with verdigris on the terminals. Remove a plug in the battery top to see if the electrolyte levels have been maintained.

## RUNNING TESTS

Earlier I suggested that it was not a good idea to buy a boat that is laid up ashore without making arrangements for all systems to be tested afloat. It is quite incredible how many new owners do not insist on engine trials even if it only means making a temporary arrangement for the engine to be run ashore by supplying a hosed cooling water supply – not an ideal situation, but provided the boat is well choked up, she should come to no harm for just a short trial. More effective trials continue afloat.

## OUTSIDE THE BOAT

Visual inspection of most of the above systems needs to be repeated while the engine is running, but do not start the engine yourself. First observe the smoke that emerges when the button is pressed. Two-stroke petrol engines will always give a hazy blue exhaust smoke as the oil in the fuel mixture is burnt. In diesel engines, except over-fuelled racing units, the smoke level at the start should be minimal. Great clouds of acrid smoke, and a continuing supply of it, may indicate cylinder bores are worn, oil consumption is high and serious mechanical attention is needed. Some diesel engine do need over-fuelling to start, but the smoke should quickly die away if they are in good condition. Check water cooled exhausts are ejecting a good supply of water and not just a trickle.

Now do the visual inspection of the engine while it warms up. If all is still looking good, check out the instrument panel to see if readings appear normal. Look particularly at the oil pressure and temperature gauges. Also check the volt and ammeters. All the senses can be used on the test. Listen to see if the engine is running evenly on all cylinders. If there is a tachometer, a glance can confirm this.

A professional can listen to an engine like a doctor, but instead of a stethoscope he uses a lump of rubber pipe which is placed on various parts of the engine to isolate the noise at one spot from the general noise of the engine. Noise from rockers should be even along the line – badly adjusted ones are soon heard. If there are odd, louder 'clicks' it may simply be a badly adjusted rocker or, more seriously, pitted tappet or cam. Some gearboxes, especially when they are not under load, rattle more than others, and this is why a test under way is necessary. Full speed trials soon find out if an engine cooling system is fully up to standard, as overheating soon occurs. Overheating on full load generally means much work has to be done to trace the cause and to put it right.

The sense of smell may also be used to trace too hot oil fumes, and even hot plastic insulation on electrical wiring. Use all the senses to help diagnose possible problems, but be careful not to put fingers or hands onto hot spots that will burn. The palm of the hand is often sufficient to differentiate between heat radiated from identical parts of a twin installation. Header tanks and heat exchangers should radiate about the same amount of heat and this can be compared.

Vibration can be observed; particular attention should be given to old engine mountings which may not be working as well as they should. At certain revolutions, most small engines have less than perfect vibration periods, but these should disappear when you open the throttle.

Finally, when the full tests are completed, the prospective buyer is fast approaching decision time. Final decisions must be based on the following considerations:

1. Whether the engine is worth buying at all. Serious faults, either mechanical or corrosion, make for a bad buy that may well be a plague for years to come. It may be possible to negotiate a much lower price for a boat so that re-engining becomes a feasible proposition, but few owners really regard their engines as scrap.

2. If less serious faults can be repaired and simple replacements made, then the engine may well be worth buying, but the cost of parts to get it back into good order should be negotiated with the seller. Your list of parts can be taken to a dealer to price them up before negotiations begin.

## Sources for basic engines to marinise

A person with reasonable mechanic's skills can save a great deal of money by building his own marine engines. Knowledge is needed to select basic power that can be matched to the special marinising kits which a number of specialist firms market. They can usually supply all the hardware needed to turn a 'land' engine, be it car, lorry or industrial, into a marine engine. Bolt-on goodies are not inexpensive, but rather than bodge things it is better to go to a specialist who produces goods within consumer law – goods fit for the purpose for which they were intended. A bonus is that some proprietors are a fount of wisdom, and their experience is well worth drawing on. To start with, he should be able to tell you which engines, within your power and price bracket, convert most easily to marine units. Some do this more easily and tidily than others. A UK firm like Lancing Marine of Portslade, East Sussex BN4 1XP is a leader in this field, and will be able to offer complete packages, but a trade directory will guide an enthusiast to all the firms who supply selected items that may be needed.

To find the base engine, local scrapyards are one possible choice. The condition of the engines there will vary enormously from those beyond all hope to almost brand new engines which have been removed from a written-off vehicle. Price will vary accordingly, but some skill and judgement is obviously necessary if you are to get a good buy.

The second possible source is from one of the many engine reconditioning firms that are found in *Yellow Pages*, or in an automotive trade directory. Here the makers often offer a completely reconditioned base engine with cylinders, pistons and connecting rods, timing train and all the basics brought up to standard. 'Standard' is important because although the engine should be as good as a factory reconditioned unit, this is not always the case. In all dealings, the reputable firm which has been long established is often worth the little bit of extra cost involved. Completely reconditioned marine engines are often available, but their price increases with the quality of the rebuild until it fast approaches that of a guaranteed factory rebuilt unit.

All in all, buying a used engine and bringing it up to standard, or marinising a land engine, is always a challenge to wisdom and skill. However, once you have had a go and achieved the expected miracle, there is a great sense of achievement.

# 9 Marine gearboxes and drive systems

Although marine power transmission systems transferring horsepower from the engine to the shaft are not strictly a part of the marine engine, I am including them here as, in the majority of inboard engines, some form of drive system is offered with the engine package – be it a conventional gearbox, out-drive or sail drive. Each type of drive has its advantages and disadvantages. The only 'best' type of drive there is, is when both boat and drive are well matched, and these coincide with the way the owner wishes to go boating. To help, I will try to point out the advantages and disadvantages of each, but the serious study should begin when the skipper decides on the kind of boating he wants to do.

Most power transmission systems are very well engineered to ensure that owners need to do a minimum of maintenance. Having said that, the basic maintenance that is needed is essential if very expensive noises, or even the sinking of a boat, are to be avoided. Among the many things owners sometimes do, is not to realise that some gearbox reduction gears have a separate oil chamber from the main part of the box. They run the reduction gear unlubricated. Other owners of out-drives and sail drives insist on saving money by not replacing the bellows or rubber seals at the recommended service interval – specified at five years or so. This might save a few pounds, but it has sunk a boat on more than one occasion.

## Gearbox trailing and unusual usage

Sailing boat owners usually know that there are limitations on how long a gearbox can be trailed – that is, left to rotate in neutral gear or 'free wheel' while the boat is sailing. The motion through the water causes the shaft to turn and rotate the gears in the box. Some gearboxes are perfectly alright and are self-lubricating in this situation, others can only be trailed for a limited number of hours, and a final group must not be trailed at all. In this case, it is usual for shafting to be fitted with a 'sailing brake' to prevent rotation. The sailing brake fitted between the engine and the propeller shaft is easy to recognise and maintain. Ensure that any brake shoes that clamp onto the shaft are in good condition. Some use a brake lining material on them that clamps against a disc which is very similar to a motor vehicle disc brake. They can even be operated remotely by hydraulic power. Others use cruder clamping systems. If fitted, they must move freely and fully away from the shaft to ensure free rotation.

In a power boat, an unusual situation of not being able to use forward gear resulted in owners proceeding to use reverse gear. Not a seagoing boat you will be glad to hear, but a narrow boat on a canal. Severe damage resulted, as the gear-box was not built to withstand this kind of usage.

Some gearboxes are equipped with emergency devices sufficient to get you home. These usually appear on hydraulic boxes where hydraulic failure would mean that the 'ahead' gear would not otherwise be able to be engaged. These are excellent for seagoing boats in particular. However, a word of warning – know exactly how they operate as once mechanical engagement has been made on some, the engine cannot be taken out of gear. To avoid the harbour wall, the engine must be stopped in good time. In the emergency state, many gearboxes must be run at a greatly reduced speed.

All owners should be thoroughly aware of the eventual damage that is done to any box by slamming the gear lever from ahead to astern at wide throttle openings. It may appear smart for a skipper to dash up to his berth at full speed, slam the box into reverse, stop and step lightly ashore. However, the clutch plates are probably screaming out in agony. With crowded berths and jam-packed marinas so common these days, the sensible skipper manoeuvres his boat slowly to avoid damage to surrounding craft as well as to his gearbox.

## Types of gearbox

The proper marine gearbox is designed for this application alone, although automotive gearboxes can be successfully converted to light duty marine applications.

The marine box is simply an ahead or astern transmission, these being engaged by a single lever or cable control operating astern or ahead clutches. The central position of the lever for either is neutral and the box nearly always has thrust bearings incorporated in it that will safely transmit the thrust from the propeller to the hull. If reduction gears are needed these are either incorporated in the box or are a bolt-on item – a reduction box which is specially designed to fit onto the aft end of the main box.

The automotive box has more gears than are necessary for marine purposes, and the reverse is usually a poor one with the wrong ratio for astern efficiency. A clutch is usually needed to operate it without unwholesome noises coming from the synchromesh gears, and it does not have a thrust bearing. There are ways to overcome these shortcomings, and I would again refer interested readers to Nigel Warren's book *Marine Conversions*.

## THE LAYSHAFT GEARBOX

This has two clutches which engage or disengage different parts of the two-gear trains used for ahead and astern. Fig 69 shows the working principle. This type of box can have the clutches operated

by mechanical advantage of a lever in older designs, but more usually by hydraulic power in the modern ones. A hydraulic pump must be built in, or onto, the box and the pressure it develops is used, actuating the pistons that move the clutches. The pump usually provides lubrication to gear wheels and bearings. Fig 70 shows cutaways of the PRM 160 box of this type.

## THE EPICYCLIC GEARBOX

I have no doubt that the workings of the epicyclic gearbox is just about the most difficult thing to explain and even more difficult to draw!

Fig 71 should go some way to explaining what an epicyclic gear train is and how its works. As the majority of marine gearboxes now use epicyclic trains, until we have the temerity to tear our own gearbox apart we can only begin to learn a little about the principles of its design.

In Fig 71 the drive shaft E turns arm D, which has an axle F, whose axis is Y–Y. Freely turning on this axis are two gear wheels, B1 and B2 – which in this case, for simplicity's sake, are joined together, although they could have a clutch between them to engage or disengage drive. As the arm D rotates, gear wheel B2 meshes with a fixed gear C1, which is part of the fixed casing in this drawing. B2 is therefore forced to turn on the axis Y–Y in the direction shown. As it is joined to B1, that gear is also driven in the same direction. However, as B1 meshes with A2 it drives it and the shaft A1 that it is fixed to in the direction shown, which is the same as that of the input shaft E.

The fixed gear C1 at the centre, about which B1 and B2 roll, is referred to as the sun wheel, and B1 and B2 which travel round it as the planet wheels. Obviously, the mass of such an arm D with the weight of axle F and B1 and B2 would be violently out of balance. What the design engineer does is to see that a number of axles like F are arranged in a cage so that, instead of a single pair of planet wheels, there are a number of planet wheels disposed round the circumference of the sun wheel. This gives greater balance to the whole system. Now the basics are understood, let us look at a proper gearbox train as used on a Self-changing Gears marine gearbox.

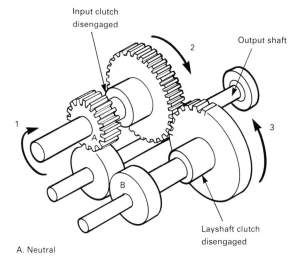

1. Input shaft from engine
turns the input clutch gear (2)
and this turns the layshaft.
Both clutches are disengaged
so the pinion A and layshaft
pinion B do not turn, and
therefore the output shaft does
not turn.

A. Neutral

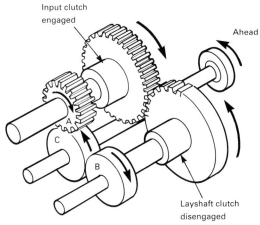

When the input clutch (ahead)
is engaged pinion A drives the
output shaft gear C. The
layshaft clutch is disengaged
so the pinion B rotates freely.

B. Ahead

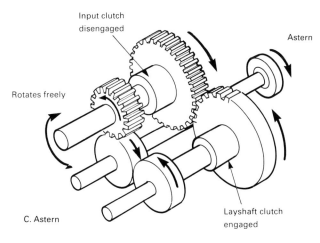

Going astern, the layshaft is
engaged to drive pinion C,
which in turn drives the output
shaft for astern rotation. As
the input clutch is disengaged,
pinion A rotates freely on the
input shaft.

C. Astern

*Fig 69  Working principle of a
layshaft gearbox.*

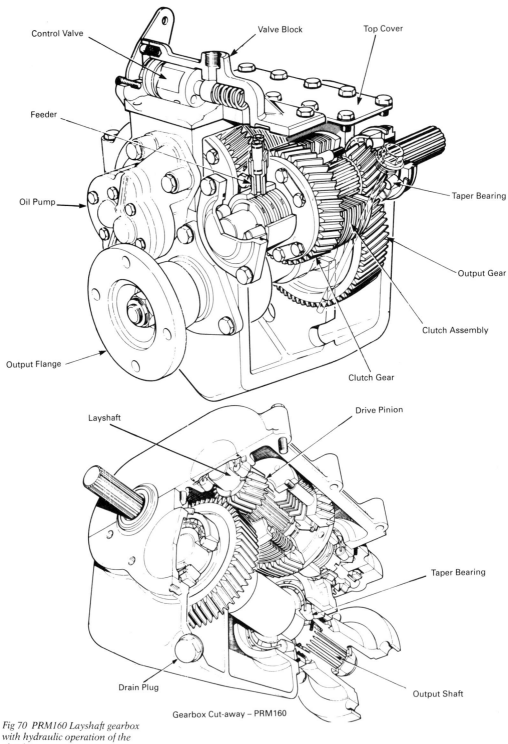

Control Valve

Valve Block

Top Cover

Feeder

Oil Pump

Output Flange

Taper Bearing

Output Gear

Clutch Assembly

Clutch Gear

Layshaft

Drive Pinion

Taper Bearing

Drain Plug

Output Shaft

Gearbox Cut-away – PRM160

*Fig 70  PRM160 Layshaft gearbox
with hydraulic operation of the
clutches.*

Fig 72 illustrates the direct drive (ahead) mode of the epicyclic box. Rotations are given from the aft end, or output shaft end, looking forward. The input engine rotation is anti-clockwise. Clutch A is operative and fully engaged. The input shaft, planet carrier and main shaft gear are therefore locked up and revolve as one solid unit to drive the output gear and shaft in a clockwise direction. The annulus gear, outside the planet wheels D and C plus two other sets shown, is free to move. The pairs of planet wheels rotate on axles which are a solid fixture on the carrier similar to Fig 71.

When reverse is required, clutch A is disengaged so that it is free and B clutch engaged. This locks up the annulus gear. With the engine input rotation in the same anti-clockwise direction, the input drive gear E rotates C planet clockwise, which in turn rotates D moving around the now fixed annulus anti-clockwise. This rotates the planet carrier clockwise driving the output shaft anti-clockwise or in reverse. The pairs of planet wheels C and D are needed to produce correct direction of rotation of the planet carrier for reverse, or as we should call it, astern gear.

It is also perhaps a little simpler now to understand why this form of gearing is generally smooth in operation, for there are either solid 'locked' up gear masses for ahead or counter-rotating gear masses during astern operation. This concept is important from the point of view of gearbox service life as, when ahead is engaged and the whole transmission locked solid, it is fully capable of

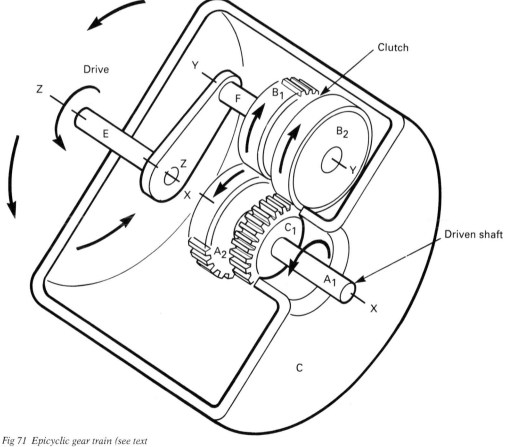

*Fig 71 Epicyclic gear train (see text for key to letters).*

transmitting the full power. When only the small planet gears are being used to transmit the astern power, it stands to reason that they are not designed to be capable of doing this for long periods of time.

The epicyclic box with oil operation is attractive as the clutch functions are easily controlled by light control cable systems. The cable only has to operate the lever which controls the hydraulic valves, which in their turn activate the two clutches, A and B. The oil system from the gear oil pump can be divided to perform two functions – clutch operation and gear lubrication.

## MAINTENANCE OF GEARBOXES

There is little maintenance to do except the following:

1. Check oil levels daily when you check the engine oil. Do not overfill past the upper dipstick mark, as extra churning oil will create excessive running temperatures. An overheated gearbox is not desirable.

2. See that oil filters are renewed. As there are no products of combustion present the oil and filter will not get as dirty as those on the engine. However, for the small cost of the filter and quantity of oil the box uses, it is worth fully servicing the box when the engine is laid up for the winter.

3. See that the cable controls actuate the hydraulic valve lever to the correct arc of movement. Check the cable terminations to see they are properly fitted and unlikely to fall off.

4. Know how to adjust any brake bands which are slipping badly. Overheating caused by

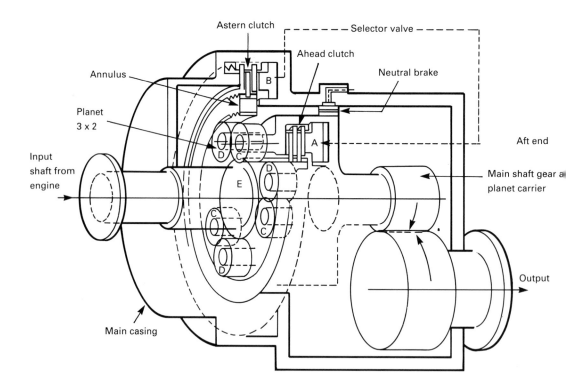

*Fig 72 Self-changing Gears schematic of the epicyclic gearbox.*

friction will damage the friction linings on clutches and can lead to overheating.

5. Flush out water-cooled gearbox castings before they are drained down during winterisation. This is usually accomplished when the raw water side of the main engine is flushed, but check to see that all water is emptied as on some boxes it collects in the lower castings and can cause damage if it freezes there.

6. Hydraulic pipes often carry great pressure. Check that they are free of chafe and terminations are tight. Chafe can happen when flexibly mounted engines rub pipes against engine beds or nearby fixed surfaces.

7. Keep an eye on the oil cooler/heat exchanger as a perished seal can allow cooling water to contaminate the gearbox oil. Treat the gearbox oil cooler exactly as you would any oil cooler on the engine itself.

## Buying a gearbox

The engine manufacturer may offer options on the gearbox provided with the engine. He will have ensured that it is capable of transmitting the full power at the maximum revolutions the engine can develop. As with the main engine, the layman should look for a neat design. This does not necessarily mean that the interior will be better engineered, but when parts that need servicing are accessible and the unit is not cluttered with accessories it is apparent that the designer has given the whole thing deep thought. Any oil filter must have easy access, and drain holes for lubricating oil should be easy to reach. If an engine has a hand-operated oil sump pump, the designer may even go so far as to fit a two-way valve which allows the engine and gearbox to be pumped out. If a reduction gear is fitted this is not usually drained by the same pump.

Like the engine, the best judgement of a box can only be made when it is running. Vibrations picked up from the cylinder firing cycle are often transmitted to the gearbox. This is just one of the factors

that can become extremely annoying on small craft at low speed tickover. There are other factors which cause this, but softening engine mounting, misaligned shafting and damaged propeller blades may contribute. Some ways to try and reduce gearbox rattle are:

1. Increase the idling speed slightly.
2. Check the alignment of the shafting when the boat is afloat.
3. Remove the propeller and have its balance checked by the manufacturer. You will soon see if blades are chipped, bent or corroded away and needing either his attention or a new propeller.

If noise persists, it may well be that there is internal damage which requires a professional to be called in. Gearbox bearings wear, but if water has been entering the box they will have corroded, and cube-shaped ball bearings never did sound good. The professional should check the flywheel face to see that it is flat and that the drive plate or damper drive coupling is properly aligned, as this can sometimes initiate gearbox rattle.

## Down angle and offset designs

Until quite recently, gearboxes used straight-through, dropped or off-set to port and starboard output shaft designs. The final drive was always parallel to, or concentric with, the crankshaft. This meant that engines always had to be tilted up at the forward end to achieve the down angle needed to get the correct clearance for the propeller under the hull, or, in single engine installation, clear of the dead wood. Correct propeller tip clearance of surrounding structures is necessary if it is to develop maximum thrust. Down angling must always be kept to a minimum, as it changes the effective pitch between the blades as they move through the top or bottom of their progression. The engine manufacturers specify the maximum installation angle so that the engine receives lubrication under all angles of pitch, roll or heel.

Today, many gearboxes are offered with the

'down angle' built into the gearbox itself. 'Straight drives' are still available even if they are not wanted on a modern installation – the replacement market must be catered for. The built-in down angle is particularly useful where the deck immediately above the engine has to be kept as low as possible to give increased or full standing head height in the accommodation above. The horizontal installation means that a few inches of engine height are saved at the forward end of the engine. In the down angle box, servicing the aft end of the engine and the gearbox is often easier since there is more space under the box itself to reach sump plugs and the like. The straight designs are sometimes poor for this kind of access, especially in single engine installations where the aft end of the box lies deep between the turn of the bilge into the keel. I have known sump plugs to be almost impossible to reach, and although this may be insignificant when buying it can later provide years of frustration when a simple oil service is necessary.

Off-set gearboxes do allow the designer to centralise twin engine beds in the boat and yet move the shaft line away from the keel area. The extra space between shafts usually contributes to better low-speed manoeuvrability.

Although all these differences in design make no contribution to the actual mechanical performance, they can make servicing easier and if full advantage is taken they can make for better engine space layouts and shafting arrangements. Finally, most gearboxes are offered with 'handed' rotation. The engine itself usually turns only in one direction, while the gearbox is able to convert this motion to either clockwise or anti-clockwise rotation for the final drive. For a single-engine installation the 'hand' of the drive does not matter. In a twin-engine installation it matters for two good reasons. First, propellers have the best water flow over them for efficiency if they are outward turning. That is, the port side propeller looking from aft towards the bow of the boat turns in an anti-clockwise direction and the starboard propeller in a clockwise direction. The balance achieved by this arrangement contributes greatly to good manoeuvring characteristics at both low and high speed. While a single engine in a high-speed craft must have a trimming device that balances out the

torque being produced by the propeller, in a handed installation opposing direction of rotation cancels this out.

## Engine drive systems

Although the various drive systems now discussed are not, strictly speaking, part of the marine inboard engine, their installation and servicing certainly has some effect on how well the engine, and especially the gearbox bearings, will last. Misalignment, vibration and badly engineered drive systems can cost the owner a great deal in the crew's frayed nerves and in money. Properly installed and looked after, they will give a lifetime of normal use.

### THE CONVENTIONAL SHAFT DRIVE (Fig 73A)

Fig 74 shows the hardware of a typical shaft drive. The diameter of the propeller shaft must be matched to the power of the engine. This is the responsibility of the builder and engine maker. Materials vary, but in recent years stainless steel has become the most commonly used material, as it stands up to the underwater environment extremely well. The best shafts are not quite like the one in Fig 74 as they have equal tapered ends, so that when the section contacting the bearing becomes worn the shaft can be turned round to extend its life. There are also variations in the aft housing. The one shown should be bolted onto the hull skeg, but sometimes the builder glasses a housing in to pass through the bottom as with a twin-engine installation. The aft housing may be water lubricated with inlets on either side of the casting, and these should be kept clear of fouling in order to let water pass through them.

The inboard bearing here is solid with a packed gland. As we will see shortly, the gland, its packing and lubrication need occasional servicing, but remote greasers or grease cups should be turned daily during use. A 'solid' inboard gland can only be used on a solidly mounted engine, unless there

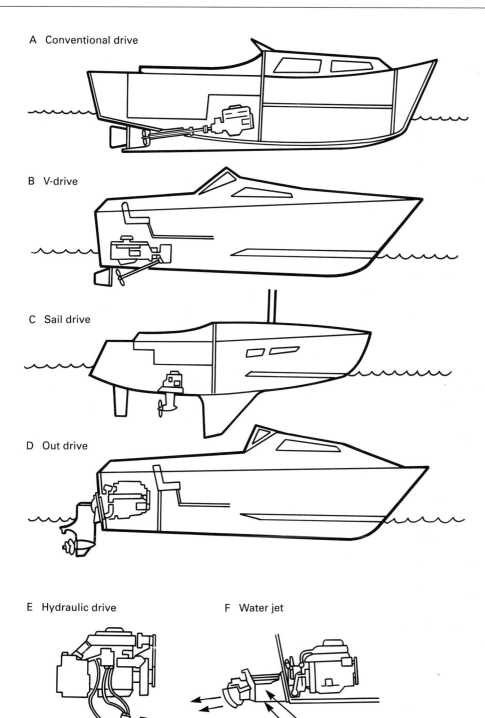

A Conventional drive

B V-drive

C Sail drive

D Out drive

E Hydraulic drive

F Water jet

*Fig 73 Engine drive systems.*

is sufficient shaft length between the engine and gland to insert a double flexible coupling which isolates them. This costs more, so it is more usual to find builders using a flexible inboard gland (Fig 75) which allows greater movement at less expense. As a flexible gland uses a length of reinforced rubber hose between the housing and gland bearing, it could be said to be more vulnerable to allowing the boat to flood if the clips holding the rubber are loose or if the rubber ruptures. However, if it is properly serviced and inspected, with the rubber section being renewed at reasonable intervals (especially if it begins to harden and crack), there should be no problems.

The half-coupling is usually held on the shaft by two devices – a key and a locking pin, but on double taper shafts there will be a castle nut and locking split pin. A good fit and proper tightness are essential to ensure that the half-coupling cannot move on the shaft, and that it is perfectly concentric when it is either bolted to its mating half or to a flexible coupling.

Sometimes instead of using grease for lubrication, the inboard gland uses water. This is usually bled from the raw water side of the engine to the gland in the same position as I have shown the lubricator tapping in Fig 73.

## V-DRIVE INSTALLATION (Fig 73B)

An alternative to the straight-through conventional propeller drive is the V-drive gearbox installation (shown in Fig 73B). This allows the weight of the engine to be kept well aft, which keeps it out of the way of accommodation space, and in planing craft over the planing area of the hull where its contribution to pitching movement is least. The main disadvantage comes when gearbox and shaft servicing is needed, for it is often impossible to reach glands and shafting running under the main body of the engine without lifting the engines out of the way. There is no need for this to happen if the engine is not so closely coupled to the V-drive gearbox, but instead uses a lay-shaft and mounts the gearbox itself further forward. This adds extra cost but it makes servicing that much easier.

## THE OUT DRIVE (Fig 73D)

Sometimes out drive units are referred to as stern drives or 'Z' drives, but whatever term is used they have proved very popular indeed over the years – from the time of their introduction for small craft in 1959 by Jim Wynne working with Volvo Penta.

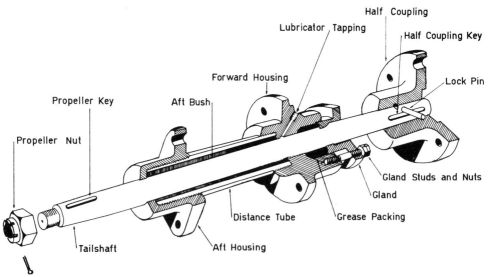

Fig 74 Conventional propeller shaft and stern gear with solid inboard gland.

Fig 76 shows the working parts of an OMC 5 or 5.7 litre petrol out drive. The degree of engineering sophistication can be gathered from the key, although by now I hope you have no trouble recognising the basic parts of a petrol engine discussed earlier in the book.

The great attraction of the out drive has been that the engine is well aft out of the way, and installation – using jigs – is very much easier and quicker for the production boat builder. Thus costs are kept down. Since the out drive leg is steerable, it also saves expense on rudder gear. There are several advantages for the owner:

1. No precision lining up of shaft and engine is required.
2. The units can be operated in shallow water using their tilt mechanism.
3. As the main bulk of the engine is inboard, it is much easier to service than a large outboard hung on the transom. Although it might at first be thought that the bulk of the drive leg immediately ahead of the propeller would reduce efficiency, this is not so as the small loss in flow is more than made up for by the

fact that the propeller stream can be kept parallel to the surface of the water through all stages of trim by means of the built-in trim mechanism, or separate trim planes. This means that both top and bottom blades of the propeller are operating at equal pitch angles. Volvo Penta has improved efficiency even further with the Duoprop system, which uses twin contra-rotating propellers.

As with all things mechanical, there are disadvantages. It is vital to ensure that the rubber bellows which protect the drive from the engine to the leg immediately outside the transom never fail. Leakage would result in very expensive damage to the drive, and would possibly flood the boat. The bellows, which are quite expensive, need to be renewed at least as often as the manufacturer's recommendations. It is essential not to store the leg in its raised position over winter on land, as this stretches the underside of the bellows and shortens their life. While the non-mechanically minded would think it a blessing that the amateur cannot carry out any major service work on the internal parts of the drive leg, the cost of professional work

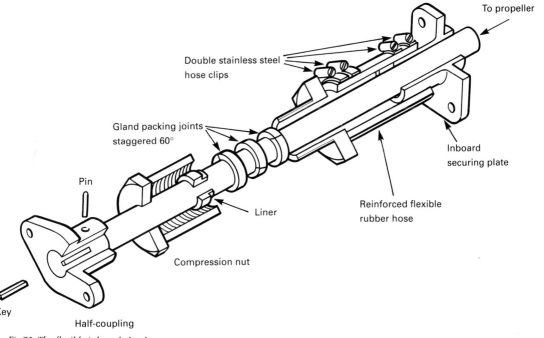

Fig 75 The flexible inboard gland.

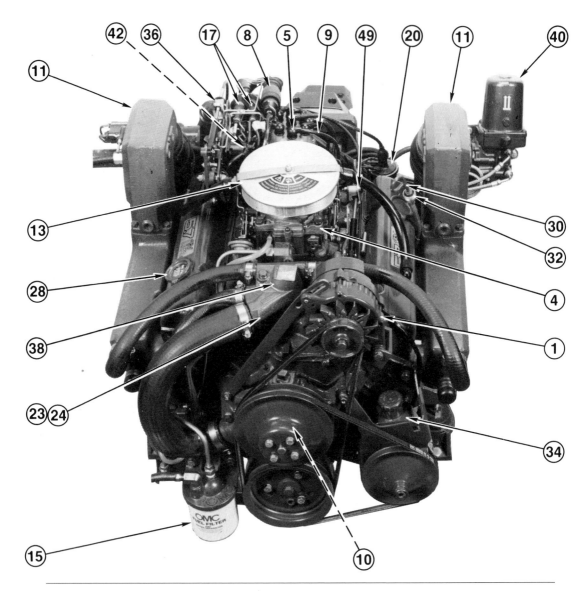

Fig 76 OMC Cobra 5 and 5.7 litre petrol outdrive based on Chevrolet block.

KEY

1. Alternator.
2. Cathodic protection anodes.
3. Anti-ventilation plate.
4. Carburettor.
5. Distributor.
6. Drain for the engine.
7. Drain for the manifold.
8. Electrical cable connector.
9. Electronic shift assist module.
10. Engine water circulation pump.
11. Exhaust elbow.
12. Exhaust relief vents.
13. Flame arrester.
14. Trim tilt cylinders (port and starboard).

15. Fuel filter.
16. Fuel pump.
17. Fuses.
18. Lower gearcase (vertical drive).
19. Upper gearcase (vertical drive).
20. Ignition coil.
21. Gimbal housing.
22. Pivot housing.
23. Model and serial number of engine (all owners should have this noted down).
24. Model and serial number (vertical drive).
25. Model and serial number (transom mount).
26. Motor mount (front).
27. Motor mount (rear).
28. Oil filler cap for engine.
29. Oil filter.
30. Oil dipstick.
31. Sump oil pan.

32. Oil withdrawal tube.
33. Power steering models: hydraulic lines.
34. Power steering models: steering pump.
35. Propeller.
36. Shift bracket and cable.
37. Starter motor.
38. Thermostat housing.
39. Thru-hub exhaust.
40. Trim/tilt pump assembly.
41. Transparent fuel pump overflow hose.
42. Trim/tilt solenoids.
43. Water drain plug.
44. Trim tab.
45. Water cooled exhaust manifold.
46. Water intake.
47. Water pump.
48. Battery ground terminal.
49. Throttle bracket and cable.

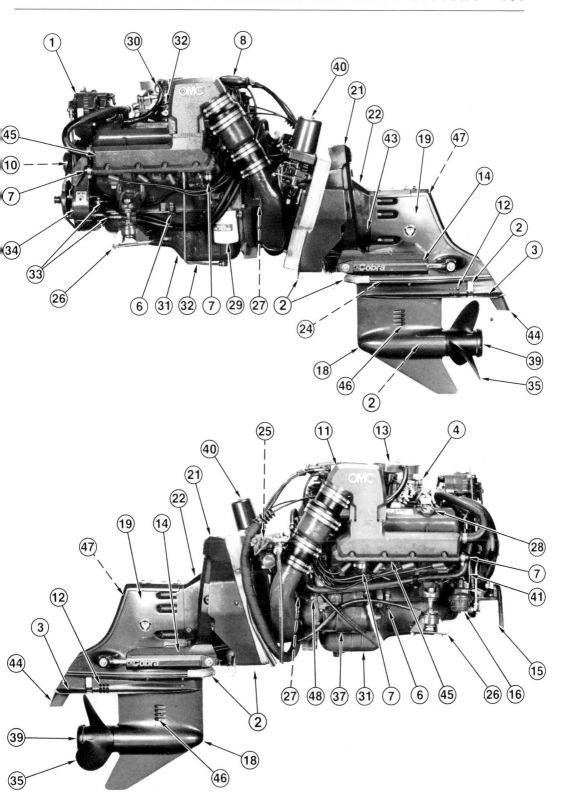

can be daunting. Legs are generally made from light alloy and thus they must be kept fully protected from corrosion, especially when they are used in sea water. Adequate cathodic protection is built onto them, but this adds to cost as it requires regular renewal – at most when 50% of the anode has been eaten away. It is important to use only anti-foulings that are safe to use on light alloy on these legs. Some owners raise the leg when the boat is in the water, assuming that this will result in less fouling. In fact, in many cases, the drive leg is

not lifted fully clear of the water and all the owner is doing is raising a greater part into the warm, light area of water where fouling grows best. Although out drive steering response is excellent at speed, it is not so good at low speed. Steerage way is quickly lost as the propeller stream decreases.

## SAIL DRIVES (Fig 73C)

These are somewhat like the out drive in that an inboard engine is coupled to a drive leg which

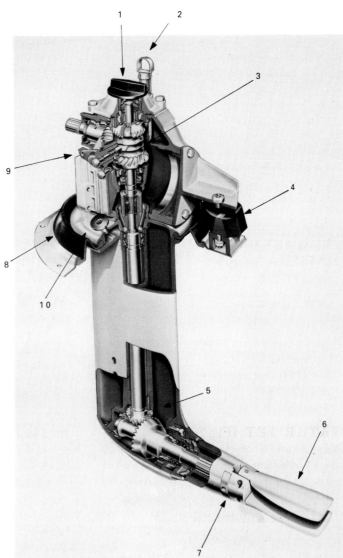

Fig 77  Volvo Penta S-drive.

KEY

1. Oil filler cap.
2. Dipstick.
3. Bevel gears and clutches.
4. Flexible rubber mounting.
5. Lower bevel drive gears.
6. Automatic folding propeller.
7. Cathodic protection – zinc anode (replaceable).
8. Rubber sealing ring leg (replace as advised).
9. Control lever.
10. Sealing casting.

transmits the power through two 90° bevel gears to the propeller. Like the out drive, the potential weakness is the rubber bellows that seal the leg as it passes through the bottom of the boat. Some sail drives have an extra rubber diaphragm as a safety measure. This may incorporate a warning device to indicate that water has penetrated into the space between the two rubber seals. As the seal sits immediately underneath the engine, this means that it is quite a job to renew the rubber seal when it becomes necessary. Like the out drive, the sail drive is made of light alloy and must be properly protected against corrosion.

The sail drive is non-steerable, but it is ideal for the modern fin-keel sailing boats. Of all the installations, the sail drive is probably the easiest for the amateur to complete as a home boat builder. As powers are available up to 45 kW (61 hp) they might also be considered for installation in a motor boat. The engines used are conventional petrol or diesel units and, as most of these are at the low end of the power range and inboard, they are usually simple to service, like the Volvo Penta unit shown in Fig 77.

## HYDRAULIC DRIVES (Fig 73E)

Although this type of drive may lose as much as 25% of the power through churning oil around, the hydraulic drive still merits consideration in some applications. The engine driving the hydraulic pump can be situated anywhere either longitudinally or athwartships in the boat. The pressurised oil is fed by pipes to an hydraulic motor which drives the propeller shaft.

## WATER JET (Fig 73F)

This again uses a conventional inboard engine to drive a water pump which directs the water taken in through the bottom of the hull aft in a powerful stream. Deflectors can change the direction of the stream for steering, and to reverse it, giving good simple control. The advantages of the water jet are that it can operate safely in shallow waters and is especially safe as there are no propellers to injure swimmers, water skiers or people being rescued.

Neither are there protrusions to catch on underwater objects or crab pot lines. However, the water inlets of jets can still become blocked by sheets of floating plastic.

## Flexible mountings

It is now almost universal practice on pleasure craft to mount the engines on flexible feet that help isolate the engine vibration from the hull. Rubber is the most common medium, but there are composites using a rubber compatible oil inside a rubber housing. It is important at the design stage to consult an engineer who is familiar with the specific characteristics of the range of mountings he produces. Simply making the rubber harder, for example, produces quite different characteristics in a mounting, and these must match the application as closely as possible. When replacing flexible mountings, it is vital that you buy exact equivalents so that the previous performance and service life will be retained.

When an engine is flexibly mounted, it is essential that the main propeller shaft is coupled in such a way as to isolate the engine from it. There are three methods used to achieve this:

1. By means of a flexible inboard propeller shaft gland that will allow the inboard shaft bearing to move in sympathy with the engine.
2. By using single or double flexible couplings between the engine half-shaft coupling and the propeller half-shat coupling.
3. By means of a marine grade constant velocity joint.

These methods will be looked at in greater detail later but, as in all things, there comes a time when even the best flexible mounting wears out. Their life is often shortened when engine fuel and oil are allowed to contaminate them. Do not imagine the engine suddenly flying off its bed when it gives up the ghost – they are 'fail-safe', the main engine bolt being captive through a base washer incorporated in the rubber.

Looked after properly, flexible mountings

should have a life of ten years plus. Some modern mountings have a cup over the rubber bush to deflect oil that may drip off the engine. There is always the problem of keeping the threaded sections of the mounting lubricated to prevent the adjusting nuts and threads becoming rusty and unmovable. Although aerosol water dispersant/lubricating aerosols are often said not to attack rubber, they do act as solvents to engine oil, and this combined oil can do damage to the rubber. A silicone-based lubricant that is compatible with rubber is best to protect both rubber and bolt.

Simple observation will indicate when deterioration of the rubber is taking place. There is increased vibration, especially at lower frequencies where an engine may vibrate the most. Well before that happens you may notice at the beginning of the season that adjustments are needed when the boat is launched and the alignment of shaft and engine is checked. As the rubber softens, so the engine needs raising to counteract the sinking. The pedestal adjustment nut needs turning to increase the height of the engine to compensate for sinkage. As many yachtsmen do not bother to disconnect couplings for the winter, this type of gradual failure will probably go unnoticed until actual failure occurs.

Total failure occurs when the flexible rubber has deteriorated to the extent that it is no longer able to hold the transverse vibration of the engine. There is extreme vibration – much more excessive than misalignment – and complete shear failure of the bonding between the rubber and metal parts of the mounting may have occurred. If this happens the engine should be shut down as soon as it is safe to do so. Where a boat needs to get home, in single-engine installations the vibration can be reduced by selecting the r/min which cause the minimum movement in engine and shaft. In a twin installation it is best to shut down the engine with the damaged mounting altogether to avoid the chance of damage to the gearbox bearings and the inboard bearing of the propeller shaft.

Flexible mountings are made to a quality that matches their price. While light duty, low-cost mounting may suit a boat that is not used much, for serious cruising boats, top quality mountings such as are usually specified on working craft and those used by government agencies are well worth the extra cost. The engine manufacturer usually specifies what is needed for the engine. Tests are carried out for rubber hardness to damp the frequency of vibration of their particular power unit. It is best always to buy properly matched mountings.

It is common to find that the rear flexible mountings, nearest the gearbox, perish first. This is probably because it is the rear end of the engine, where the flywheel is often housed on modern engines that vibrates the most. A full set of flexible mountings should always be used. This is because new ones will certainly not have matching characteristics to the old, soft ones.

The ease with which mountings can be replaced is very much dependent on the original design of the engine beds. In Fig 78 the engine is simply levered up and two wedges slipped under the gearbox and wooden blocks under the forward end. In other less helpful designs the engine must be lifted completely clear of the bearers so that the new mountings can be positioned.

## Lining up engine and shafting

No matter what type of mounting an engine is on – solid or flexible – it must be properly lined up with the propeller shafting. The only exception is when constant velocity joints are employed. Thus, even when flexible couplings are employed between the gearbox half-shaft and the propeller half-shaft couplings, they must still be lined up even though some manufacturers say they will withstand some little degree of misalignment. In solidly mounted engines (Fig 79A) a feeler gauge is used to check the gap is the same in all positions through 360 degrees of the half-couplings. Where flexible couplings are used, especially double flexibles, it is impossible to get alignment without them being completely removed and a 'dumb-bell' made up to fill the gap solidly between gearbox and half-shaft couplings. Once the dumb-bell is in position the feeler gauge is used as for solid couplings.

## Flexible couplings (Fig 80)

We have already seen why a flexibly mounted engine must have either a flexible stern gland to the propeller shaft, or a flexible or double flexible coupling between the engine and the propeller. This is yet another simple looking mechanical device which needs a fairly technical specification and installation, so it is best left to be decided between the engine maker and stern gear manufacturer as it will vary from one application to

another. The variations are, of course, in the power and r/min that has to be carried by the coupling, shaft length between gland and engine, and the type of inboard gland being used.

The flexible coupling allows it to take loads in several directions. Thus it not only absorbs the flexing of the engine, but takes up the movement of the hull, transmits the torque of the engine and the thrust of the propeller. It also protects the gearbox bearings and inboard propeller shaft bearing from excess loading and distortion of the propeller shaft, which could lead to fatique fracture. The manufacturer will advise on specifications to suit both petrol and diesel engines over the full power

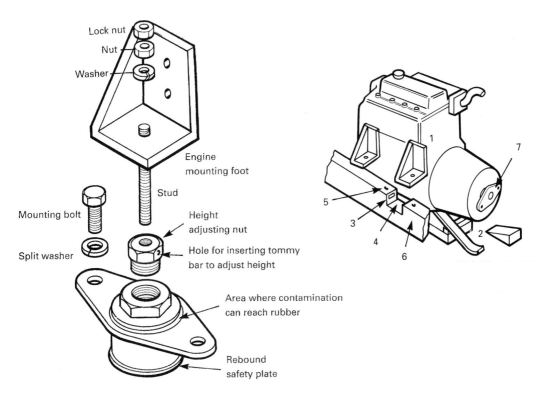

Lock nut
Nut
Washer
Engine mounting foot
Stud
Mounting bolt
Split washer
Height adjusting nut
Hole for inserting tommy bar to adjust height
Area where contamination can reach rubber
Rebound safety plate

1
7
5
3
4
6
2

*Fig 78 Flexible engine mountings and design for easy replacement.*

KEY

1. Engine mounting feet.

2. Wood blocks and wedge with lever for raising the aft end.
3. Steel reinforcing bar glassed in.
4. Slot so that new mounting is easily slid into position.
5. Tapped holes in steel reinforcing

bar to fit flexible mounting.
6. Engine beds.
7. Engine and shaft half-couplings undone so that engine can be raised.

range, but like flexible engine mountings, the hardness of the rubber and the deflection characteristics must be matched to the application. Do not simply buy a rival manufacturer's replacement without knowing that it matches the original one exactly.

The makers offer different service grades for marine applications and they require maximum rated power output, engine speed or propeller shaft speed if coupled through a reduction gear, and the maximum torque output. To ensure a satisfactory working life, boats that are in regular use – like workboats – need heavy-duty couplings, while most pleasure boats can manage with lighter duty units. However, although they are usually a 'fail-safe' product, for the extra money involved I would always specify a heavy-duty model rather than some of the low-cost and (to my mind) flimsy products one sometimes finds on the pleasure boat market. Two makes I have used over many years satisfactorily are made by Silentbloc and Metalastic in the UK.

## LOOKING AFTER FLEXIBLE COUPLINGS

Although these couplings will take some misalignment of shafting, it is bad practice to allow them to do so. They should be lined up as carefully as a solidly mounted engine with a solid inboard gland. Fig 79B shows how the shafting is lined up and the use of a dumb-bell. As they contain rubber, oil and fuel should be kept off them. On some couplings punch marks in the outer casing indicate that the halves of the couplings should always be reconnected in exactly the same place.

## Constant velocity joints (GKN Aquadrive)

An alternative to flexible couplings is the use of a constant velocity joint placed between the engine

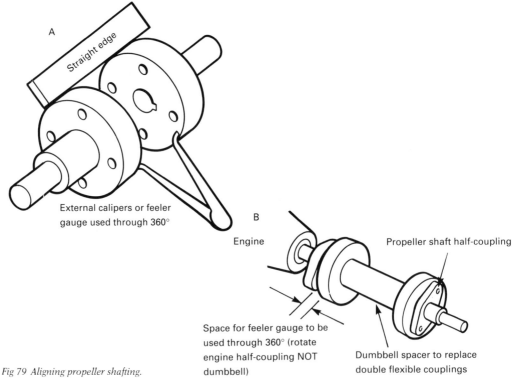

*Fig 79 Aligning propeller shafting.*

A

Straight edge

External calipers or feeler gauge used through 360°

B

Engine

Propeller shaft half-coupling

Space for feeler gauge to be used through 360° (rotate engine half-coupling NOT dumbbell)

Dumbbell spacer to replace double flexible couplings

and the inboard gland. Although the initial installation costs are higher, this type of drive has several worthwhile advantages. In today's high performance fast craft, construction weight is kept to a minimum, and as a result hulls tend to be more flexible than ever before. Not that hulls in the past were in themselves as rigid as some might imagine, for even lifeboat hulls flex and twist in a storm.

The Aquadrive allows the engine and gearbox to be installed at any safe operational angle, with as much as 16 degrees between that of the engine and the shaft line. It allows an engine to be installed with lower height, or when a new engine is being installed the mounting alignment has no need to be precisely the same as the old engine. The cost of the drive can often be saved in not having to make costly alterations to the engine beds.

The working parts are shown in Fig 81. It is possible to use the Aquadrive with an inboard engine with out drive leg, remote 'V' drive, or for coupling a jet drive. As the drive will take much greater movement without distress, the engine can be mounted on much softer rubber mounts, and this should contribute to a quieter engine installation.

## Repacking a stern gland

From time to time, the stern gland on boats with conventional shafting will need to have the gland repacked. A small leak of water at the shaft will not go amiss, as it gives a little extra lubrication. A dripping gland will either sink the boat if you are absent for long, or on boats fitted with an automatic bilge pump it will keep cycling this and run down the battery.

On boats with a solid inboard shaft bearing the forward housing is solid cast metal. The bearing surfaces, as we have seen, may be either lubricated with water from a bleed on the engine's cooling water system, or with grease from a remote

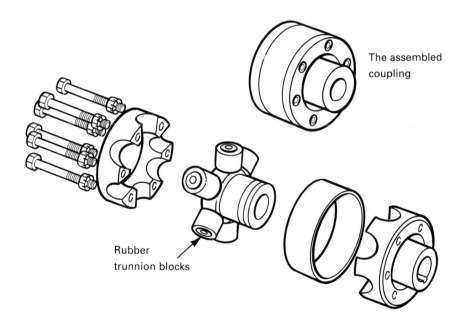

The assembled coupling

Rubber trunnion blocks

*Fig 80 A Silentbloc radial flexible coupling.*

greaser or grease cup. As the bearing is likely to be wet from water which moves up the distance tube from the aft housing, the grease would soon emulsify and provide less efficient lubrication. Water and emulsified grease would also tend to enter the forward housing in messy, if not disastrous, quantities. The answer is to have grease impregnated or sometimes PTFE gland packing in the forward housing, which retains lubrication but keeps out quantities of water.

If a shaft has been allowed to run hot this will rapidly harden gland packing so that it will not be able to function properly. In severe cases when the gland has been over-tight and not lubricated it can cause serious overheating and severe damage to the bearing surfaces of both propeller shaft and gland. A hardened seal, over compressed, certainly takes years of service life off the shaft.

The time to repack is, of course, when the boat is on land for the winter, or slipped for some other repair. The worst job is removing the old packing – a job done more easily if the shaft is taken right out. First disconnect the engine and propeller half-shaft couplings. A pin or Allen screw on the prop

half-shaft coupling usually needs to be removed before it will slide off. The fiddly job is fishing out the old hardened packing with a hooked implement. Gland packing manufacturers usually offer a special tool for this job.

## GLAND PACKING SPECIFICATION

Gland packing is made to suit various diameter shafts and the size must be specified. Not all gland packings are of the fibre/grease type. Although not so common in UK built boats, PTFE and graphite tapes are used. Graphite has excellent low-friction qualities, but it can produce electrolytic corrosion in metals. Since other excellent packing materials are readily available, this one is best avoided.

## REPLACING CONVENTIONAL PACKING

The new gland packing (Fig 82) is wrapped around the propeller shaft several times so that rings can be made from the strip. Take care that the Stanley

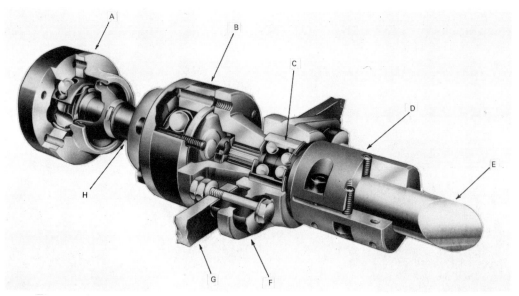

Fig 81 The Aquadrive constant
velocity drive system.

KEY

A)  Forward constant velocity joint.
B)  Aft constant velocity joint.

C)  Double thrust bearing.
D)  Clamp coupling to propeller shaft.
E)  Propeller shaft.

F)  Thrust bearing joint mounting plate.
G)  Hull mounted thrust plate.
H)  Shaft between joints (can be up to 1.5 m long).

knife does not scratch the smooth shaft. It is best to work on a section of the shaft away from the main bearing area. The space for gland rings will vary from one forward housing to another, but you need only sufficient rings to allow the gland to have a reasonable bearing surface within the housing. About half the length of the gland needs to be inserted into the housing.

Without getting the rings out of shape, rub a generous amount of grease onto each ring before inserting it into the housing. Be certain to arrange the joint in each ring at about 120 degrees to the previous one. This is to avoid making a neat passage for the ingress of water.

With the shaft back in place and the gland nuts screwed into the forward housing (if they have been removed), slide the gland down the shaft to start compressing the new packing. Replace the gland nuts and take care to tighten them down equally just finger-tight onto the gland packing. New packing takes a little time to settle, but as you have all winter for this to happen there is no rush. Inspect the nuts after a week or two and again tighten them down just by hand. When they seem as finger-tight as they are going to be, finally tighten them an extra half turn with a spanner. The lock nuts are there to see that the gland does not come adrift, so check that they are tightened down

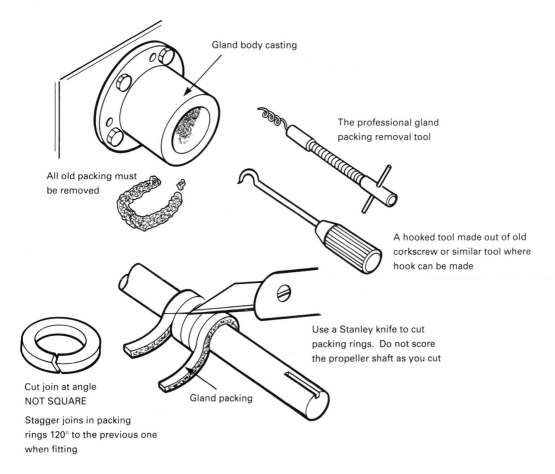

Gland body casting

The professional gland packing removal tool

All old packing must be removed

A hooked tool made out of old corkscrew or similar tool where hook can be made

Use a Stanley knife to cut packing rings. Do not score the propeller shaft as you cut

Cut join at angle NOT SQUARE

Gland packing

Stagger joins in packing rings 120° to the previous one when fitting

*Fig 82 Replacing propeller shaft gland packing.*

without giving any extra turns on the main nut. After replacing the rest of the stern gear, wait until afloat for the final lining up of the engine and propeller shaft half-couplings. When she goes afloat again, the first job will be to check that the new gland is not leaking. If you live away from your boat and use a yard to launch for you, don't forget to let them know loud and clear that they are to inspect the gland when the boat is launched. As the new gland packing is run in it might need a little more tightening, so keep an eye on it for a week or two once boating has started in earnest.

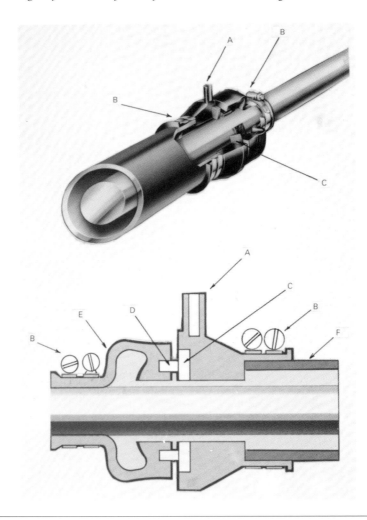

*Fig 83  Deep sea seal for propeller shafts.*

KEY

A) Water injection spigot for lubrication where normal water pressure to lubricate the seal is reduced when the boat moves through the water. The water can be bled from the raw water side of the engine's cooling system.

B) Double stainless steel hose clips.

C) Fixed seat containing the stationary bronze seal.

D) Rotating bronze seal which is pushed down the shaft by the shape of the rubber seal compressing it against the fixed seal.

E) Rubber seal housing fixed to rotating propeller shaft by stainless steel hose clips.

F) Stern tube must have minimum of 1 inch circular bearing area to fix the stationary seal to.

The deep sea seal has to be matched to the engine r/min and bearing spacing as well as the diameter of the shafting.

## The deep sea seal

The modern answer to the conventional shaft seal is the deep sea seal, which has been used on fighting and commercial craft for many years. The working principle is shown in Fig 83, which shows how the two sealing surfaces – one rotating with the shaft and the other fixed to the stern tube – are kept under watertight pressure by the force exerted by the rubber sleeve that encases the moving seal. An inboard shaft gland must still have a plain minimum length of one inch on it to accommodate the fixed section of the deep sea seal. The initial cost is therefore considerably more than for a gland with conventional packing, but it is watertight down to a proven 25 feet water pressure.

# 10 Tools and treatments

The extremely confined space allowed for the engine on an average boat means that the mechanic always has great difficulty working safely or quickly on it. This is often why the professional bill is high as so much time can be wasted simply gaining access to some parts of the engine installation. The selection of tools that can be comfortably used to work quickly and efficiently in engine spaces is important for both the professional and the amateur. Many of us get a great deal of pleasure out of this side of the hobby – provided the pain from barked knuckles is not too severe. There are temptations to be avoided, however.

First there is the temptation to have only one set of tools for the family banger, the home workshop and your boat. Inevitably, this means that you will never have the right tool in the right place just when it is wanted. As the safety of a boat often depends on having the right tools immediately to hand, the boat should have its own set of tools which are always kept aboard during the season.

The second temptation is to buy the cheapest tools for the boat because they are going to be used relatively little and will, in any case, rust in the damp atmosphere of the boat. I detest cheap tools as they are usually made of inferior steels and break, or they are a poor mechanical fit and contribute to ruining slots and hexagon heads on screws and bolts. Tools need not rust on a boat if they are kept properly (preferably in a strong plastic tool box), and occasionally sprayed and wiped over with a rust inhibiting spray such as WD-40. I usually do this after the engine has been laid up for the winter and again after it has been made ready for the season. Surely not too great a task – one which has so far preserved my own set for some 25 seasons.

## Precise fit is important

Although readers may well suspect that I have some kind of a hang up about standards committees I have just one more to mention.

There is an international committee that is supposed to unify the world's fastener threads on screws, bolts and nuts so that minimum trouble will be caused to the mechanic trying to find a spanner to fit them. Unfortunately, the standards committee seems to have mistaken its job and has simply come up with new standards for hexagonal head nuts and fastener threads which no one really wants to adopt. The result is you find a plethora of different sizes, few of which your set of spanners fits perfectly.

When buying a marine engine, parts nearly always seem to be fastened by a confusing selection of threads and nuts so that it is hardly to be wondered at that one tool manufacturer makes an 'All-sorts' set. Generally speaking, engines from the USA and the UK, derived from the automotive industry, have American Fine (A/F) threads on the main base unit, while European engines use metric sizes and there is a growing use of the European ISO standard threads.

However, mechanical parts away from the main engine still use a frightening number of redundant (Whitworth) and bastard threads. Electrical equipment and carburettors, in particular, often use peculiar thread sizes although BA and metric are still favourites for the electrics. It is important to establish exactly which threads and hexagonal heads are used so that the wrenches always fit the head as perfectly as possible.

Similarly, the width of a screwdriver blade should always fit the full width of the slot, and the handle should be as long as will fit into the working space to allow full torque to be applied. The danger always present when using a screwdriver is for it to cam-out of the slot. This damages both the blade and the slot. When working in small spaces it is often helpful to purchase specially short spanners and screwdrivers. After a season or two working on a particular boat engine, you will soon realise where special tools are particularly handy and these will build up into a kit.

As well as conventional slot screwdrivers, a selection of cross-head drivers is needed. Cross-head designs vary from Phillips, Pozidriv to GKN Supadriv. The variations in the cross-head design mean that any one driver is not a perfect fit in the other, so again, care is needed to avoid cam-out damage.

## Types of spanners or wrenches

Both *open ended* and *ring spanners* should be included in a kit and the off-set type will help get into awkward corners. The ring spanner spreads the torque around the circumference of the nut, and this makes it better for the job if it can be used in the available space. Although *adjustable* wrenches help deal with difficult heads, they never fit perfectly. Therefore care is always needed to avoid damage.

One of the best buys of my DIY mechanic's life has been a comprehensive socket set by Britool consisting of A/F, Whitworth, metric and square sockets, and a host of items to drive them. They were expensive, but no engine fastener has defeated me yet – and they are still as good as the day they were bought. I also have a metric/BA small socket set for electrics and the flexible drive is ideal for reaching really awkward fasteners. I repeat, good tools, like beauty, are a joy forever.

For serious engine overhauls a *torque wrench* to use with the basic socket set is needed. James Neill, who make Britool, also make an excellent range of torque wrenches which are accurately calibrated.

Multiple calibrations are helpful as torques may be given in lb/ft, kilogram/metre or the now more universally adopted Newton metres. Over tightening fasteners puts an undue strain on them and may even damage the stud or casting they are holding. This is particularly true when fasteners are inserted into light alloy engine blocks and outdrive castings from which many are made. Although owners' manuals seldom state the correct tightening torques, workshop manuals usually do. For major jobs, such as tightening down the cylinder head onto the gasket properly and fastenings on crankshafts and rockers, the torque wrench is indispensable.

A *feeler* or *thickness gauge* has a number of blades of different thicknesses which are unfolded from the hollow handle. Each blade is etched with the thickness to which it has been accurately ground. A single blade or combination of blades is inserted between two surfaces to determine the thickness of the space left between them. The gauge is used for adjusting the rockers and the spark plug gap. The aim in measuring is to get a nice tight, but still sliding, fit on the blades to determine the measurement.

## Test instruments and specialised tools

Often a visit to a car accessory store will reward the keen marine mechanic with a selection of inexpensive but very useful test instruments and specialised tools. Fig 84 shows a selection which I have found useful in my own workshop and boat.

A) Gunson's 'Clik-adjust' is a two-handed micrometer rocker (or, if you must have it, 'tappet') adjuster. You may well have noticed how a three-handed mechanic is usually needed for this job as a feeler gauge, screwdriver and lock nut spanner all have to be used at the same time. Sod's law dictates that the feeler gauge falls into the bilge as you wrestle with the other two. This tool can be used with both petrol and diesel engines of different cylinder configurations, and even differing thread pitches on their adjusting screws, for both inch and millimetre clearances.

B) Gunson's 'Testune multimeter' is a sophisticated meter but there are any number of auto-electrical testing meters available – from those costing just a few pounds to the semi-professional one shown, which is still under £50. The difference in price indicates

*Fig 84  Special tools for the more advanced mechanic's kit.*

KEY

A) Gunson's Clik-adjust micrometer tappet adjuster.

B) Testune analogue diagnostic multimeter.
C) Halfords' 12V spark plug cleaner.
D) Armstrong Fastening's Heli-coil thread repair tools and thread inserts.

E) Gunson's Colortune tune up window plug for petrol engines.
F) Neill 'Britool' stud remover.
G) Impact driver for removing stubborn cross head or slot head fastenings.

the range and sophistication of tests that can be completed. A circuit voltage electric light bulb will test a circuit to see whether power is flowing or not, but these modern instruments are a boon for testing electrical circuits on diesel starting equipment and for keeping both the starting and ignition circuits tuned on petrol engines.

Most of these instruments are designed for the automotive market and are therefore 12 V, but some can be adapted to use on 24 V systems. The Testune, for example, provides a range of tests including tachometer (r/min), dwell meter, battery leakage, ultra-low voltage, battery charge, high voltage, low voltage, resistance and current measurement up to 10 amps.

Before buying, check just what the meter will do and only buy the instrument with the functions that you feel capable of using within the foreseeable future. Check the size of the calibrated scales – the larger the better as they will then be much easier to read accurately, especially on the small hand-size meters. On a poor scale, small voltage differences which may be significant could be barely noticeable.

C) A portable *spark plug cleaner*, which is simply filled with an abrasive dust into which the dirty plug is inserted, and the motor wires clipped onto the battery terminals. This can be a worthwhile item to carry aboard if an old engine is burning oil and sooting up its plugs. It is useful for the outboard, too. Otherwise, a small wire brush will clean the electrodes, but it will not be able to reach into the body where a great deal of dirt finds a home.

D) The *heli-coil* is used extensively by some quality marine engine manufacturers such as BMW and Mercury. These thread inserts are used in light alloy engine castings and outdrives to prevent the thread being corroded or stripped out by the harder stainless steel fasteners in the relatively soft metal. They certainly save the day when a thread in any metal has been accidentally stripped or badly corroded. When a cylinder head spark plug thread has been accidentally stripped, a new insert will restore it and save the cost of a new cylinder head. The Heli-coil thread repair packs are expensive but are very much cheaper than buying new parts for an engine or outdrive. The kits are sold in specific thread sizes, so you need to know which thread to order.

The set consists of a tap, insert threading tool and the insert threads. The only extra the buyer needs is a drill bit the same size as the thread insert designation, i.e. a ⅜ in for a ⅜ in screw thread. Full instructions are included in the pack. After drilling out the old thread hole, tap it with the tap that is supplied, then use the special tool to thread in the insert – a job even the beginner can do easily.

E) The Gunson's 'Colortune' is designed for tuning up petrol engines. Many years ago, Ricardo did a great deal of research into combustion chamber design on diesel engines. For these experiments he used quartz inserts into the cylinder head to see and photograph what was going on. The Colortune works in much the same way, but it is a spark plug which is inserted in place of one in the engine and connected by an adapter lead to the normal HT lead from the distributor. When the engine is started, a 'window' in the plug allows the mechanic to see the colour of the combustion flame, allowing correct adjustment of the carburettor jets to be made to produce one which indicates the greatest efficiency. The plug can be used for both two-stroke and four-stroke petrol engines and is an excellent diagnostic tool to achieve fuel economy and efficiency or to check ignition faults. It can be used to adjust all fixed choke and variable jet carburettors and sets of adapters are available for using the basic plug in a variety of plug hole sizes. The standard Colortune plug is 14 mm and adapters are available for 18, 12 and 10 mm sizes.

## Tools for drastic situations

While a small hacksaw may be useful for severing a rusted hose clip or even cutting a new slot in a screw head, there are many situations during mechanical work which call for special tools. I am not thinking of the special tools catalogued by engine manufacturers which are vital for the professional mechanic to service a particular engine. For most of us, it would be uneconomic to buy these. What I have in mind are a small selection of tools which are often needed to cope with the one big enemy – corrosion.

As far as the average engine is concerned, rusted and corroded fastenings which cannot be undone easily are far too common. All corroded threads or studs are best soaked in a penetrating oil for as long as possible before attempting to undo them. Occasionally, a stud will corrode in the casting to such a degree that it snaps off, leaving part totally inaccessible in the casting. In this case a pilot hole can be drilled and a special square tap extracting drift driven in, which can then be turned with a spanner. Care is needed to make sure that when driving in the extracting drift it does not simply expand the stud and make it produce an even fiercer grip. Incidentally, to avoid this problem there are thread isolating compounds available which will prevent studs and bolts jamming in corroded threads, but a waterproof grease usually serves just as well for fasteners that are fairly regularly undone. There are thread sealants which are designed to prevent a thread undoing, but for general use they tend to fasten things just a bit too tightly. They then need a lot of 'undoing' to get them apart. Do not, therefore, confuse thread isolating compounds with thread sealants.

The *nut-splitter* is the final remedy for a totally unmanagable nut that has produced bleeding knuckles, frayed tempers, and which has wasted the first beautiful day of the boating season. This tools slips over a corroded nut and a spanner is used to tighten up an acme thread, which has a hardened steel chisel point on the end. This is screwed into the recalcitrant nut, splitting it off the thread for easy removal.

## Stripped threads

When working in the space of a workshop a stripped thread is an easy matter to remedy, but in the confines of a boat's engine space the difficulty of making a repair can be a nightmare. Beware the strong-armed mechanic exerting too much muscle power! Light alloys are particularly soft metals, and threads in them may already be damaged because they are corroded. The usual sign is a powdery white deposit around them. Even when the correct stainless steel fasteners are inserted dry into light alloy some corrosion still takes place. To prevent this, the best practice is to use a thread isolating compound (mentioned above). One such as Llewellyn Ryland DTD 369 St is used in the aircraft industry to lubricate and passivate two dissimilar metals.

If a thread is stripped there are two ways to get around the problem. We have already discussed the Heli-coil thread insert; the second method is to drill out the damaged thread, retap to a larger size and then get a fastener or plug to fit the new tapping. Sump plugs inserted into light alloy are always a problem when – through sheer fear of losing all the engine or gearbox oil – they are over-tightened.

## Corroded screw threads

Sometimes it is possible to free a dry thread by heating it with a small gas blow-lamp. Obviously, great care is needed to avoid fire or explosion, or the destruction of any nearby gasket, but when the metal is expanded the threads sometimes loosen sufficiently to be moved. Fig 84G is a safer way. On slot-headed screws use an *impact driver*. This is a screwdriver which is hit with a soft head mallet, the blow being transferred into sharp torque at the driver bit that is inserted. Care is needed to make sure that the blow does not smash the casting, but with care impact drivers work very well.

# Canned mechanics

It really is amazing these days what can be put into an aerosol can to help a mechanic. Most products found in car accessory shops are fine for use on a marine engine. Always read the labels, as they often contain health warnings. Products that may be safely used in the open air may not be totally safe to use in the confines of a small engine space.

Some products which may be of help are the following:

*Cleaning and degreasing agents.* A clean engine is essential to work on comfortably, and you need to be sure that dirt will not drop into places where it is not wanted. Most of these products are 'spray on, wash off' and care is needed in the washing stage to see that water does not get where it is not wanted – particularly into the carburettor, or any electrics such as starter motor and generator. I use 'cling-film' to waterproof the electrics before washing down or even draining cooling water. Use a roll of kitchen foil for wrapping up parts such as injectors that have been removed from the engine and which need to be kept clean. Do not use foil near electrics as it conducts electricity.

Special electrical cleaning sprays do an excellent job cleaning small amounts of oil and carbon off electrical items.

*Lubricating and corrosion inhibiting* sprays – perhaps one of the best known being WD-40 – abound in DIY stores and car accessory shops. Most do a great job and should be used regularly on the outside of the engine and then given a wipe off or for lubricating small internal parts. Be sure to check that they are totally compatible with the materials, particularly rubbers and plastics, onto which they are sprayed. Most are safe on electrical insulating materials, but not necessarily on gasket materials. Perkins Powerparts make a good preservative wax spray which is ideal for use on the outside of the engine over winter. All engine surfaces can be cleaned off with white spirit (turpentine substitute) and a fluffless rag.

*The silicone* family are good waterproofers and compatible with most rubbers. However, some sealants have an acidic content which can attack metal. More acid-free silicones are now being produced, but products sold for producing gasket-free joints and for insulating electrical terminations and sealing junction boxes are excellent. Silicones are very persistent on surfaces once they are applied, so care should be taken not to apply them to GRP surfaces which might need to be repaired, or to any surface that might need painting in the future. Silicones can be removed, but only with great difficulty. All silicones must be used only for applications which suit their temperature range.

*Plastic metals* are available, most being based on very tough epoxide resin compositions. For the amateur they can achieve a satisfactory temporary repair, but they depend on perfectly clean surfaces before their ultimate bond strength can be achieved. An amateur is seldom able to achieve the standard of cleanliness required, but the potential strength of plastic metals should not be doubted, as many aircraft are literally glued together these days using epoxide formulations. Repairs in castings can be strong enough to be drilled and tapped.

# Metal treatments

Restoration of a corroded engine is time well spent during the winter. Work is easier if major parts have been disassembled, as castings have many nooks and crannies on the outside where it is difficult to reach and remove the corrosion. After degreasing, surfaces should be perfectly dry before mechanical abrasion takes place, otherwise dust is attracted to the nooks. Care must always be taken to ensure that dust and dirt are kept out of working parts, and all orifices into an engine must be totally sealed. Corks make excellent hole sealers – even if it means drinking a few extra bottles of wine to get them!

The electric drill, using wire brushes and abrasive flap wheels, is speedy, but a wire brush may reach parts that the drill does not. The problem that power tools create is polishing the metal surface when speed is excessive. The best drills to use are those with electronic speed controls on them. Coarse grit flap wheels using 40 to 60 grit are good for removing serious surface pitting or on rough castings. Decrease the grit size to produce a finer finished surface, using anything up to 180 grit. For hand-finishing emery cloth grade 3 to 2 corresponds with the above flap-wheel grits for coarse surfaces and FF (150 grit) for the finer finishing grade.

It is anticipated that when you use electric tools you will take precautions to ensure they are used safely – preferably in a dry workshop. Any power used in a damp place, particularly in a boat is highly dangerous and the least that can be done is to ensure the power line is fitted with a working circuit breaker that will cut current before it can kill.

## Surface chemical treatments

Once metal has a totally clean surface with all loose particles of corrosion removed, it should be chemically treated. Ferrous metal that has rusted will still have minute pockets of rust below the surface. If these are not to develop and lift paint off very quickly, chemical treatment is needed to make certain that they are inert. Care is always needed when using them – goggles and some protection for the hands are highly recommended. Some people's skin is particularly prone to dermatitis. In fact, when working on engines it is a good idea for everyone to use a skin barrier cream, which will protect the hands from fuel and oil. All paint systems usually come with health warning advice. Heed the warnings, in particular, when using solvents and paints which contain isocyanates (most two-can polyurethanes) and use them only in well ventilated spaces.

Acidic treatments for ferrous metals that are successful and easy for the amateur to use are based on either phosphoric or tannic acid. Many proprietary 'potions' exist – wonder rust cures that nobody should be fooled by. The best ones simply state that they contain either of these two acids which will effectively neutralise the minute rust pockets. My own preference for ferrous metals are ones based on phosphoric acid, and after the application has thoroughly dried, follow up with one of

the two-can high-performance painting systems.

Both the two-can polyurethanes and epoxy coating systems produce a very hard, long-lasting finish which will stand up to most temperatures on the engine except the very hottest parts. They both have excellent impact abrasion and water resistance. Chlorinated rubber paints are often used as an inexpensive engine finish, but they are not as effective as the high-performance range already mentioned. If not all paint has been removed from a surface and it is intended to use a high-performance coating, it is as well to test the old paint to ensure that it is totally compatible with the new. Try out a little of the thinner on a patch to see if it loosens or blisters the old paint. If it does, you must remove every trace of the old.

After cleaning and abrasion, light alloys need an etching primer. These are again based on phosphoric acid and some also contain cadmium, which acts as a passive corrosion inhibiting barrier and primer for succeeding paint coatings. These etching primers can be used safely on steel, stainless steels, cast iron, light alloys and copper. As the total removal of paint from an engine is seldom necessary, it is helpful if the engine manufacturer can supply 'touch up' quantities of the original specification and colour. Engine paints need to be able to stand up to the temperature of the parts they are used on. There are proprietary high-temperature paints which are used in the automotive trade, and these can be used to spruce up an engine very nicely.

On light alloy out drives it is essential to touch-up paint coating damage as soon as is practicable, since exposed areas of light alloy will have a higher rate of corrosion. Most owners of out drives will already know that copper-based anti-foulings will induce a very high rate of corrosion, and that they must be avoided at all costs.

Painting the hardware on your boat is not simply cosmetic, therefore. A clean engine allows the mechanic to spot leaks very quickly, it is much more pleasant to work on and it will most definitely be preserved for a long time to come. Enjoy *pleasure* boating rather than *worry* boating, and believe me, one of the nicest things in life to hear is 'Gee, aren't your engines smart!'

# Appendix A  Conversion tables and formulae

| To convert | into | multiply by |
|---|---|---|
| °C | °F | (t degrees C × 1.8) + 32 |
| °F | °C | (t degrees F − 32) ÷ 1.8 |
| Cubic centimetres | Cubic inches | 0.3937 |
| Cubic inches | Cubic centimetres | 16.39 |
| Imperial feet | Metres | 0.305 |
| Gallons | Litres | 4.546 |
| Grammes | Ounces | 0.03527 |
| lbs | Grammes | 453.6 |
| Imperial gallons | US gallons | 1.205 |
| Inches | Centimetres | 2.5399 |
| Inches | Millimetres | 25.4 |
| Kilograms | lbs | 2.205 |
| Kilograms | Ounces | 35.37 |
| Litres | Cubic inches | 61.0 |
| Litres | Gallons | 0.220 |
| Metres | Feet | 3.28 |
| Metres | Inches | 39.37 |
| Millimetres | Inches | 0.039 |
| US gallons | Imperial gallons | 0.834 |
| lb/ft torque | kg/m | 0.138 |
| kg/m torque | lb/ft | 7.233 |
| lb/inch torque | N-m (Newton-metres) | 0.1129 |
| lb/ft torque | N-m | 1.3558 |
| Kilo Pascal | lb/in² | 0.14508 |
| Bars | lb/in² | 14.5037 |
| Tonnes | Imperial tons | 0.984206 |

*Horsepower*

| | | |
|---|---|---|
| Horsepower (hp) | Kilowatts (kW) | 0.746 |
| hp | metric hp | 1.014 |

*Approximate weights of various liquids*

| | Pounds per US gallon | Specific gravity |
|---|---|---|
| Diesel fuel | 6.88 to 7.46 | 0.825 to 0.895 |
| Ethylene glycol | 9.3 to 9.6 | 1.12 to 1.15 |
| Petrol (gasoline) | 5.6 to 6.3 | 0.67 to 0.75 |
| Lubricating oil (medium) | 7.5 to 7.7 | 0.90 to 0.92 |
| Water | 8.34 | 1 |

# Appendix B   Ford engine marinisers worldwide

The following list, kindly supplied by the Ford Motor Company, gives details of most of the major firms on both sides of the Atlantic which marinise or use Ford parts for their marine engines.

*United Kingdom*

Beta Marine Ltd,
Merrerts Mills Industrial Estate,
Bath Rd,
South Woodchester,
Nr Stroud, Gloucestershire

'C' Power (Marine) Ltd,
22 Bridge End Rd,
Grantham NG31 6JQ

C T Marine,
Blue Lias Marina,
Stockton,
Rugby, Warwickshire

Dolphin Marine Engineering,
2 Armstrong Rd,
Manor Trading Estate,
Benfleet, Essex

Lancing Marine Ltd,
51, Victoria Rd,
Portslade,
Sussex

Mermaid Marine Engines Ltd,
Ferndown Industrial Estate,
70/72 Cobham Rd,
Wimborne,
Dorset BH21 7RN

Sabre-Lehman Engines Ltd,
Ferndown Industrial Estate,
Wimborne,
Dorset BH21 7PW

Tempest Diesels Ltd,
Foundry Rd,
Stamford,
Lincolnshire

Thornycroft Marine Ltd,
PO Box 2,
Hurst Lane,
Tipton,
West Midlands DY4 9AD

Water Mota Ltd,
Abbotskerswell,
South Devon TQ12 5NF

*Europe*

Fornaut SA,
45 rue Charles Nodier,
933310 Le Pre Saint Gervais,
France

Motor AB N Gustavson Eftr.,
Box 6053,
S-181-06 Lidingo,
Sweden

Nedalo BV,
Industrieweg 4-1422 AJ
 Uithoorn,
Postbus 30-1420 AA Uithoorn,
Netherlands

Nuova Motonautica,
Via Toscanelli,
47042 Cesenatico,
Forli, Italy

Sabb Motor A/S,
Postbox 2728,
N-5010 Bergen,
Norway

TM Marine,
Bunninassa,
Dromod,
Co. Leitrim, Eire

*United States of America*

Chrysler Marine and
 Ind. Products,
151 Industrial Drive,
Beaverdam WI 53916
(460 Diesel only)

Commander Marine
Corporation,
4780 N.W. 128th St,
Miami, Florida 33054

Hardin Marine,
1711S Claudia Way,
Anaheim,
California

Indmar Products Co,
2820 Fite Rd,
Millington, TN 38127

Mercury Marine,
1939 Pioneer Rd,
Fond du Lac, EWI 54935
(Part of 224 4 cyl diesel)

OMC Stern Drive,
3145 Central Avenue,
Waukegan, IL 60085

Pleasurecraft Marine,
7515 Hill Road,
Canal Winchester, OH 43110

Redline Marine,
1101 Main,
Lewsiston, ID 83501

US Marine Corporation,
105 Marine Drive,
Hartford, W1 53027

# Appendix C  Part suppliers (UK) for engines and gearboxes

Spares and advice on old or obsolete engines and gearboxes (UK) is listed in *Sell's Marine Market* under 'Engines' (old and obsolete).

**Bollinder**
Mr Perris,
24 Mayfield Rd,
Moseley ,
Birmingham B13 9HJ, UK

**Foden FD4 and FD6 2-stroke diesels**
Mr Alan Dixen,
Rolls Royce Cars,
Crewe, UK

**Gardner Vintage Engines – drawings**
Mr D. Houghton,
Oldfield Cottage,
Itchenor,
Chichester PO20 7AB, UK

**Ruston Hornsby (engines) and Parsons gearboxes**
Lipscombe and Hessey,
Boveney,
Windsor, Berks, UK

**Stuart Turner**
Fairways Marine Engineers,
Bath Place Wharf,
Downs Rd,
Maldon,
Essex CM9 7HU, UK

**TMP Gearboxes (TMP 12000)**
Mr O'Brien,
TMP Gearboxes,
96 Thames St,
Weybridge,
Surrey KT13 8JW, UK

**Volvo Penta**
Volvo Penta UK Ltd,
Otterspool Way,
Watford, Herts WD2 8HW, UK

**Watermota**
Watermota Ltd,
Abbotskerswell,
Newton Abbot,
Devon TQ12 5NF, UK

**Wortham Blake**
Wortham Blake and Co.,
The Forum,
High St,
Edgware, Middx, UK

# Appendix D   Manufacturers of marine petrol engine carburettors

| Carburettor type[1] | Application[2] | Manufacturer |
|---|---|---|
| Solex 4A1 | BMW-6 cylinder | Pierburg GmbH and Co. KG, Leuschstrasse 1, Postfacn 838, D–4040 Neussl, W. Germany |
| Solex 44PHN3 | Volvo Penta 140 and 145, BMW-4 cylinder | La Society des Carburateurs Solex, 19 rue Lavoisier, 92002, Nanterra Cedex, France |
| Solex 26NV | Stuart Turner, Newage Lion, Some Volvo Penta, Albin, Mandal and Marstal | |

The 26NV was replaced by 26VBN2 on the later models of some of the above engines.

| | | |
|---|---|---|
| Solex 44PA1 | A whole range of Volvo Penta including AQ 115A/100B, AQ 130D/280D, AQ 130D/270TD, AQ 140/280D, AQ 170C/280C, AQ 170C/280TC | |
| Solex 45PHH | Volvo Penta racing application | |
| Zenith | Some engines of French origin | Zenith Société Européen de Carburation, 17 rue Louise Michel, F–92300 Lerallois-Perret, France |
| Rochester 2GE | Volvo Penta AQ 200 | General Motors Corporation Rochester Products Division |
| | OMC 140 | 1000 Lexington Avenue Rochester, NY, USA |
| Rochester 2BBL | OMC Cobra 2.3, 3, 4.3 and 5 lt | |
| Rochester 4BBL | OMC Cobra 4.3, 5, 5.7 lt | |
| | Chevrolet 350, 450-2, 454-4 | |

| Carburettor type[1] | Application[2] | Manufacturer |
|---|---|---|
| Tillotson HL Series | Vire | Marvel-Schebler Tillotson Division, 707 Southside Drive, Decatur, IL 162525, USA |
| | *Also* | Tillotson Ltd, Clash Industrial Estate, Tralee, Co. Kerry, Eire |
| Zenith-Stromberg 175CD | Volvo Penta AQ B18 CD Rover V-8 | Originally Zenith Carburettor Co. |
| VN Series[3] Solex 30AHG[3] | Volvo Penta MB18B and BB100 Volvo Penta MB18F and BB30 Wortham Blake | *Now* Hobourn SU Ltd, Wood Lane, Erdington, Birmingham, UK |
| Ford Motorcraft IV (Manual choke) | UK Ford 2206/2270 Ford 2305D and 2305F | Ford Motor Company Ltd, Industrial Power Products, Arisdale Avenue, South Ockenden, Essex RM15 5TJ, UK |
| SU HD6 | Rover V-8 | Originally SU Carburettor Co. *Now* Hobourn SU, Wood Lane, Erdington, Birmingham, UK |
| Weber | Some Ford 2350D and 2305F | UK Weber Concessionaires, Sunbury-on-Thames, Middlesex, UK |
| | | Weber SpA, Via delle Casse, I–40100 Bolognia, Italy |
| Carter carburettors | | Carter Automotive Co. Inc., 9666 Olive Boulevard, St Louis, MO 63132, USA |

| Carburettor type[1] | Application[2] | Manufacturer |
| --- | --- | --- |
| Holley[4] 2300/2bbl | Ford 302 CID | Holley Carburettor Division, |
| 4160/4bbl | Ford 351 CID | 11955 East Nine Mile Rd, |
| | Ford 460 CID | Warren, |
| | Ford 351W CID | Michigan 48089, USA |
| | Ford 429 CID | |
| | Chris Craft 307 and 350 CID | |
| | Ford 460 CID Low Output | |
| | Ford 302 CID High Output | |
| 4150/4bbl | Volvo Penta 350 CID High Ouput | |
| | Mercury Marine 454 CID | |
| 1904/1bbl | Chrysler 225 CID | |
| 2210/2bbl | Ford 302 CID | |
| 4011/4bbl | Volvo Penta 454 CID | |

[1] *Carburettor type.* This indicates only the basic model and each model may have many small variations which need much more precise matching (part numbers) than the basic model indicated.

[2] *Application guide.* Engine manufacturers always reserve the right to change specifications and this list does not constitute a precise guide as to which carburettor was, or is, being used on any of the listed engines. (In fact, one engine builder stated that he never knew which carburettor was to be fitted to engines arriving at his marinising works – it very much depended on what was in stock at the time of dispatch!) However, carburettors are usually engraved with the name of the manufacturer, and might have the model number on them. The addresses were kindly supplied by the Motor Research Association, Watling Street, Nuneaton, Warwickshire CV10 0TV, UK.

[3] UK Solex Company went out of business some years ago and parts were sold off. It is therefore much more difficult to trace exact sources for specific engine carburettors. An owner in difficulty should first contact the engine maker, then one of the addresses given above to track down the actual carburettor manufacturer.

[4] Holley have been manufacturing marine engine carburettors for over 50 years and carry an exact Parts Carb. List numbering (not shown here) for engines generally manufactured over the last 20 years which are included in the above list.

'C' on Ford designation means Cleveland Foundry – typically high performance units.

'W' on Ford designation means Windsor Foundry – general use engines.

bbl indicates number of throttle bores on the carburettor.

# *Appendix E   Companies mentioned in the text*

Listed below are the names and addresses of companies which I have mentioned in the text (some of which have representation in the USA).

Alexander Duckham and Co. Ltd (Oils),
Duckhams House,
157/159 Masons Hill,
Bromley,
Kent BR2 9HU, UK

Deep Sea Seal and Aquadrive,
Halyard Marine,
2 Portsmouth Centre,
Quartermaine Rd,
Old Airport,
Portsmouth PO3 5QT, UK

Ega Ltd (Plastic Conduit),
Glascoed Rd,
St Asaph,
N. Wales LL17 0ER, UK

Eurogauge Co. Ltd,
Imberhorne Lane,
East Grinstead,
Sussex RH19 1RF, UK

Frank W. Murphy (Instruments),
PO Box 470248,
Tulsa,
Oklahoma, USA;
also at Blackmoor Road,
Ebblake Industrial Estate,
Verwood,
Dorset BH21 6AY, UK

Gunson's Ltd,
Pudding Hill Lane,
Stratford,
London E15 2PU, UK

Llewellyn Ryland Ltd,
Hayden St,
Birmingham B12 9DB, UK

Lucas Marine Ltd,
Unit E,
Albany Park Industrial Estate,
Frimley Rd,
Camberley,
Surrey GU15 2PL, UK;
also Lucas Automotive,
5500 New King St,
PO Box 7002,
Troy,
Michegan 48007–7002, USA

Metalastik Vibration Control Systems,
Dunlop Ltd,
PO Box 98,
Evington Valley Rd,
Leicester LE5 5LY, UK

Perkins Engines (Powerparts products),
Eastfield,
Peterborough PE1 5NA, UK

Sell's Marine Market,
55 High Street,
Epsom,
Surrey KT19 8DW, UK

Silentblok Ltd,
Manor Royal,
Crawley,
Sussex RH10 2QG, UK

Stuart Pilot Ltd,
Ashley House,
Hurlands Close,
Farnham,
Surrey GU9 9JF, UK

Turner Newall Ltd,
PO Box 40,
Rochdale OL12 7EQ, UK

VDO Instruments Ltd,
Holford Way,
Birmingham B6 7AX, UK

James Walker and Co. Ltd,
Lion Works,
Woking,
Surrey GU22 8AP, UK

# *Appendix F Diesel engine fault finding chart*

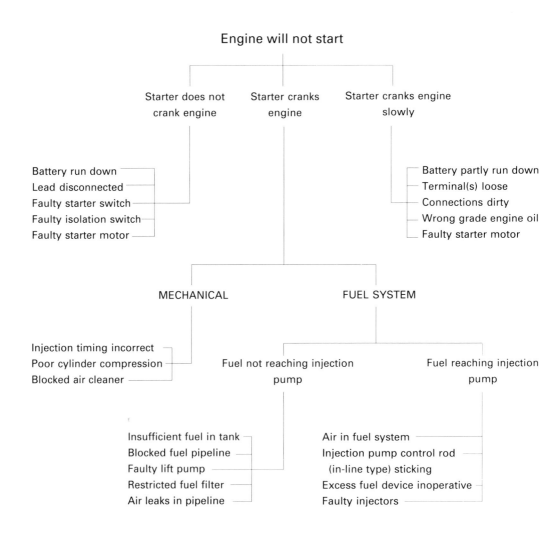

Engine will not start

Starter does not crank engine | Starter cranks engine | Starter cranks engine slowly

Battery run down
Lead disconnected
Faulty starter switch
Faulty isolation switch
Faulty starter motor

Battery partly run down
Terminal(s) loose
Connections dirty
Wrong grade engine oil
Faulty starter motor

MECHANICAL | FUEL SYSTEM

Injection timing incorrect
Poor cylinder compression
Blocked air cleaner

Fuel not reaching injection pump | Fuel reaching injection pump

Insufficient fuel in tank
Blocked fuel pipeline
Faulty lift pump
Restricted fuel filter
Air leaks in pipeline

Air in fuel system
Injection pump control rod
(in-line type) sticking
Excess fuel device inoperative
Faulty injectors

| | MECHANICAL | FUEL |
|---|---|---|
| ENGINE OVERHEATS | Insufficient water<br>Insufficient lubricating oil<br>Fan belt to pump slack or broken<br>Blocked heat exchanger tubes<br>Thermostat sticking<br>Faulty water pump; blocked inlet<br>Injection timing incorrect<br>Engine needs top overhaul | Faulty injectors |
| ENGINE KNOCKS | Bearings worn<br>Piston slap<br>Sticking valve rocker(s)<br>Broken valve spring(s)<br>Injection timing incorrect | Faulty injector(s)<br>Air in system |
| EXHAUST EMITS EXCESSIVE SMOKE | Maximum stop screw out of adjustment<br>Excess fuel device out<br>Poor compression | Incorrect pump timing<br>Faulty injector(s)<br>Faulty pump |
| ENGINE MISFIRES | Sticking valve(s)<br>Sticking piston rings<br>Top overhaul needed<br>Broken injector pipe | Faulty injector(s)<br>Air in system<br>Faulty pump |
| ENGINE STARTS AND STOPS | Valve(s) sticking<br>Governor idling setting incorrect | Air in system<br>Faulty lift pump<br>Fuel filter restricted<br>Insufficient fuel in tank |
| ENGINE DOES NOT GIVE FULL POWER | Sticking valve(s)<br>Worn piston rings and bores<br>Incorrect valve clearance<br>Sticking piston rings<br>Injection timing incorrect<br>Engine overheating | Air in system<br>Faulty lift pump<br>Fuel filter restricted<br>Faulty injector(s)<br>Insufficient fuel in tank<br>Dirty air cleaner<br>In-line pump control rod sticking<br>Stop control pulled out slightly |
| ENGINE IDLES IMPERFECTLY | Governor idling setting incorrect<br>Injection timing incorrect<br>Air leak in governor system<br>Sticking valve(s)<br>Broken valve spring(s) | Air in system<br>Fuel filter restricted<br>Faulty injector(s)<br>Faulty lift pump<br>Faulty pump<br>Insufficient fuel in tank |

# Appendix G  Petrol engine fault finding chart

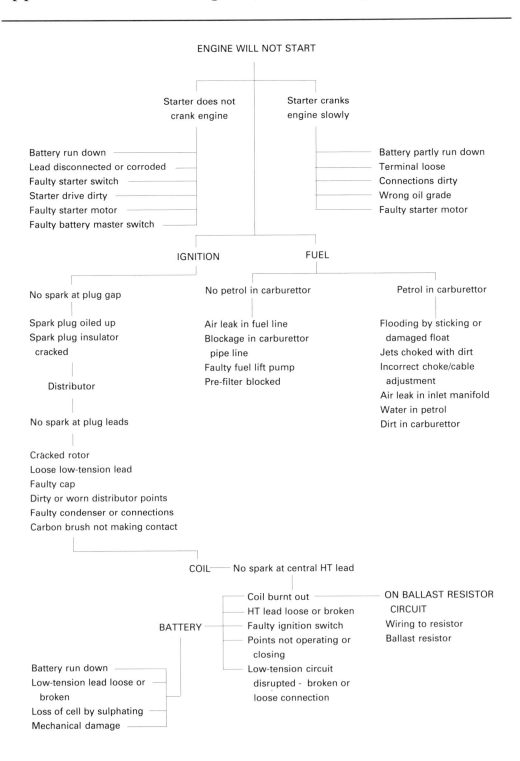

ENGINE WILL NOT START

Starter does not crank engine

Starter cranks engine slowly

Battery run down
Lead disconnected or corroded
Faulty starter switch
Starter drive dirty
Faulty starter motor
Faulty battery master switch

Battery partly run down
Terminal loose
Connections dirty
Wrong oil grade
Faulty starter motor

IGNITION

FUEL

No spark at plug gap

No petrol in carburettor

Petrol in carburettor

Spark plug oiled up
Spark plug insulator
  cracked

Air leak in fuel line
Blockage in carburettor
  pipe line
Faulty fuel lift pump
Pre-filter blocked

Flooding by sticking or
  damaged float
Jets choked with dirt
Incorrect choke/cable
  adjustment
Air leak in inlet manifold
Water in petrol
Dirt in carburettor

Distributor

No spark at plug leads

Cracked rotor
Loose low-tension lead
Faulty cap
Dirty or worn distributor points
Faulty condenser or connections
Carbon brush not making contact

COIL—— No spark at central HT lead

Coil burnt out
HT lead loose or broken
Faulty ignition switch
Points not operating or
  closing
Low-tension circuit
  disrupted - broken or
  loose connection

ON BALLAST RESISTOR
  CIRCUIT
Wiring to resistor
Ballast resistor

BATTERY

Battery run down
Low-tension lead loose or
  broken
Loss of cell by sulphating
Mechanical damage

| | IGNITION | CARBURETTOR | MECHANICAL |
|---|---|---|---|
| ENGINE MISFIRES | HT leads to spark plugs shorting<br>Incorrect spark plug gap<br>Cracked spark plug insulator<br>Battery connection to coil loose<br>Faulty or damp distributor cap | Water in carburettor<br>Fuel line partially choked<br>Fuel lift pump pressure low<br>Fuel pump or pre-filter choked<br>Needle valve dirty or damaged | Valve sticking<br>Valves burnt<br>Valve spring broken<br>Incorrect valve clearance |
| ENGINE STARTS AND STOPS | Low-tension connection loose<br>Faulty switch contact<br>Dirty contact points | Air leaks<br>Fuel line blocked<br>Water in fuel<br>Needle valve sticking/ flooding, or no fuel<br>Fuel pump faulty | |
| ENGINE DOES NOT GIVE FULL POWER | Fuel supply faulty<br>Air leaks in inlet manifold<br>Jet partly choked | Ignition retarded<br>HT lead shorting<br>Valve sticking or wrongly adjusted<br>Valve burnt or badly seated<br>Valve spring broken<br>Wrong or faulty distributor cap | |
| ENGINE RUNS ON FULL THROTTLE ONLY | Slow-running jet blocked<br>Slow-running adjustment screw out of adjustment | Valve sticking<br>Valve burnt<br>Valve spring broken | |
| ENGINE RUNS IMPERFECTLY | Weak mixture<br>Fuel feed faulty<br>Inlet valves not closing<br>Ignition timing incorrect<br>Carburettor flooding | | |
| ENGINE KNOCKS OR RUNS ON | | | Timing too far advanced<br>Excessive carbon deposit<br>Loose bearing or piston<br>Plug leads crossed<br>Cylinder head gasket blown |

# Index

# Other Adlard Coles Titles of Interest

## PILOTAGE

*Adlard Coles Pilot Packs Volumes 1, 2 and 3* by Brian Goulder
*Vol 1* Great Yarmouth to Littlehampton and IJmuiden to Carentan
   ISBN 0 229 11798 8
*Vol 2* Chichester to Portland, the Channel Islands, and St Vaast to Erquy
   ISBN 0 229 11799 6
*Vol 3* Bridport to Isles of Scilly and Le Légué to Ushant
   ISBN 0 229 11800 3
A major new pilotage series for sail and power covering the most popular sailing grounds in Europe. Every harbour has a two colour navigational pilotage chart accompanied by port and pilotage information. The only series with a computerised update facility.

*Normandy and Channel Islands Pilot – 7th Edition* by Mark Brackenbury
   ISBN 0 229 11826 7
A highly respected pilotage guide from Calais to St Malo including the Channel Islands. Thoroughly researched and updated.

*North Brittany Pilot – 5th Edition Revised* by K Adlard Coles and the RCC Pilotage Foundation
   ISBN 0 229 11696 5
A thoroughly revised edition covering the French coast from St Malo to Ushant.

*North Biscay Pilot – 3rd Edition Revised* by the RCC Pilotage Foundation
   ISBN 0 229 11661 2
Detailed information from Brest to the Gironde Estuary, with clear charts of ports and harbours.

*South Biscay Pilot – 3rd Edition Revised* by Robin Brandon
   ISBN 0 229 11680 9
From the Gironde Estuary to La Coruna. Thoroughly updated to include the many recent changes that have taken place in this area.

*The Atlantic Crossing Guide – 2nd Edition* by the RCC Pilotage Foundation
   ISBN 0 229 11828 3
The second edition of this extremely popular book has been totally updated with many new charts and photographs. Full of practical advice, it covers the complete North Atlantic circuit.

*World Cruising Routes* by Jimmy Cornell
   ISBN 0 229 11793 7
A brilliantly comprehensive guide to nearly 300 cruising routes around the world. All the necessary information for planning an extended cruise in any of the world's oceans has been brought together for the first time in a single volume.

## BUILDING, REPAIR AND MAINTENANCE

*Metal Corrosion in Boats* by Nigel Warren
    ISBN 0 229 11796 1
The only book available on a subject of vital importance to owners.

*The Care and Repair of Small Marine Diesels* by Chris Thompson
    ISBN 0 229 11813 5
The owner's handbook of basic care and advanced servicing of marine diesel engines up to 150 h.p.

*Surveying Small Craft – 2nd Edition* by Ian Nicolson
    ISBN 0 229 11710 4
A guide to examining boats for faults. Tells what to look for, how to spot it and where.

*Build A Simple Dinghy* by Ian Nicolson and Alasdair Reynolds
    ISBN 0 229 11806 2
The ideal book for all amateur builders, explaining clearly how to build a dinghy for less than half the price of the same size good quality inflatable.

## NAVIGATION

*Start to Navigate* by Conrad Dixon
    ISBN 0 229 11706 6
An excellent introduction for young and old alike.

*Coastal Navigation* by Gerry Smith
    ISBN 0 229 11709 0
This programmed learning course designed for the beginner comes complete with practice chart.

*Radio Position Fixing for Yachtsmen* by Claud Powell
    ISBN 0 229 11788 0
An introduction to the art of navigation by Decca, Loran, Omega and Transit.

*Radar Mate* by Lt Cdr G A G Brooke and Capt S Dobell
    ISBN 0 229 11789 9
Spiral-backed for open-flat convenience, this practical manual is designed to help readers identify images shown on a radar screen.

*VHF Yachtmaster* by Pat Langley-Price and Philip Ouvry
    ISBN 0 229 11720 1
A complete self tutor (book plus cassette) for those wishing to pass the compulsory examination.

## WEATHER

*Instant Weather Forecasting* by Alan Watts
    ISBN 0 229 11724 4
Twenty-four colour cloud photographs with facing explanations provide a brilliant short-term forecasting guide.

*Reading the Weather: Modern Techniques for Yachtsmen* by Alan Watts
    ISBN 0 229 11774 0
A definitive work on using weather fax and reading the weather by other practical means.

## COMING IN FEBRUARY 1989

*OSMOSIS and the Care and Repair of Glass Fibre Yachts* by Tony Staton-Bevan
    ISBN 0 229 11837 2
In the revised and expanded edition of this highly acclaimed book the author sets out to deal with the prevention and cure of problems with hulls, decks and fittings, with cracking and blistering, stress crazing, fading gel-coats and collision damage.

## COMING IN MAY 1989

*Fast Boats and Rough Seas* by Dag Pike
    ISBN 0 229 11840 2
A more advanced follow-up to *Practical Motor Cruising*, designed to explain advanced handling techniques for fast boats. It will cover high speed handling as well as operating techniques in rough weather, all based on personal experience. Peppered with entertaining anecdotes, it is a very practical book which will be welcomed by fast boat skippers and crew.

8/21/12

⑧

7/24/06